Endogenous

Previous titles in this series:

Endogenous Growth

Edited by
Torben M. Andersen
and
Karl O. Moene

BLACKWELL
Oxford UK & Cambridge USA

Copyright © Scandinavian Journal of Economics 1993

ISBN 0-631-18975-0

First published 1993
Reprinted 1995

Blackwell Publishers
108 Cowley Road, Oxford OX4 1JF, UK
and
238 Main Street,
Cambridge, MA 02142, USA

British Library Cataloguing-in Publication Data.

A catalogue record for this book is available from the British Library.

Library of Congress Cataloging-in Publication Data.

Endogenous Growth/edited by Torben M. Andersen and Karl O. Moene.

p.c.m. Articles from the Scandinavian Journal of Economics.
ISBN 0-631-18975-0 (pb)

1. Economic development. 2. Economic development – Mathematical models.
I. Andersen, Torben M., 1956–   . II. Moene, Karl Ove.

HD75.E53   1994   94.5928

338.9 – dc20   CIP

Printed and bound by Athenæum Press Ltd.,
Gateshead, Tyne & Wear.

Contents

Endogenous Growth

Preface

Growth theory is currently changing direction. The orthodox neoclassical approach is being modified and extended by models of endogenous growth. This volume provides a survey of the topic, along with fresh contributions in the field.

Growth performance differs widely among countries and, as demonstrated in this volume, the usual empirical tests of convergence of growth rates are blurred by Galton's classical fallacy of regression to the mean. In addition, judging theories by simple correlations may be flawed if shocks are not properly accounted for. Appropriate empirical methods show a tendency towards divergent growth rates. A consensus is emerging among scholars whereby divergent growth experiences are better accounted for by the new growth theory than by the old. As shown in this collection of papers, endogenous growth models may, for instance, give rise to multiple equilibria, implying that economies with identical structures may have different growth rates. Due to these findings, as well as to national and international spillover effects, optimal growth cannot easily be achieved without coordination inside and among countries.

An important insight of the new theory is that economic institutions and short-term policies have long-run effects on growth. Other contributions in this volume cover the growth effects of different trade, interest rate, tax and public investment policies, as well as lobbying activities. Moreover, the relationships between growth, talent and income distribution are explored from different perspectives. The emphasis is on the effects of egalitarianism both within and across generations.

Financial support from the Aarhus University Research Foundation and the Bank of Norway Fund for Economic Research is gratefully acknowledged.

Torben M. Andersen
Karl O. Moene

On Endogenizing Long-Run Growth*

Peter J. Hammond

Stanford University, Stanford, CA, USA

Andrés Rodríguez-Clare

Universidad de Costa Rica, San José, Costa Rica

Abstract

This assessment of recent theoretical work on endogenous growth identifies three different engines of long-run growth: (i) the asymptotic average product of capital is positive; (ii) labor productivity increases as an external effect of capital accumulation; (iii) there are feedback effects on the cost of accumulating knowledge or innovating. A general model encompassing all three is considered, and then used to review different proposed determinants of long-run growth rates. The contribution of endogenous growth theory has been to create a framework in which to explain why economic institutions and policies can have long-run effects on growth rates.

I. Introduction

Progress in economic science often takes the form of explaining what was previously inexplicable. That is, variables which had earlier been treated as exogenous become endogenized. Their values become determined, at least in principle, within an economic model.

Much early economic analysis restricted itself to the short run, in which the stock of capital equipment and workers' skills were treated as exogenously fixed by history. Progress toward a theory of growth came from adding a theory of investment which would determine endogenous

---

*We would like to thank Stanford Economics Ph.D. students Joshua Gans, Thomas Hellman, Giovanni Maggi, editors Torben Andersen and Karl Moene, as well as Joaquim Silvestre, Philippe Aghion and Frank Hahn for their helpful comments on a previous rough draft of this paper. Rodríguez-Clare is also grateful to the Alfred P. Sloan Foundation for financial support in the form of a Dissertation Fellowship in the Stanford Economics Department that allowed him to concentrate on his research during the academic year 1992-3. Of course, we accept responsibility for all remaining errors.

changes in capital stocks, and a comparable theory of skill or "human capital" acquisition for workers. In the medium term, rates of economic growth are obviously affected by a vast range of factors, including saving behavior, measures to stimulate private investment, provision of public goods whose benefits extend into the future, and policies affecting banking, finance, international trade, health, education, etc. Hence there is no shortage of ways to explain why growth occurs in the medium term, or how fast such growth can be. Accordingly, there is no shortage of medium term endogenous growth models.

In the long run, however, the situation is quite different. For 30 years, overlapping generations of students have been taught by their predecessors that long-run growth rates, if they are not zero, are determined by exogenous, non-economic factors such as population growth and the rate of scientific discovery. Indeed, as is well known, the orthodox neoclassical model of growth with no exogenous technological progress implies that the economy will reach a steady state in the long run with zero growth in income per head. Thus, according to this model, measures to promote growth can only enhance short- and medium-run growth rates, as well as long-run levels of consumption and output; it became the prevailing view that long-run growth rates could not really be affected at all by economic policy. In this sense, the engine of growth was seen as entirely exogenous. The long-run rate of growth was endogenous only in a trivial sense, since it was entirely determined by exogenous technical progress or population growth.

Recently, a serious challenge to this orthodoxy has been mounted. Actually, related ideas could already be found in earlier work on growth theory and development by Stigler (1951), Haavelmo (1954, 1956), Tobin (1955), Solow (1956), Myrdal (1957), Schultz (1961, pp. 5–6; 1962) and Arrow (1962), among those we know now were destined to win Nobel prizes later on.[1] Yet it took the recent work of Romer (1986, 1987, 1990), Prescott and Boyd (1987a, b), Lucas (1988) and others to set off a revolution. These authors developed various models in which long-run growth rates could be determined by the same kind of factors that had previously been regarded as affecting only short- or medium-term growth. In the process, they created what has come to be called "endogenous growth theory" in which the engine of growth has become part of the model itself: it results from the maximizing actions of individual economic agents. This is like the transformation from a carriage with an exogenous horse to a

---

[1] See Gunnar Myrdal's "principle of circular and cumulative causation". One distinguishing feature of the new theory is its reliance on external economies of scale. This is an idea that had been explored by Alfred Marshall, Allyn Young, Tibor Scitovsky, Nicholas Kaldor, Albert Hirschman, Nathan Rosenberg, and many others besides those whose works we mention explicitly in the paper.

horseless carriage or automobile with its own built-in source of motive power.

This paper surveys these recent developments in the theory of economic growth. In our view, three major themes have emerged. The first concerns how to modify the orthodox neoclassical model so that endogenous long-run growth in income per capita becomes possible. The classic works in the new growth literature, including Romer (1986, 1990), Lucas (1988), Jones and Manuelli (1990), Rebelo (1991), and Grossman and Helpman (1991a), all emphasize this theme.

Second, there has been considerable analysis of how the growth rate can be affected by variables such as public goods, finance, trade, taxes, demographic parameters, income distribution and social norms, all of which played no role in the traditional neoclassical theory. Recently, many papers have appeared that take an endogenous growth model, extend it to incorporate at least one of these extra variables, and then perform a comparative static analysis of how these variables influence long-run growth.

The third major theme concerns how growth can be propagated across countries that are linked through flows of goods, capital and ideas. For instance, if technological innovation is the engine of growth, then it would seem that the growth potential of countries that have not reached the technological frontier is larger than for the innovating countries. These issues, however, are far from being well understood.

As can readily be appreciated, the new growth literature is already enormous. Indeed, several other symposia and surveys have already appeared, or will do so shortly.[2] For this reason, and due to limitations of space and time, our survey is restricted in many ways. First, we will not review systematically the literature on the third major issue concerning how growth is propagated internationally, though our discussion of the relation between trade and growth is of some relevance. In some sense, this means that we leave aside the development issues that are most pertinent to relatively poor countries. Second, given our own comparative advantage, we focus on the theoretical part of the literature, virtually excluding all mention of its very important empirical side. Finally, the survey attempts to be self-contained and to derive most of its results analytically; as a consequence, the number of models and papers which can be

---

[2] We have noticed surveys or prominent lectures by Lucas (1988, 1993), Romer (1991), Stern (1991), Sala-i-Martin (1990a,b), Helpman (1992), Hahn (1992), Solow (1993), and other symposia in a supplementary issue of the *Journal of Political Economy*, 1990, in the May 1991 issue of the *Quarterly Journal Economics*, in the Winter 1992 issue of the *Oxford Review of Economic Policy* and in the December 1992 issue of the *Journal of Economic Theory*. There have even been newspaper articles in the *Economist* (January 4, 1992, p. 17) by Brittan (1993).

reviewed in any detail is quite small and many important contributions will not be mentioned at all. We believe that this is a price worth paying, however, since it permits us to be more rigorous and didactic in explaining what we think is most important.[3]

In what follows, Section II begins by reviewing the orthodox neoclassical growth model. Then Sections III, IV and V are devoted to the first major theme. They present three different and fundamental departures from the orthodox model that allow endogenous long-run growth of income per capita. These three sections cover the major basic features of the new growth theory.

Next, Section VI develops a more general model that embodies all these three different approaches. It also derives some general results about how several different exogenous variables affect the growth rate. This allows a better understanding of the essential aspects of the three different approaches to endogenous growth that were outlined in Sections III–V. Thereafter, Section VII briefly reviews the main literature on specific determinants of growth, linking its predictions to the results of Section VI wherever possible. The final Section VIII is a concluding assessment.

II. The Orthodox Neoclassical Model of Purely Exogenous Growth

Neoclassical growth theory has many significant predecessors. These include the "classical" growth theories of Smith, Ricardo, Malthus, Marx, etc.; see Harris (1987). There are also the "Keynesian" growth models of Harrod (1939) and Domar (1946).[4] Tobin's (1955) paper was a significant addition to this line of work, as it made the growth rate depend on the elasticity of labor supply, amongst other variables. Modern endogenous growth theory, however, takes as its point of departure the very similar orthodox neoclassical equilibrium growth models of Solow (1956) and Swan (1956).[5] In their purest form, these predict that the capital–labor ratio converges to some long-run equilibrium value, as do the real wage, the rate of return to capital, and the level of income per capita. These long-run equilibrium values do depend on the saving rate. But the long-run rate of growth of output is in a sense exogenous, being equal to the rate of population growth. In the long run, consumption per capita converges to a

---

[3] For a much more extensive survey, see Gans (1989).

[4] This is actually somewhat preceded by the work of Fel'dman (1928), as Domar (1957) eventually acknowledged.

[5] See also the collections of articles by Newman (1968), Stiglitz and Uzawa (1969), and Sen (1970), as well as the thorough survey by Hahn and Matthews (1964).

stationary equilibrium value. Policies to enhance growth can only influence the short term.

Let L denote the amount of available labor. In many growth models it is assumed that L grows at a fixed exponential exogenous rate. Yet, as biologist Paul Ehrlich (1968) for one has pointed out so strikingly, were population growth to continue indefinitely without the physical size of our heirs shrinking to zero, then ultimately the human race could not be contained within any sphere expanding more slowly than the speed of light! In any case, since the question is whether income per head can grow, this exogenous population growth rate will not materially affect most of our results.[6] So, for simplicity, most of the rest of the paper will simply assume it is zero. Moreover we will often refer to L as a non-reproducible resource because it has an exogenous supply that is fixed in the long run. Indeed, a somewhat similar model, with L representing the rate of depletion of an exhaustible resource rather than labor supply, was used by writers such as Dasgupta and Heal (1974), Solow (1974), and Stiglitz (1974). In their analysis of growth with exhaustible resources, the value of this L had to converge to zero in the limit. It turns out that the possibilities for long-run growth are much the same as when L is a fixed quantity of labor.

To see why income per capita cannot grow for ever in the orthodox neoclassical growth model, note first that it postulates a constant returns to scale (CRS) production function. Specifically, when output Y is measured net of capital depreciation, it is given by a function

$$Y = F(K, L) \tag{1}$$

of L and of a single capital good K. In this one sector growth model, net investment is given by

$$\dot{K} = F(K, L) - C, \tag{2}$$

where C denotes consumption and a dot over any variable is used to denote its time derivative. Differentiating (1) with respect to time gives

$$\dot{Y} = F_1(K, L)\dot{K}, \tag{3}$$

where F_i will always denote the partial derivative of F with respect to the i-th argument. Suppose that net investment $\dot{K}$ is a positive constant proportion s of net output Y. Hence, using (3), and indicating the proportional growth rate of any variable by a hat, output grows at rate

$$\hat{Y} = \dot{Y}/Y = sF_1(K, L). \tag{4}$$

---

[6] In some endogenous growth models such as Romer (1990), population growth may lead to an explosive rate of output growth. See Jones (1993).

A growth model in which s is determined by the intertemporal maximization of infinitely lived representative agents is presented in Section VI. For the purposes of this section, however, the original and only slightly cruder assumption (due to Harrod, Domar, Solow and Swan) of a fixed s for all time is sufficient to establish the main points.

At this stage, in order to ensure existence of a steady state with a positive level of output, neoclassical growth theory has usually invoked the Inada (1963) conditions. There are two of these. The first *lower* condition requires that $F_1(K, L) \to \infty$ as $K \to 0$. More interesting for us, however, is the second *upper* condition requiring that

$$F_1(K, L) \to 0 \text{ as } K \to \infty. \tag{5}$$

Given this upper condition, (4) implies that the rate of growth of output tends to zero in the limit. This is true no matter what the value of s may be, and it remains true even when $s(t)$ varies with t.

The next three sections consider three different modifications of the neoclassical model that make long-run growth possible. Of these, the first involves simply dropping the crucial upper Inada condition (5). The second modification asserts that a by-product of capital accumulation is an increase in the productivity of labor or of other non-reproducible factors. Reasons given for this have included: (i) learning by doing; (ii) government provision of public services financed out of taxation; (iii) capital accumulation allowing a deeper division of labor. The third modification also relies on an accumulation process having a by-product, but emphasizes how increasing knowledge or "human capital" makes innovation and/or education less costly.

III. Inessential Non-reproducible Factors

The simplest departure from the previous model with no technical change is to relax the upper Inada condition (5), so that the marginal productivity of capital does not tend to zero as the capital–labor ratio goes to infinity. This assumption means that only reproducible factors are "essential" in the sense that, as their input levels approach zero, so the marginal products of other factors also converge to zero.

In a prominent example of this approach, Jones and Manuelli (1990) explicitly assume that

$$F_1(K, L) \to \mu > 0 \text{ as } K \to \infty. \tag{6}$$

In this case, (4) and (6) together imply that the growth rate of Y is bounded away from zero and becomes $s\mu > 0$ in the limit. The long-run rate of output growth is endogenous, being determined by the rate of capital accumulation.

A notable example that satisfies (6) is the constant elasticity of substitution (CES) function

$$F(K, L) = [aK^\rho + (1 - \alpha)L^\rho]^{1/\rho}, \qquad 0 < \rho \leq 1. \tag{7}$$

Of course, (7) takes on the Cobb–Douglas form $F(K, L) = K^\alpha L^{1-\alpha}$ when $\rho = 0$. As is well known, the condition $\rho \leq 1$ is necessary for F to be concave. Moreover, $\rho > 0$ implies that, as $K \to \infty$, so

$$F_1(K, L) = \alpha K^{\rho-1}[aK^\rho + (1 - \alpha)L^\rho]^{(1/\rho)-1}$$

$$= \alpha[\alpha + (1 - \alpha)(L/K)^\rho]^{(1/\rho)-1} \to \alpha^{1/\rho} > 0. \tag{8}$$

On the other hand, it is easily checked that $F_1(K, L) \to 0$ as $K \to \infty$ when $\rho \leq 0$. In fact $\rho > 0$ ensures that the elasticity of substitution $\sigma = (1 - \rho)^{-1}$ exceeds 1: this is necessary for the share of capital in output to be bounded away from zero as the capital–labor ratio goes to infinity. Actually, Solow (1956, p. 77) himself considers this possibility (especially when $\rho = 1/2$), and describes the economy as "highly productive" in this case.

Another simple example satisfying (6) is

$$F(K, L) = \mu K + BK^\alpha L^{1-\alpha}, \qquad 0 < \alpha < 1, \qquad \mu > 0. \tag{9}$$

Rebelo (1991), as well as Barro and Sala-i-Martin (1992), postulate a model in which the production function is as in (9), but with $B = 0$, so that only reproducible resources are used as inputs. This is often referred to as the "AK model" because the production function can be expressed as $F(K, L) = AK$. Of course, it gives the same asymptotic properties as if $B > 0$ in (9), since the second term becomes relatively unimportant in the limit as $K \to \infty$.

Rebelo also shows that even when non-reproducible resources are essential in production, as they are in the Cobb–Douglas case, growth is still possible as long as there is at least one capital good whose production uses only reproducible resources. This can be seen in a two-sector growth model, with output C of the consumption good being produced according to a Cobb–Douglas production function using capital K_C and labor L, so that

$$C = K_C^\alpha L^{1-\alpha}, \qquad 0 < \alpha < 1 \tag{10}$$

while the investment sector uses only capital and exhibits CRS, so that

$$\dot{K} = aK_I, \qquad a > 0, \tag{11}$$

where $K_C + K_I = K$. To see how growth is then possible in the long run, just note that if a constant fraction ϕ of the capital stock goes to produce investment goods, then $K_I = \phi K$, while $K_C = (1 - \phi)K$. Hence (10), (11) and ϕ jointly determine the constant growth rate

$$\hat{C} = a\hat{K}_C = a\hat{K} = aa\phi. \tag{12}$$

The same principle lies behind the Lucas (1988) model of growth through skill acquisition or human capital accumulation. In his model, which is based in turn on work originally carried out by Uzawa (1965), skill augments the efficiency of labor. Moreover, skill is passed from generation to overlapping generation. In additon, externalities allow individuals to accumulate skill more easily when their parents' human capital stock is higher. Also, individuals spend fractions u of their time producing output and $1 - u$ increasing their human capital H. So the model is described by

$$\dot{K} + C = Y = F(K, uLH) \tag{13}$$

$$\dot{H} = \xi(1 - u)LH, \tag{14}$$

where ξ is a positive parameter that indicates how effective is time spent learning.[7] For any $u < 1$, long-run balanced growth is obviously possible at a rate g given by

$$g = \hat{C} = \hat{K} = \hat{H} = \xi(1 - u)L \tag{15}$$

provided that u and the savings ratio $s = \dot{K}/Y$ can both be chosen to satisfy

$$\dot{K} = gK = sY = sF(K, uLH) \tag{16}$$

for all time. Thus, according to (15), the long-run rate of growth is determined by: (i) the exogenous supply of labor L; (ii) the proportion $1 - u$ of labor effort that goes into acquiring skills; (iii) the rate of learning parameter ξ.

IV. Increasing Labor Productivity as an External Effect of Capital Accumulation

The second modification of the neoclassical growth model is most clearly expressed by introducing a continuum of identical representative agents.

---

[7] Lucas also assumes that the productivity of any worker's own human capital increases with the social average level of human capital. Concretely, he assumes a production function of the form $y = F(K, uLH)g(H)$, where $g' > 0$. This is done to make the results of the model appear more realistic. It is not necessary for the economy to be able to grow in the long run. Another difference from our formulation is that Lucas also has another reproducible asset — physical capital. Again, this is not the main insight of his model and so we omit it from this discussion. Both physical and human capital do appear, however, in the general model we set out in Section VI.

Each agent's output is assumed to be given by a CRS production function

$$y = F(k, E\ell), \tag{17}$$

where, for that agent, k is the stock of available capital and ℓ is the input of labor. Here E represents the efficiency of labor, which is common to all agents. In fact it is assumed that

$$E = A(K), \tag{18}$$

where $A(K)$ is an increasing function of the aggregate capital stock K. That is, labor (or any other non-reproducible resource) becomes more productive as a direct external effect of capital accumulation; cf. Swan (1956, p. 338). Aggregating over all identical agents implies that

$$Y = F(K, A(K)L). \tag{19}$$

Three main justifications for this assumption will be discussed in the ensuing subsections. First, however, we investigate the conditions under which this general one-sector model allows long-run growth. When investment is a constant fraction s of output, (19) implies that the growth rate of aggregate ouput is

$$\hat{Y} = \dot{Y}/Y = (F_1 + F_2 A'(K)L)\dot{K}/Y$$
$$= sF_1(K, A(K)L) + sF_2(K, A(K)L)A'(K)L. \tag{20}$$

Supose that, because of the usual upper Inada condition (5), the term sF_1 in (20) tends to zero as $K \to \infty$. Even so, there can still be long-run growth provided that the term $sF_2 A'(K)L$ is bounded away from zero. Because of CRS, the partial derivative F_2 is homogeneous of degree zero, and so

$$F_2(K, A(K)L)A'(K)L = F_2(1, A(K)L/K)A'(K)L. \tag{21}$$

A sufficient condition for the expression in (21) to be bounded away from zero is that $A'(K)L$ converges to $b > 0$ as $K \to \infty$. For then $A(K)L/K \to b$ also, and so $F_2(1, A(K)L/K)A'(K)L$ tends to $F_2(1, b)b$. Finally, therefore, the asymptotic growth rate of output is

$$\hat{Y} = sF_2(1, b)b > 0 \tag{22}$$

which depends once again on the asymptotic rate of saving s, as well as on the parameter b.

Learning by Doing and Social Knowledge

One justification for the technological possibilities described by (19) was originally offered by Haavelmo (1954; 1956, pp. 36–39) in a growth model with a single aggregate linear production function. He postulated that aggregate learning by doing results from the investment process, so that the present level of education or knowledge of the workforce is a function of the capital stock. This was before Arrow (1962) gave prominence to the same idea in a more plausible growth model with vintage capital and fixed coefficients, along the lines that had recently been pioneered by Johansen (1959), Salter (1960) and Solow (1960).[8]

Thereafter, following Levhari (1966), Sheshinski (1967) reformulated Arrow's model to exclude vintage effects, so that it became described by (19). He then imposed both the upper and lower Inada conditions on the function F — as Arrow had done in an extreme way by assuming fixed coefficients. Sheshinski also assumed that there would be diminishing returns to cumulative investment in the generation of knowledge, in the sense that $A(K)/K \to 0$ as $K \to \infty$. In this case, if σ denotes the rate of growth of L, while $A(K) = K^\eta$ with $\eta < 1$, then it is possible for both Y and K to grow at any common rate g satisfying

$$Y_0 e^{gt} = F(K_0 e^{gt}, K_0 L_0 e^{(g\eta + \sigma)t}) \tag{23}$$

for all t. This makes it clear that constant growth is only possible at a rate satisfying $g = g\eta + \sigma$, and so $g = \sigma/(1 - \eta)$. Hence the growth rate in income per capita, which is $g - \sigma = \sigma\eta/(1 - \eta)$, must be increasing in the population growth rate and zero when there is no population growth.

In his 1986 paper Romer made the accumulation of knowledge result at least in part from private decisions, and not simply remain an unintended consequence of aggregate past investment as it had been in Arrow's interpretation. In effect Romer regarded K, the aggregate stock of knowledge, as a public good from which individual producers could benefit directly. More importantly, Romer considered the possibility that $\eta > 1$. Then $A(K)/K = K^{\eta - 1} \to \infty$ as $K \to \infty$ and so, as shown above, there can be positive long-run growth even when population is constant. Indeed, long-run growth is also possible in the possibly more plausible case when $\eta = 1$.

In these models it should be noted that, even though there may be increasing returns to scale in the aggregate, each agent remains with a production function that is concave and has constant returns to scale in the variables under that agent's control. As Chipman (1970) and Romer (1986) point out, perfect competition therefore remains possible, with each producer taking both prices and the aggregate capital stock (or labor productivity) as fixed. In fact, capital accumulation is like a public good to which each producer contributes privately by investing. Evidently the resulting equilibrium allocation will usually be far from efficient.

---

[8] Arrow cites other closely related ideas that had appeared previously, including Verdoorn's (1949, 1980) law and the Swedish "Horndal effect" (dating back to the 1830s) noted by Lundberg (1961); see also David (1975, Ch. 3).

Public Services

Another justification for (18), inspired by Barro (1990), is that E represents public services which enhance labor productivity. For simplicity it is assumed that these services are produced with the same production function as private goods and are financed by a proportional income tax, so that $E = \tau Y$. Then the aggregate form of equation (17) implies that $E = \tau Y = \tau F(K, EL)$. Thus $1 = \tau F(K/E, L)$ because of CRS. Therefore $E = cK$, where c is the positive constant given implicitly by $1 = \tau F(1/c, L)$. This is a special case of (18), of course.

Notice that this formulation makes public services non-rivalrous. This is because an increase in L that leaves E constant would not cause each worker to have fewer public services. However, having these services be public is not a necessary condition for this formulation to allow long-run growth. For if instead public services were to become private to each worker, with G as the total level of such services, then we would have $E = G/L$. It is easy to check that with this modification the results are similar to those above, except that the constant c is given by $1 = \tau F(1/c, 1)$.

Division of Labor

The final justification to be considered here holds that a deeper division of labor between different specialized tasks increases the productivity of non-reproducible resources. But, to borrow from the memorable title of Ch. III of Adam Smith's *Wealth of Nations*, "the division of labour is limited by the extent of the market".[9] And of course the market can be expected to become more extensive if the capital stock increases. Thus, it is assumed that capital accumulation allows an increase in the productivity of non-reproducible resourses — an increase that will actually occur if production is organized efficiently.[10]

A simple formulation of this idea postulates that output is produced from capital K_Y in the final output sector and from an intermediate input Z according to a CRS production function

$$Y = F(K_Y, Z). \tag{24}$$

---

[9] Of course, Stigler (1951) honored Smith by choosing the very same title.

[10] The model presented in this section is adapted from Rodríguez-Clare (1993). It is related to Becker and Murphy (1992), though they give quite different interpretations. The model differs from Romer (1990) who assumes that the fixed requirement to produce a new variety of z involves essential non-reproducible factors and hence externalities in the research sector are needed to generate the possibility of long-run growth. Yang and Borland (1991) also give the division of labor an essential role in the growth process, but let growth itself be driven by learning by doing.

Following Dixit and Stiglitz (1977), assume that Z is produced using quantities $z(j)$ $(0 \le j < \infty)$ of a continuum of varieties of an intermediate good according to a strictly concave production function

$$Z = \left[\int_0^\infty z(j)^\alpha \, dj \right]^{1/\alpha}, \qquad 0 < \alpha < 1, \tag{25}$$

with constant elasticity of substitution exceeding one. Assume also that each variety of intermediate good $z(j)$ is produced from $K(j)$ units of capital and $L(j)$ units of labor according to

$$z(j) = \begin{cases} 0 & \text{if } K(j) < 1 \\ L(j) & \text{if } K(j) \ge 1. \end{cases} \tag{26}$$

Since producing $z(j)$ involves set-up costs, perfect competition is no longer possible; instead, there will be a monopolistically competitive equilibrium. In fact, this section will only investigate the conditions under which growth is possible. Accordingly we focus on allocations that are instantaneously efficient at each time, rather than going through the more involved derivation of equilibrium that can be found in Rodríguez-Clare (1993). Of course we do not assume intertemporal efficiency, since dynamic externalities generally make that goal unattainable in equilibrium.

Another implication of set-up costs is that instantaneous efficiency requires not all varieties of the intermediate good to be made available. Since all varieties require the same technology and enter the production of Z symmetrically, it loses no generality to represent the set of available varieties by the interval $[0, n]$ of the real line. Given that the unit of capital is defined as the amount needed to produce each variety of intermediate good, it follows that n must be equal to K_Z, the quantity of capital used in the intermediate goods sector.

In fact the production functions (25) and (26) imply that there are returns from the division of labor in the production of intermediate goods. To see this note that, because of strict concavity $(0 < \alpha < 1)$ and the symmetric way in which different varieties of z appear in (25), instantaneous efficiency requires all firms producing final goods to use the same quantity of all available varieties. Thus $z(j) = z$ for all $j \le n$. Then (26) implies that $L(j) = z$ for all such j. Hence the total amount of labor devoted to the production of intermediate goods must be $L_Z = nz$. Because $L_Z = L$, it follows that $z(j) = z = L/n$ for all $j \le n$. Thus (25) implies that

$$Z = \left[\int_0^n z^\alpha \, dj \right]^{1/\alpha} = n^{1/\alpha} z = n^{1/\alpha}(L/n) = n^\phi L, \quad \text{where } \phi = (1 - \alpha)/\alpha. \tag{27}$$

Finally then, the production relation (24) can be written as

$$Y = F(K_Y, n^\phi L) = F(K_Y, K_Z^\phi L) \tag{28}$$

which shows how an increase in the measure $n = K_Z$ of varieties available increases the efficiency of labor in producing final goods. This property of the production function in (25) and (26) is commonly referred to as love of variety for inputs. It arises because different inputs are imperfect substitutes for each other. So, if fewer varieties of intermediate goods are made available, then the firm will have to use those that are available more intensively. There is a loss of output due to imperfect substitution.[11]

In the special case when $F(K_Y, Z) = K_Y^\beta Z^{1-\beta}$ it follows from (28) that $Y = K_Y^\beta K_Z^{\phi(1-\beta)} L^{1-\beta}$. Then it is easily shown that instantaneously efficient capital allocation requires $K_Y = K - K_z = \tau K$, where $\tau \equiv \beta/(\beta + \phi(1-\beta))$.[12] In this case the maximum production of Y given K is

$$Y = F(\tau K, [(1-\tau)K]^\phi L). \tag{29}$$

It is obvious that (29) is a special case of the general model described by equation (19). The corresponding micro version of (29) is given by $y = F(\tau k, [(1-\tau)K]^\phi \ell)$, which is a particular form of (17).

V. Feedback Effects on the Cost of Learning or Innovation

A third departure from the neoclassical growth model postulates that a by-product of earlier accumulation is a decrease in the cost of later accumulation. For instance, the higher is the "stock of knowledge", the lower is the cost of accumulating more knowledge. Formally

$$Y = F(K, L, H_Y) \tag{30}$$

$$\dot{K} = G(H_I) h(K), \tag{31}$$

where L is the size of the labor force, H_Y is the amount of human capital devoted to producing output, and H_I is the level of human capital devoted

---

[11] One alternative modelling strategy would be to assume that each firm producing a final good needs different inputs at different times. At any time, a given producer of the final good wants an ideal specialized input; if, however, that input is not available in the market, the firm will buy the "closest" one it finds and transform it, at a cost, into the desired input. The more varieties of the input that are available, the less the firm will have to spend on this transformation and hence the more efficient the firm will be. This alternative model is based on a reinterpretation of Lancaster (1979) proposed by Weitzman (1991).

[12] With a more general production function F, even one that is homothetic, the amount of capital K_Y allocated directly to producing output Y would not be proportional to K, and would also depend on L. Then (19) would need replacing by $Y = F(K, A(K, L)L)$, but with L fixed the difference is trivial. Here we restrict ourselves to the Cobb–Douglas case in order to simplify the exposition.

to the accumulation sector. Of course $H_Y + H_I = H$, where H is the total stock of human capital in the economy. In addition, it is assumed that F and G are both concave CRS production functions, while the function h is increasing. In this formulation, K usually stands for the stock of knowledge. The model has no externalities.

It is clear from (31) that if $h(K)/K$ is bounded away from zero and $G(H_I) > 0$, then

$$\hat{K} = G(H_I) h(K)/K \tag{32}$$

will be positive in the limit as $K \to \infty$. So a positive and constant asymptotic growth rate of K is possible. But notice then how (30) implies that

$$\hat{Y} = \dot{Y}/Y = F_1(K, L, H_Y) \dot{K}/Y = [KF_1(K, L, H_Y)/Y] \hat{K}. \tag{33}$$

So when $\hat{K}$ is positive in the limit, a necessary and sufficient condition for a constant and positive rate of growth of output to be possible is that the ratio $KF_1(K, L, H_Y)/Y$, which represents the "share of knowledge" in the value of output, should be bounded away from zero in the limit as K goes to infinity.

Two important special cases of this model are now discussed.

Expanding Input Variety

Romer (1990) assumes that some firms undertake research with the deliberate intention of "discovering" new varieties of intermediate inputs. But an unintentional consequence of this research is that it becomes easier for other firms to innovate. His model can be expressed by means of the accumulation equation (31) together with the following three equations, whose meaning should be clear from the preceding analysis:

$$Y = L_Y^\beta H_Y^{\delta - \beta} Z^{1 - \delta}, \qquad 0 < \beta < \delta < 1 \tag{34}$$

$$Z = \left[\int_0^\infty z(j)^\alpha \, dj \right]^{1/\alpha}, \qquad 0 < \alpha < 1 \tag{35}$$

$$z(j) = \begin{cases} 0 & \text{if } K(j) < 1 \\ L(j) & \text{if } K(j) \geq 1. \end{cases} \tag{36}$$

Here L and H represent the levels of unskilled and skilled labor respectively. As before, we represent the set of varieties available on the market by the interval $[0, n]$, where now $n = K$ since K is only used to produce intermediate goods. Therefore, K can be interpreted as the measure of both the stock of knowledge and the variety of intermediate goods.

As in the previous section, the production system (34)–(36) exhibits love of variety for inputs. Also as in the derivation of (27) above, it can be seen that instantaneously efficient production here requires $z(j) = z = L_Z/K$ for all $j \le K$. Hence $Z = [\int_0^n (L_Z/K)^\alpha \, dj]^{1/\alpha} = [n(K_Z/K)^\alpha]^{1/\alpha} = K^\phi L_Z$, where ϕ is the constant $(1 - \alpha)/\alpha$. So

$$Y = L_Y^\beta H_Y^{\delta - \beta} (K^\phi L_Z)^{1 - \delta}. \tag{37}$$

Now an efficient allocation of labor requires that $L_Y = \zeta L$, with ζ given by $\beta/(\beta + 1 - \delta)$. The system (34)–(36) can therefore be reduced to a version of (30) given by

$$Y = aK^{\phi(1 - \delta)} L^{\beta + (1 - \delta)} H_Y^{\delta - \beta}, \tag{38}$$

where $a \equiv \zeta^\beta (1 - \zeta)^{1 - \delta}$. This must be supplemented by the accumulation equation (31), of course.

Improving Input Quality

Romer's approach postulates innovation of new capital goods that make production of final goods less costly. In contrast, Grossman and Helpman (1991b,c), together with Aghion and Howitt (1992), have developed "quality ladder" models where innovation improves the quality of existing varieties of capital goods.[13] Since Grossman and Helpman assume that innovation increases the quality of each good by some fixed proportion, in effect they obtain an equation for "knowledge accumulation" similar to (31). This can be seen in the following simple model that captures their main insights.

Output is assumed to be produced with a Cobb–Douglas production function

$$Y = D^\beta L_Y^{1 - \beta}, \qquad 0 < \beta < 1 \tag{39}$$

that uses labor L_Y and a composite input D. The latter is "assembled" from a continuum of varieties of inputs according to the function

$$D = \exp \int_0^1 \ln[\lambda^{m(j)} x(j)] \, dj = K \exp \int_0^1 \ln[x(j)] \, dj \tag{40}$$

where K is the stock of knowledge, which is given by

---

[13] In Aghion and Howitt, technical progress improves the quality of intermediate goods. Together with Segerstrom, Anant and Dinopoulos (1990) and Segerstrom (1991), they emphasize the links between endogenous innovation and Schumpeter's process of "creative destruction". Most of Grossman and Helpman's work postulates upgrading the qualities of consumer goods. Such formulations are formally equivalent to ours because what matters in the end is the efficiency of capital goods in producing Gorman-Lancaster consumption characteristics. The capital goods formulation is more natural for our discussion, since we have been emphasising intertemporal production possibilities throughout.

$$K = \exp \int_0^1 \ln[\lambda^{m(j)}]\, dj = \lambda \exp \int_0^1 m(j)\, dj. \tag{41}$$

In these last two equations λ represents the proportional quality improvement that each innovation brings to input variety j, while $m(j)$ measures the number of innovations that have happened to input variety j. Hence $\lambda^{m(j)}$ represents the quality of input variety j, measured as usual in efficiency units per physical unit.

Each input $x(j)$ is produced from labor according to the simple production function $x(j) = L(j)$, where $x(j)$ and $L(j)$ should be interpreted as output and input density functions on the interval $[0, 1]$. As before, (40) implies that it is instantaneously efficient to spread labor evenly across the different varieties. Thus $x(j) = x = L(j) = L_X$ for all j in $[0, 1]$. Then (39) and (40) imply that

$$D = KL_X \quad \text{and} \quad Y = (KL_X)^\beta L_Y^{1-\beta}. \tag{42}$$

Instantaneous efficiency then requires that labor be distributed between sectors in constant proportions, with $L_X = \beta L$ and $L_Y = (1-\beta)L$. It follows that

$$Y = bK^\beta L, \qquad \text{where } b \equiv \beta^\beta (1-\beta)^{1-\beta}. \tag{43}$$

In the research sector, human capital is used to generate innovations to the different varieties of the input x. The innovation process is random, and described by a particular Poisson process. Putting $H(j)$ units of human capital into research on variety j for a small time interval of length dt produces a quality upgrade with marginal probability $aH(j)\, dt$, where a is some positive constant. This quality upgrade increases $m(j)$ to $m(j) + 1$.[14] Because the different varieties of the input x enter (40) and (41) symmetrically, and because quality improvements are all proportional, it is instantaneously efficient to spread human capital evenly across varieties. Thus $H(j) = H$ for all j. From (34) and the properties of the Poisson distribution, see Grossman and Helpman (1991a, p. 97), it can then be shown that the stock of knowledge grows according to

$$\dot{K} = aHK. \tag{44}$$

Summary

Recapitulating, we see that all three models (30)–(31), (31) with (34)–(36), and (43)–(44) basically amount to one common specification of tech-

---

[14] The more mathematically inclined reader may realize that there is a technical difficulty here, because a continuum of independent random variables produces non-measurable outcomes in a way that makes the integrals in (40) and (41) almost surely ill-defined. There are technical remedies, however, the easiest of which involves abandoning strict stochastic independence so as to make these formulae still applicable.

nology. This requires final goods to be produced according to (30), where K represents the "stock of knowledge", which grows according to the equation $\dot{K} = G(H_I)h(K)$, as in (31) above.

VI. Endogenizing the Growth Rate

A More General Growth Model

This section attempts to integrate into one single model the three types of growth models explored in Sections III–V above. Moreover, Section VII below will use the general analysis of this section in order to interpret earlier results on particular determinants of growth such as trade, finance, fiscal policy, social norms, etc.

The more general model we are about to present still uses very special functional forms, even though Hahn (1992) and others have rightly seen these as a serious limitation of most endogenous growth theory. However, what really matters for long-run growth is the asymptotic behaviour of the model as the economy becomes large. So it would actually be possible to reach similar conclusions after replacing the specific global functional forms we use with more general functions, while concentrating on their asymptotic elasticities and marginal products, etc. Such techniques are illustrated by the careful work of Brock and Gale (1969) and McFadden (1973) on the existence of optimal growth paths.

In our general model, but with specific functional forms, ℓ_Y is the amount and $u\,(=\ell_Y/\ell)$ is the proportion of labor which each agent devotes to production of final output (as opposed to education). Each agent's output y is assumed to depend on own physical capital k, own knowledge h, and efficiency units of labor $E\ell_Y$, where E is the common level of efficiency for all producers. As in Section IV, labor has its efficiency enhanced by aggregate capital accumulation according to the equation

$$E = K^\phi, \qquad \phi > 0. \tag{45}$$

Here it is important to recall that ϕ can be greater than one.

Each agent's concave production function is assumed to have a constant elasticity of substitution among factors that is greater than one. Thus

$$y = F(k, h, E\ell_Y) = A[\beta k^\alpha + \delta h^\alpha + (1 - \beta - \delta)(K^\phi u\ell)^\alpha]^{1/\alpha}, \tag{46}$$

where α, β, $\delta \in [0, 1]$ with $0 < \alpha < 1$. Later, we shall also consider the Cobb–Douglas case when $\alpha \to 0$, and so $y = Ak^\beta h^\delta (K^\phi u\ell)^{1-\beta-\delta}$ with elasticity of substitution equal to one.

Output can either be consumed or invested to accumulate capital, so $y = c + \dot{k}$. Also, apart from being used to produce output, labor can also be allocated to each agent's own research sector, where it increases the stock of knowledge according to the equation

$$\dot{h} = \xi(\ell - \ell_Y)h^\gamma = \xi(1-u)\ell h^\gamma, \quad \xi > 0, \quad \gamma \in [0, 1]. \tag{47}$$

As in the particular models of Section V, a higher aggregate stock of knowledge makes research less costly. If one interprets h as the stock of human capital instead of knowledge, and $(1-u)\ell$ as the quantity of labor allocated to education, this formulation also captures the most important aspects of models in which skill acquisition is the engine of growth.

Compared to the neoclassical growth model, (46) and (47) incorporate all three departures that were considered in Sections III to V. For example: if $\alpha > 0$, then none of the factors is essential for production; if $\phi > 0$, then the productivity of labor in the Y sector increases as a by-product of capital accumulation; while if $\gamma > 0$, then the productivity of labor in research increases as a by-product of previous research. If the three parameters α, ϕ, and γ were zero, however, the corresponding features would revert to those in the neoclassical model of Section II.

Endogenous Growth

In order to determine the growth rate, this section also introduces, for the first time in this paper, an explicit intertemporal utility function. The continuum of identical and infinitely lived representative agents each maximize a utility integral over time by choosing independently how much income to save at all times, as well as what proportion u of labor time to devote to producing output. This kind of assumption has become standard in endogenous growth theory. It allows the equilibrium growth rate to be determined as a function of more fundamental demand side parameters, especially the discount rate and the degree of aversion to changes in consumption.

Let $\varepsilon \geq 0$ denote each representative agent's constant rate of relative fluctuation aversion (cf. the usual measure of relative risk aversion), and $\rho > 0$ the common instantaneous discount rate. Then each agent wants to maximize the intertemporal utility integral

$$U = \int_0^\infty e^{-\rho t}v(c)\,dt, \text{ where } v(c) = (1-\varepsilon)^{-1}c^{1-\varepsilon}, \varepsilon > 0, \varepsilon \neq 1. \tag{48}$$

The special case $\varepsilon = 1$, in which the instantaneous utility function $v(c)$ reduces to $\ln c$, has received much attention in the recent literature.

Since E in (45) and (46) represents an externality, each agent does not take into account how this will be affected by private actions: instead, the time path $K(t)$ of aggregate capital is taken as given. Therefore, each agent faces the same optimal control problem whose present value Hamiltonian

$v(c) + r\dot{k} + q\dot{h}$ can be epxressed as

$$(1 - \varepsilon)^{-1}c^{1-\varepsilon} + r\{A[\beta k^a + \delta h^a + (1 - \beta - \delta)(K^\phi u\ell)^a]^{1/a} - c\}$$
$$+ q\xi(1 - u)\ell h^\gamma. \tag{49}$$

Here r and q are the co-state variables of k and h, respectively. Thus r is the shadow price of capital, while q is that of knowledge. As in Romer (1986) and Lucas (1988), an equilibrium can now be characterized by holding fixed the aggregate capital stock K in the usual conditions for this optimization problem, and then imposing the condition that $K = k$ because all agents make the same choices in equilibrium. Necessary conditions for an equilibrium are that

$$c^{-\varepsilon} = r \tag{50}$$

$$rA^a(1 - \beta - \delta)(K^\phi\ell)^a u^{a-1}y^{1-a} = q\xi\ell h^\gamma \tag{51}$$

and also

$$\dot{r} = \rho r - rA^a\beta k^{a-1}y^{1-a} \tag{52}$$

$$\dot{q} = \rho q - rA^a\delta h^{a-1}y^{1-a} - q\xi(1 - u)\ell\gamma h^{\gamma-1}, \tag{53}$$

where y is given by (46). Here, of course, (50) and (51) are the first order conditions for maximizing the Hamiltonian with respect to c and u respectively, while (52) and (53) are the co-state equations for K and h respectively.[15] Because (49) is concave in the current choice variables c and u, equations (50) and (51) are sufficient for an appropriate global maximum at each instant of time. Sufficient conditions for intertemporal optimality are more subtle because the awkward last term $(1 - u)\ell h^\gamma$ in (49) creates a non-concavity. However, it follows from the results of Seierstad and Sydsæter (1977) that the path derived will be optimal provided that: (a) the maximized Hamiltonian is concave in the two state variables k and h; (b) the standard transversality condition

$$e^{-\rho t}(rk + qh) \to 0 \text{ as } t \to \infty \tag{54}$$

is also satisfied. Unfortunately condition (a) in particular seems quite hard to verify in this model, except in special cases.

Recall the general notation $\hat{x}$ for the growth rate of any variable x. Then (50) implies that

$$\hat{c} = -\hat{r}/\varepsilon. \tag{55}$$

---

[15] It should be pointed out that really (51) is necessary only for an interior equilibrium, with $0 < u < 1$. But we shall be more concerned with (51) as one of a set of sufficient conditions.

Some manipulation of (52) together with (46) and the equilibrium condition $K = k$ gives

$$\hat{r} = \rho - A\beta[\beta + \delta(h/k)^\alpha + (1 - \beta - \delta)(k^{\phi-1}u\ell)^\alpha]^{(1-\alpha)/\alpha}. \tag{56}$$

Equation (55) implies that for steady growth with $\hat{c}$ constant, the r.h.s. of (56) must be constant. It is then obvious that there can never be balanced growth in this model, since no constant growth rate of h and k leaves this expression constant.

First Case: $\alpha > 0$ and $\gamma < 1$

In this case, the growth rate of h necessarily tends to zero because $\gamma < 1$. In the long run agents may as well choose $u = 1$. Then, if there is sustained growth of output, the economy necessarily approaches an asymptotic state in which c, y and k all grow at the same constant proportional rate g while h/k approaches zero. Moreover, as long as $-\rho + \hat{r} + g < 0$ so that the transversality condition $e^{-\rho t}rk \to 0$ as $t \to \infty$ is satisfied, the sufficient conditions for optimality described above will be met by any path satisfying (50)–(53): the awkward last term of (49) becomes zero.

In the subcase when $\phi < 1$ also, the term k^ϕ becomes relatively insignificant in the limit, and so we are essentially left with the "AK model" of Section III. Then (55) and (56) imply that as $k \to \infty$, so $\hat{r}$ tends to $\rho - A\beta^{1/\alpha}$ and $\hat{c} \to g$, where

$$g \equiv (A\beta^{1/\alpha} - \rho)/\varepsilon. \tag{57}$$

The transversality condition requiring that $-\rho + \hat{r} + g < 0$ is also satisfied asymptotically in case $g < \rho - \hat{r} = A\beta^{1/\alpha}$. This requires that $A\beta^{1/\alpha} - \rho < \varepsilon A\beta^{1/\alpha}$ and so $\rho > (1 - \varepsilon)A\beta^{1/\alpha}$. Hence, when ϕ and γ are both strictly less than one, sustained consumption growth at rate $g > 0$ occurs on a guaranteed optimal path if and only if $A\beta^{1/\alpha} > \rho > (1 - \varepsilon)A\beta^{1/\alpha}$. Of course, when $\varepsilon \geq 1$ it is sufficient that $A\beta^{1/\alpha} > \rho > 0$, a condition similar in spirit to that derived by Jones and Manuelli (1990). This says that equilibrium consumption grows if and only if the marginal product of physical capital remains above the discount rate as the capital stock goes to infinity. On the other hand, if $0 < A\beta^{1/\alpha} \leq \rho$, then the rate of discount is so high that equilibrium consumption will not grow, even though such growth is feasible. But when $\rho \leq (1 - \varepsilon)A\beta^{1/\alpha}$, the transversality condition (54) is violated, and the utility integral diverges on the asymptotic growth path. Then it is likely that no equilibrium exists because it is not optimal for any agent to follow the path whose asymptotic properties we have characterized given that all other agents follow the same path.

A knife-edge subcase occurs when $\gamma < 1$ and $\phi = 1$. The analysis is very similar to that in the previous paragraph, with the difference that the asymptotic growth rate becomes

$$g = (A^* - \rho)/\varepsilon, \text{ where } A^* \equiv A\beta[\beta + (1 - \beta - \delta)\ell^a]^{(1-a)/a}. \tag{58}$$

Furthermore, the revised condition for existence of a growth equilibrium is $A^* > \rho > (1 - \varepsilon)A^*$.

The last subcase to be considered is when $\gamma < 1$ and $\phi > 1$. Provided that $k \to \infty$ as $t \to \infty$, (55) and (56) imply that $\hat{r} \to -\infty$ and so $\hat{c} \to \infty$. Then (46) and the equilibrium condition $K = k$ together imply that $\hat{y} = \phi\hat{k}$. Therefore any equilibrium path must have all the growth rates $\hat{y}$, $\hat{k}$ and $\hat{c}$ converging to infinity as $t \to \infty$. Perpetual increasing returns lead to ever accelerating growth. As long as $a > 0$ there is no (finite) asymptotic growth rate to determine in this case. Indeed, as Solow (1993) has observed in a very similar connection, there is even the possibility that output, consumption, and capital could all become infinitely large in a finite time.

Second Case: $a \to 0$

Since our aim is to determine steady-state growth rates, we now restrict our analysis even further to the special case in which the production function is Cobb–Douglas. The equilibrium conditions (50)–(53) then need to be expressed in their limiting forms as $a \to 0$, which we denote by (50′)–(53′). Imposing the equilibrium condition $K = k$ on (52′) gives

$$\hat{r} = \rho - \beta yk = \rho - A\beta k^{-\Psi} h^\delta (u\ell)^{1-\beta-\delta}, \tag{59}$$

where $\Psi \equiv 1 - (1 - \beta - \delta)\phi - \beta = (1 - \beta)(1 - \phi) + \delta\phi$. Because of (55), steady growth of consumption at rate $g = \hat{c} = -\hat{r}/\varepsilon$ requires

$$\Psi \hat{k} = \delta \hat{h}. \tag{60}$$

To avoid rather perverse cases in which one of the variables h and k is required to shrink while the other expands, analysis will be restricted to the case when $\Psi \geq 0$ because $\phi \leq (1 - \beta)/(1 - \beta - \delta)$.

The first subcase is when $\phi = (1 - \beta)/(1 - \beta - \delta)$ and so $\Psi = 0$. Then a steady state requires h to be constant and so (47) implies that $u = 1$. When $\gamma \geq 1$ steady state growth is impossible, since it would not be an equilibrium to have $u = 1$. So we consider what happens when $\gamma < 1$.

Because $u = 1$ and $\Psi = 0$, it follows from (46) and the condition $K = k$ that $y = Akh^\delta \ell^{1-\beta-\delta}$. So a steady state evidently requires growth at rate $g = \hat{c} = \hat{y} = -\hat{r}/\varepsilon$. In addition, when $a \to 0$, (51′) becomes

$$r(1 - \beta - \delta)y = q\xi u\ell h^\gamma. \tag{61}$$

Taking the growth rates of all the variables in this equation when $u = 1$ and h is constant implies that $\hat{q} = \hat{r} + \hat{y} = g(1 - \varepsilon)$. Since equation (53′) gives

$\hat{q} = \rho - r\delta y/qh$ when $u = 1$, it follows that

$$(1 - \varepsilon)g = \rho - r\delta y/qh. \tag{62}$$

Eliminating the ratio ry/qh from equations (61) and (62) then gives

$$(1 - \varepsilon)g = \rho - \frac{\delta \xi \ell h^{\gamma - 1}}{1 - \beta - \delta}, \tag{63}$$

when $u = 1$. Imposing the conditions $g = -\hat{r}/\varepsilon$, $\Psi = 0$ and $u = 1$ on equation (59) then gives

$$-\varepsilon g = \rho - A\beta h^\delta \ell^{1 - \beta - \delta}. \tag{64}$$

Here (63) and (64) are two simultaneous equations in g and in h^*, the asymptotic stationary level of h. By subtracting (64) from (63) it is easy to see that

$$g = A\beta h^\delta \ell^{1 - \beta - \delta} - \frac{\delta \xi \ell h^{\gamma - 1}}{1 - \beta - \delta} \tag{65}$$

but in the general case there is no analytical solution for h^*. In the special case when $\varepsilon = 1$, however, (63) implies that, for $\gamma < 1$, the stationary value of h is

$$h^* \equiv [\delta \xi \ell / \rho (1 - \beta - \delta)]^{1/(1 - \gamma)} \tag{66}$$

and then (64) determines the steady state growth rate as

$$g = A\beta (h^*)^\delta \ell^{1 - \beta - \delta} - \rho. \tag{67}$$

Finally, when $\varepsilon = 1$, it is easy to check that the transversality condition (54) is satisfied provided that $\rho > 0$.

The second subcase is when $\phi < (1 - \beta)/(1 - \beta - \delta)$ and so $\Psi > 0$. Then (60) implies that $\hat{h}$ must be positive if the economy is growing. So $\gamma < 1$ would make long-run growth impossible. In the case $\gamma = 1$, however, we look for balanced growth at a rate satisfying $g = \hat{c} = \hat{y} = \hat{k} = \delta \hat{h}/\Psi = -\hat{r}/\varepsilon$ (where the last two equations follow from (47) and (60)), and with u constant. Then using (47), (59) and (60) yields

$$\hat{r} = -\varepsilon g = -\varepsilon (\delta/\Psi) \xi (1 - u)\ell, \text{ and so } g = (\delta/\Psi) \xi (1 - u)\ell$$

$$\text{while } \xi u \ell = \xi \ell - \Psi g/\delta. \tag{68}$$

Moreover, (53') together with (51') (or (61) with $\gamma = 1$) implies that

$$\hat{q} = \rho - \xi (1 - u)\ell - r\delta y/qh = \rho - \xi (1 - u)\ell - \xi u \ell \delta/(1 - \beta - \delta). \tag{69}$$

Next, differentiating (51') or (61) with $\gamma = 1$ and u constant gives $\hat{r} + \hat{y} = \hat{q} + \hat{h}$ and so

$$(1-\varepsilon)g = \hat{q} + \Psi g/\delta = \hat{q} + \xi(1-u)\ell = \rho - \frac{\xi u \ell \delta}{1-\beta-\delta} = \rho - \frac{\xi \ell \delta - \Psi g}{1-\beta-\delta}. \quad (70)$$

Solving (70) for g gives the result that

$$g = \frac{(1-\beta-\delta)\rho - \xi \ell \delta}{(1-\varepsilon)(1-\beta-\delta) - \Psi} = \frac{\xi \ell \delta - (1-\beta'-\delta)\rho}{(1-\beta-\delta)(\varepsilon-\phi)+\delta}, \quad (71)$$

where the second equality was derived using the definition of Ψ. This solution is valid, and gives a positive growth rate, in case both numerator and denominator are positive, which they could be even if $\phi > 1$.

Finally, the transversality condition (54) is satisfied provided that $-\rho + \hat{r} + \hat{k}$ and $-\rho + \hat{q} + \hat{h}$ are both negative. It is routine to check that the second of these conditions is automatically satisfied because $u > 0$, while the first is also satisfied in case

$$\rho > \frac{(1-\varepsilon)\xi \ell \delta}{(1-\beta-\delta)(1-\phi)+\delta}. \quad (72)$$

Summary of Results

The most important clear cut results of this section are as follows:

Case (i) $\gamma < 1$, $\phi < 1$, $\alpha > 0$: In this case there is no equilibrium with long-run growth when $A\beta^{1/\alpha} \leq \rho$ or when $\rho \leq (1-\varepsilon)A\beta^{1/\alpha}$. But when $A\beta^{1/\alpha} > \rho > (1-\varepsilon)A\beta^{1/\alpha}$, the growth rate converges in the limit to $(A\beta^{1/\alpha} - \rho)/\varepsilon > 0$. This case corresponds to a model like those of Jones and Manuelli (1990) or Rebelo (1991) in which capital accumulation by itself generates long-run growth; that is, a neoclassical growth model without the upper Inada condition.

Case (ii) $\gamma < 1$, $\phi = (1-\beta)/(1-\beta-\delta)$, $\varepsilon = 1$ *and* $\alpha \to 0$: Here the steady state growth rate is

$$g = A\beta[\xi \delta \ell / \rho(1-\beta-\delta)]^{\delta/(1-\gamma)} \ell^{1-\beta-\delta} - \rho \quad (73)$$

provided that $\rho > 0$. In this case accumulation of h eventually stops, and the long-run engine of growth is a balance of capital accumulation with learning by doing; this is what makes ϕ equal to $(1-\beta)/(1-\beta-\delta)$. This case is formally equivalent to Romer (1986).

Case (iii) $\gamma = 1$, $\phi < (1-\beta)/(1-\beta-\delta)$ and $\alpha \to 0$: Here the steady state growth rate is

$$g = \frac{\delta \xi \ell - (1-\beta-\delta)\rho}{\delta + (\varepsilon-\phi)(1-\beta-\delta)} \quad (74)$$

provided that (72) is satisfied. In this case capital accumulation is only possible in the long run because h grows, and this is the true engine of growth.

In all three cases, when there is a steadily growing equilibrium, the long-run growth rate of consumption is decreasing in the discount rate, as is hardly surprising. Other parameters affect growth differently for the different cases. In cases (i) and (ii) capital accumulation is the engine of growth, and so it is intuitively reasonable that growth should be increasing in A. In cases (ii) and (iii), however, growth is increasing in both the size of the economy, as measured by each agent's stock of the fixed factor ℓ, and productivity of labor in education, as measured by ξ. This happens for different reasons in the two cases.

In case (ii), where capital accumulation combined with learning by doing is the engine of growth, a higher ℓ affects growth by increasing the steady state value h^* of h, as indicated by (66). In turn, this occurs because a higher ℓ increases the marginal product of h, and hence in equilibrium more resources will be devoted to increasing h. A similar argument explains why and how ξ affects the growth rate in case (ii).

On the other hand, in case (iii), human capital accumulation is the engine of growth. In this case either a higher ℓ or a higher ξ affect the growth rate through a simpler mechanism: for each given $1 - u$, they both increase the growth rate of h. Finally, note that in case (iii) growth is increasing in the externalities from physical capital accumulation (ϕ) and, except possibly in rare cases when $\varepsilon < \phi$, is decreasing in the share $1 - \beta - \delta$ of E in final output. The explanation for this last result is that a higher share of E in final output causes a reallocation of labor from this sector to the education sector, thus decreasing the rate of growth of h.

VII. Fundamental Determinants of the Rate of Growth

The previous section showed how the long-run growth rate is determined by such parameters as the discount rate (ρ), the productivity of resources in production (A), the size of the economy (L), the intensity with which fixed resources are used in production ($1 - \beta - \delta$), the productivity of the research sector (ξ), as well as the strength of externalities in production (ϕ) and in research (γ). Indeed, we have come a long way from the standard neoclassical growth model, where all these factors could have at most level effects.

The fundamental determinants of the rate of growth have not yet been properly considered, however, since it can be argued that many of these parameters are really determined endogenously by more fundamental variables like fiscal, trade and financial policy, the efficiency of the financial system, demographic variables and social norms. This section reviews some of the literature that has attempted to open up these black boxes. Wherever possible, these ideas will be linked to the general growth model of the previous section.

Trade and Growth

Here the topic that has received most attention concerns how growth is affected by trade through its impact on the allocation of resources across sectors. Lucas (1988) captures this in a simple model in which growth arises from learning by doing. He postulates a fixed quantity of labor L, which the economy allocates between the production of two goods z_1 and z_2. Producing one unit of good z_i requires q_i units of labor. Because of learning by doing in each sector, $dq_i/dt = -v_i L_i q_i$, where L_i is the quantity of labor allocated to the production of good i and v_i is a positive parameter that measures the rate of learning by doing in sector i. Suppose that $v_1 > v_2$. In this case, equilibrium in a closed economy involves a growth rate of output at an intermediate rate between v_i and v_2. If the economy is too small to affect international prices, then as it opens up to international trade, preferences in the economy no longer matter for the allocation of labor in equilibrium. Indeed, the economy will specialize in the good for which it has a static comparative advantage. If for some reason the comparative advantage of the economy is initially in good 2, the growth rate will decrease to v_2. If the comparative advantage is in good 1 instead, the growth rate will increase to v_1. In terms of the model developed in Section VI, this is similar in spirit to having trade affect the learning-by-doing parameter ϕ. Young (1991) develops a more detailed and complete model along these lines.

In Grossman and Helpman (1991a, Ch. 6), trade affects growth through a similar mechanism. Growth arises because new varieties of non-tradable intermediate goods are introduced, then used to produce two final goods. Innovation uses human capital intensively, and so does one of the final goods. If the economy has a static comparative advantage in the human capital-intensive good, then as the economy opens up to international trade, human capital will flow from the innovation sector to the production of this final good, thereby lowering the rate of growth. Of course, if the comparative advantage is in the good that uses human capital with low intensity, the growth rate will increase as the economy opens up to international trade. In terms of our model of Section VI, trade affects growth by altering the share $(1 - \beta - \delta)$ of labor in the production of final goods.

A different effect of trade on growth is analysed by Stokey (1991). She considers a model in which growth arises from investment in education, which allows workers to produce more sophisticated (i.e., valuable) goods. Opening the economy up to international trade changes the relative prices of different goods, thus also changing the incentives for education. For instance, suppose the economy starts with a relatively low human capital stock. Then international trade will cause the prices of more sophisticated goods to drop relative to those of simpler goods for this economy, thus lowering both the incentives to become educated and the growth rate. The relation between this result and the analysis of Section VI is harder to explain. However, the effect of trade on growth in this model is like the effect of a change in the share of human capital in the production of final goods (δ): that is, it affects the returns to human capital accumulation.

A different link between trade and growth is analysed by Grossman and Helpman (1991a, Chs. 7 and 8) and by Rivera-Batiz and Romer (1991). The latter show that in a model similar to (39)–(44) in Section V where innovation is the engine of growth, integrating two identical economies into one single market unambiguously increases the growth rate, since it increases the returns to innovation. This happens for the same reason that an increase in L increases the growth rate in case (iii) of Section VI. If integration involves only trade, however, with no free flow of ideas, the authors show that it does not affect growth. But if innovation uses intermediate goods, then trade would increase the rate of growth because love of variety for inputs makes innovation less costly. This is analogous to a fall in ξ in the model of Section VI. Grossman and Helpman also derive more general results along similar lines for the case in which the two economies are not identical.

Financial Intermediation and Growth

A strong consensus among economists is that countries with healthier financial systems generally grow faster. Yet the model developed in Section VI has identical representative agents and must therefore lack individual uncertainty. This makes it impossible for financial intermediation to play any role in the growth process. Some recent papers nevertheless do analyse this phenomenon through growth models in which capital accumulation is the sole engine of growth. In terms of our growth model of Section VI, all these models have the result that a more developed financial sector increases the value of the parameter A in (43). This is like output augmenting technical change, which leads to a higher growth rate as in cases (i) and (ii).

The financial system is given two main roles in these models. First, it encourages agents to invest a higher proportion of their wealth in more productive but riskier assets, as it reduces the need to keep wealth in liquid assets. This has been formalized recently by Bencivenga and Smith (1992), who allow agents to invest their wealth in two types of project: one with a high return and low liquidity; and another with a low return and high liquidity. In addition, agents face the possibility that in future they may need wealth in liquid form to meet an emergency. The authors show that, compared to a situation in which agents must finance their own projects, a better financial system allows more resources to be devoted to the high return investment, since it can meet the liquidity needs of agents without forcing them to invest in the low return projects.[16]

The other main role of financial intermediation is to allow agents with funds they do not need immediately to lend to other agents who have more pressing needs. It is crucial in modelling this role that there be lumpiness in project size and/or constraints on the maximum project size that an entrepreneur can manage. For otherwise investors could just invest all their own wealth without any need for borrowing and lending. Financir intermediation of this type introduces problems of asymmetric inforr ,-tion, so that agents who borrow may not behave in a socially optimal ay. For instance, as analysed by Aghion and Bolton (1991), agents who borrow will not devote as much effort to increasing the probab'ity of success of the project. This makes wealth distribution matter for financial intermediation and growth. Note that this also has implications for the pattern of income inequality as the economy develops: the distribution of wealth at time t is a function of the distribution at time $t-1$. The authors discuss possible limits to this distribution.[17]

Demographics, Education and Growth

The Uzawa–Lucas model of growth was reviewed in Section III, and is similar to case (iii) of Section VI. It involves human capital being effectively transferred from generation to generation. Individuals spend the early part of their life acquiring skill, a process that is easier for individuals with well educated parents.[18] These models include a dynastic intertemporal utility function with discounting at the same rate over the lifetime of each (apparently single) parent as over that of each descendant.

---

[16] Another model along these lines is presented in Saint-Paul (1992). Also, Greenwood and Jovanovic (1990) develop a model in which the financial system increases the average productivity of investment and the growth rate, while growth reinforces the development of the financial system.

[17] Banerjee and Newman (1991) consider a related model. See Pagano (1992) and Stiglitz (1992) for more extensive analyses of the relationship between finance and growth.

[18] A similar but richer model appears in Stokey (1991), with the difference that a higher "social" level of human capital makes it easier for individuals to build their own human capital.

Becker, Murphy and Tamura (1990) and Ehrlich and Lui (1992) extend these growth models to study the intergenerational process of growth in more detail. In Becker *et al.*, parents are altruistic and care about both the number of children they have and their education. Ehrlich and Lui assume that parents have children in order to receive care in their old age; the amount of care they get depends positively on the number of children and their education. In both these models better educated parents find it easier to educate their children. This leads them to opt for more education and fewer children. Therefore, as the economy grows and the average education increases, parents devote more time to education and less to bringing up many children. In turn, this reinforces the growth process. An interesting result derived by Ehrlich and Lui is that as the probability of children reaching maturity increases, parents invest more in education and so growth increases. On the other hand, when the probability of mature agents reaching old age increases, the effect on growth is ambiguous. In terms of our model in Section VI, this work shows how the discount rate and hence the incentives to invest time in education depend on more fundamental demographic parameters.

Fiscal Policy and Growth

The effect of exogenous fiscal policy on the actual growth rate of an economy depends on how revenues are raised and on how the government spends those revenues. When the engine of growth is capital accumulation, and provided that the substitution effect dominates the income effect, income taxes that include taxation of interest income decrease incentives to accumulate capital, since owners can only obtain a fraction of the benefits — see Jones and Manuelli (1990) and Rebelo (1991). Such income taxes therefore have effects identical to those of lowering A in cases (i) and (ii) of the growth model in Section VI. This differs drastically from the case where the engine of growth is human capital accumulation, as in case (iii) of Section VI where taxes on consumption expenditures and on investment in physical capital have no effect on the growth rate. For again the effect of a proportional tax on consumption and physical investment is identical to a decrease in A, which in case (iii) of Section VI has no effect on the growth rate.

On the other hand, as Barro (1990) argues, government expenditures in services that enhance productivity in the private sector will increase the growth rate. However, if revenues are used to finance government services that have no effect on productivity, or if they are wasted by bureaucrats, then growth of consumption will decrease. Of course, if the government services are desired by consumers, the implications for welfare remain ambiguous.

Social Norms, Politics and Income Inequality

Many other organizations and institutions besides the market can affect growth. Perhaps most research has been devoted to understanding the effect of governments, whose powers may be used for income redistribution and abused by rent-seekers. In contrast to the previous subsection, the models we review here endogenize government policy decisions such as those affecting taxation.

Murphy, Shleifer and Vishny (1991) consider how the most talented people in society choose between becoming entrepreneurs, or rent-seekers whose activities reduce growth. It is shown that in making this choice, the most talented individuals in society will consider the size of the market in both activities, the size of the firm they can manage, and the type of contracts that can be enforced. In general, the smaller the market for goods (say, because of poor infrastructure), or the smaller the size of the firm that can be effectively managed (say, because the capital market is underdeveloped), or the less that entrepreneurs can appropriate from the surplus they generate (say, because of unclear property rights and/or lack of patent protection), the more likely are the most talented individuals to become rent-seekers who lower the growth rate.

The government may also be used as an agency for income redistribution. Alesina and Rodrik (1991) and Persson and Tabellini (1991) both consider democracies in which fiscal policy that affects growth is decided by voting. The growth engine of Alesina and Rodrik's model is similar to Barro's (1990). In Persson and Tabellini's paper, however, growth is driven by the accumulation of knowledge in an economy where individuals have different abilities. Also, their fiscal policy involves only income redistribution. Both papers reproduce the traditional result that, when the distribution of income is skewed to the right, implying that the median of the distribution is smaller than the average, then there is more taxation or more income redistribution. The new feature is that this leads to a lower growth rate rather than just to a lower level of aggregate income.

Perotti (1992) explores a more complex link between income distribution and growth. Growth results from accumulating human capital, but in his model some individuals cannot afford the fixed cost of acquiring education. Nor are loans available to finance investment in education. When the economy is poor, fiscal policy that makes the distribution of income more unequal may increase growth, as a bigger proportion of the population can then afford education. However, when the economy is rich, increasing growth requires making the distribution of income more equal, since this decreases the proportion of the population who cannot afford education.

In all the models reviewed so far, growth arises because agents desire to increase future consumption either for themselves or for their descendants. However, in reality people care about things other than market goods, like being able to marry well. Usually such goods cannot be bought in the market, but are acquired "through status". Cole, Mailath and Postlewaite (1991) develop an interesting model in which people may save in part to acquire the status that will lead themselves or their children to enjoy more valuable non-market goods. The authors show that if social norms base status on wealth, growth is higher than if social norms make status independent of wealth. Of course, an alternative model based on Veblen's notion of conspicuous consumption is likely to have lower growth.

VIII. Conclusion

To evaluate the importance of the new endogenous growth theory, we must first recognize that there is long-run growth in the real world. For instance, according to Maddison (1982) the average growth rate of income per capita in the United States between 1890 and 1970 was 2.3 per cent per year. Solow (1957) showed how only an eighth of this growth (up to the time when he wrote) could be explained by increases in the capital–labor ratio due to capital accumulation; the rest was the famous Solow residual.[19] Following Solow, this residual can be explained as the result of continual technology shocks, each of which increases the level of steady state income per capita. The observed growth rate is then no more than the result of continuous adjustment of the system to these exogenous shocks. It seems much more fruitful, however, to *explain* how these technological shocks arise: this is what endogenous growth theory has attempted to do. In a sense, the word "endogenous" is even redundant: for if growth is not endogenous, then really there is no growth *theory*, but only a sophisticated accounting system. Note that some earlier growth theories, such as Arrow's learning by doing model or Shell's (1967, 1974) model of publicly financed technological growth, are endogenous in this sense.[20]

This paper has concentrated on the *theory* of growth, to the virtual exclusion of its empirical side. So it would be rash to "summarize" what the new growth theory teaches us about real economies. However, there is one theoretical point general enough to deserve emphasis. This is that a common feature of many growth models is their reliance on positive externalities in one form or another. This is important, because it implies

---

[19] This estimate has since come under repeated critical scrutiny. Some of the most recent re-estimates are presented and discussed in Boskin and Lau (1992).

[20] For another early model of endogenous technical progress, see Conlisk (1969).

that growth rates will in general be lower than optimal and that there is a role for good government to play in encouraging appropriate growth. It also marks a clear, if minor, departure from the heavy use macroeconomists have been making of optimal growth models.

A final remark is in order. There is an important sense in which almost none of these recent results are really new: it was already well known that trade, finance, fiscal policy, income inequality and social norms could affect macroeconomic performance. Before the appearance of endogenous growth models, however, these variables would generally have only level effects, which would show up in growth rates only during the adjustment phase. Of course, as Atkinson (1969) and others pointed out, this adjustment phase could easily last for rather a long time, even several generations. Nevertheless, the main contribution of the new literature is that it explains how these same variables can also affect the long-run rate of growth. Although modest in fundamentally new insights, this is still an important contribution. For instance, since we are unable to measure welfare effects with sufficient precision, it is probably better to limit taxes to those that depart from the always unattainable first best further in their short-run than in their long-run effects. In particular, we should try to avoid destroying the incentives for agents to promote long-run growth. Furthermore, we should be emphasizing the long-run growth benefits of supply side policies such as freer international trade and market integration, while readily conceding the possible short-run damage to those who work in or own parts of uncompetitive industries, and the general desirability of arranging some short-run compensation for those who do suffer short-run damage.

References

Aghion, P. & Bolton, P.: A trickle-down theory of growth and development with debt overhang. Mimeo, Nuffield College, Oxford and London School of Economics, 1991.

Aghion, P. & Howitt, P.: A model of growth through creative destruction. *Econometrica 60*, 323–51, 1992.

Alesina, A. & Rodrik, D.: Distributive politics and economic growth. NBER WP 3668, 1991.

Arrow, K. J.: The economic implications of learning by doing. *Review of Economic Studies 39*, 155–73, 1962; reprinted in *Collected Papers of Kenneth J. Arrow, Vol. 5: Production and Capital*, Ch. 7, 157–80, Belknap Press of Harvard University Press, Cambridge, MA, 1985.

Atkinson, A. B.: The time-scale of economic models: How long is the long run? *Review of Economic Studies 36*, 137–52, 1969.

Banerjee, A. V. & Newman, A. F.: Occupational choice and the process of development. Manuscript, Harvard University and Northwestern University, 1991.

Barro, R.: Government spending in a simple model of endogeneous growth. *Journal of Political Economy 98*, S103–S125, 1990.

Barro, R. & Sala-i-Martin, X.: Public finance in models of economic growth. *Review of Economic Studies 59*, 645–61, 1992.

Becker, G. S. & Murphy, K. M.: The division of labor, coordination costs, and knowledge. *Quarterly Journal of Economics 107*, 1137–60, 1992.

Becker, G. S., Murphy, K. M. & Tamura, R.: Human capital, fertility, and economic growth. *Journal of Political Economy 98*, S12–S39, 1990.

Bencivenga, V. & Smith, B.: Financial intermediation and endogeneous growth. *Review of Economic Studies 58*, 195–209, 1991.

Boskin, M. J. & Lau, L. J.: Capital, technology and economic growth. In N. Rosenberg, R. Landau & D. C. Mowery (eds.), *Technology and the Wealth of Nations*, Ch. 2, 17–55, Stanford University Press, Stanford, 1992.

Brittan, S.: Endogenous growth — treat with care. *Financial Times*, March 4, 1993.

Brock, W. A. & Gale, D.: Optimal growth under factor augmenting progress. *Journal of Economic Theory 1*, 229–43, 1969.

Caballé, J. & Santos, M.: On endogenous growth with physical and human capital. Southern European Economics Discussion Series, DP 96, 1992.

Chipman, J. S.: External economies of scale and competitive equilibrium. *Quarterly Journal of Economics 84*, 347–85, 1970.

Cole, H. L., Mailath, G. J. & Postlewaite, A.: Social norms, savings behavior and growth. *Journal of Political Economy 100*, 1092–1125, 1992.

Conlisk J.: A neoclassical growth model with endogenously positioned technical change frontier. *Economic Journal 79*, 348–62, 1969.

Dasgupta, P. & Heal, G. M.: The optimal depletion of exhaustible resources. *Review of Economic Studies (Symposium of the Economics of Exhaustible Resources)*, 3–28, 1974.

David, P. A.: *Technical Choice, Innovation, and Economic Growth: Essays on American and British Experience in the Nineteenth Century.* Cambridge University Press, Cambridge, 1975.

Dixit, A. K. & Stiglitz, J. E.: Monopolistic competition and optimum product diversity. *American Economic Review 67*, 297–308, 1977.

Domar, E.: Capital expansion, rate of growth and employment. *Econometrica 14*, 137–47, 1946.

Domar, E.: *Essays in the Theory of Economic Growth.* Oxford University Press, New York, 1957.

Ehrlich, I. & Lui, F. T.: Intergenerational trade, longevity, and economic growth. *Journal of Political Economy 99*, 1029–59, 1991.

Ehrlich, P.: *The Population Bomb.* Ballantine Books, New York, 1968; revised 1971.

Ethier, W. J.: National and international returns to scale in the modern theory of international trade. *American Economic Review 72*, 389–405, 1982.

Fel'dman, G. A.: K teorii tempov narodnogo khozyaistva (On the theory of the rates of growth of national income). *Planovoe khozyaistvo, 11 and 12*, 1928; translated in N. Spulber (ed.), *Foundations of Soviet Strategy for Economic Growth*, 174–99 and 304–31, Indiana University Press, Bloomington, 1964.

Gans J.: *The Role of Knowledge in Economic Growth: Towards a General Theory of Economic Growth.* Bachelor's Honours Thesis, University of Queensland, 1989.

Greenwood, J. & Jovanovic, B.: Financial development, growth and the distribution of income. *Journal of Political Economy 98*, 1076–1107, 1990.

Grossman, G. M. & Helpman, E.: *Innovation and Growth in the Global Economy.* MIT Press, Cambridge, MA, 1991a.

Grossman, G. M. & Helpman, E.: Quality ladders in the theory of growth. *Review of Economic Studies 58*, 43–61, 1991b.

Grossman, G. M. & Helpman, E.: Quality ladders and product cycles. *Quarterly Journal of Economics 106*, 557–586, 1991c.

Haavelmo, T.: *A Study in the Theory of Economic Evolution*. North-Holland, Amsterdam, 1954; 2nd. edn. 1956.

Hahn, F. H.: On growth theory. Forthcoming in *Economics in a Changing World* (Proceedings of the Tenth International Economic Association World Congress in Moscow, 1992). Macmillan, London, 1993.

Hahn, F. H. & Matthews, R. C. O.: The theory of economic growth: A survey. *Economic Journal 74*, 779–902, 1964; reprinted in *Surveys of Economic Theory, Vol. II: Growth and Development*. Macmillan, London and St. Martin's Press, New York, 1967.

Harris, D. J.: Classical growth theory. In the *New Palgrave Dictionary of Economics*. Macmillan, London, 1987.

Harrod, R. F.: An essay in dynamic theory. *Economic Journal 49*, 14–33, 1939.

Helpman, E.: Endogenous macroeconomic growth theory. *European Economic Review 36*, 237–67, 1992.

Inada, K.: On a two-sector model of economic growth: Comments and a generalization. *Review of Economic Studies 30*, 119–27, 1963.

Inada, K.-I.: Endogenous technical progress and steady growth. *Review of Economic Studies 36*, 99–107, 1969.

Johansen, L.: Substitution versus fixed production coefficients in the theory of economic growth: A synthesis. *Econometrica 27*, 157–76, 1959.

Jones, C.: Time series tests of endogenous growth models. Manuscript, Department of Economics, Massachusetts Institute of Technology, 1993.

Jones, L. & Manuelli, R.: A convex model of equilibrium growth: Theory and policy implications. *Journal of Political Economy 98*, 1008–38, 1990.

Lancaster, K.: *Variety, Equity, and Efficiency*. Columbia University Press, New York, 1979.

Levhari, D.: Extensions of Arrow's 'learning by doing'. *Review of Economic Studies 33*, 117–31, 1966.

Lucas, R. E.: On the mechanics of economic development. *Journal of Monetary Economics 22*, 3–42, 1988.

Lucas, R. E.: Making a miracle. *Econometrica 61*, 251–272, 1993.

Lundberg, E.: *Produktivitet och Räntabilitet* (Productivity and Profitability). P. A. Norstadt och Söner, Stockholm, 1961.

Maddison, A.: *Phases of Capitalist Development*. Oxford University Press, Oxford, 1982.

McFadden, D.: On the existence of optimal development programmes in infinite-horizon economies. In Mirrlees and Stern, Ch. 12, 260–82, 1973.

Mirrlees, J. A. & Stern, N. H. (eds.): *Models of Economic Growth*. Macmillan, London, 1973.

Murphy, K. M., Shleifer, A. & Vishny, R. W.: The allocation of talent: Implications for growth. *Quarterly Journal of Economics 106*, 503–30, 1991.

Myrdal, G.: *Economic Theory and Underdeveloped Regions*. Duckworth, London, 1957.

Newman, P. R.: *Readings in Mathematical Economics, Vol. II*. John Hopkins Press, Baltimore, 1968.

Pagano, M.: Financial markets and growth: An overview. Financial Markets Group DP 153, London School of Economics, 1992.

Perotti, R.: Income distribution, politics, and growth. *American Economic Review (Papers and Proceedings) 82*, 311–6, 1992.

Persson, T. & Tabellini, G.: Politico-economic equilibrium growth. Mimeo, Institute of International Economic Studies, Stockholm, 1990.

Prescott, E. C. & Boyd, J. H.: Dynamic coalitions, growth and the firm. In E. C. Prescott, N. Wallace (eds.), *Contractual Arrangements for Intertemporal Trade*, Ch. VII, 146–60, University of Minnesota Press, Minneapolis, 1987a.

Prescott, E. C. & Boyd, J. H.: Dynamic coalitions: Engineers of growth. *American Economic Review (Papers and Proceedings) 77*, 63–7, 1987b.

Rebelo, S.: Long run policy analysis and long run growth. *Journal of Political Economy 99*, 500–21, 1991.

Rivera-Batiz, L. A. & Romer, P. M.: Economic integration and endogenous growth. *Quarterly Journal of Economics 106*, 531–55, 1991.

Rodríguez-Clare, A.: The division of labor and economic development. Preprint, Department of Economics, Stanford University, 1993.

Romer, P. M.: Dynamic competitive equilibria with externalities, increasing returns, and unbounded growth. Unpublished Ph.D. dissertation, University of Chicago, 1983.

Romer, P. M.: Increasing returns and long run growth. *Journal of Political Economy 94*, 1002–38, 1986.

Romer, P. M.: Growth based on increasing returns due to specialization. *American Economic Review (Papers and Proceedings) 77*, 56–62, 1987.

Romer, P. M.: Endogeneous technological change. *Journal of Political Economy 98*, S71–S103, 1990.

Romer, P. M.: Increasing returns and new developments in the theory of growth. In W. Barnett, (ed.), *Equilibrium Theory and Applications: Proceedings of the 6th International Symposium in Economic Theory and Econometrics*, Ch. 5, 83–110. Cambridge University Press, Cambridge, 1991.

Saint-Paul, G.: Technological choice, financial markets and economic development. *European Economic Review 36*, 763–81, 1992.

Sala-i-Martin, X.: Lecture notes on economic growth, I: Introduction to the literature and neoclassical models. NBER WP 3563, 1990a.

Sala-i-Martin, X.: Lecture notes on economic growth, II: Five prototype models of endogenous growth. NBER WP 3564, 1990b.

Salter, W. E. G.: *Productivity and Technical Change*. Cambridge University Press, Cambridge, 1960.

Schultz, T. W.: Investment in human capital. *American Economic Review 51*, 1–17, 1961.

Schultz, T. W.: Reflections on investment in man. *Journal of Political Economy 70*, S1–S8, 1962.

Scott, M. F. G.: *A New View of Economic Growth*. Clarendon Press, Oxford, 1989.

Scott, M. F. G.: Policy implications of "A New View of Economic Growth". *Economic Journal 102*, 622–632, 1992.

Segerstrom, P. S.: Innovation, imitation, and economic growth. *Journal of Political Economy 99*, 807–27, 1991.

Segerstrom, P. S., Anant, T. C. A. & Dinopoulos, E.: A Schumpterian model of the product life cycle. *American Economic Review 80*, 1077–91, 1990.

Seierstad, A. & Sydsæter, K.: Sufficient conditions in optimal control theory. *International Economic Review 18*, 367–91, 1977.

Sen, A. K. (ed.): *Growth Economics: Selected Readings*. Penguin Books Ltd., Harmondsworth, 1970.

Shaw, G. K.: Policy implications of endogenous growth theory. *Economic Journal 102*, 611–21, 1992.

Shell, K. (ed.) *Essays on the Theory of Optimal Economic Growth*. MIT Press, Cambridge, MA, 1967.

Shell, K.: A model of inventive activity and capital accumulation. In Shell, 67–85, 1967.

Shell, K.: Inventive activity, industrial organisation and economic growth. In Mirrlees and Stern, Ch. 4, 77–96, 1973.

Sheshinski, E.: Optimal accumulation with learning by doing. In Shell, 31–52, 1967.

Solow, R. M.: A contribution to the theory of economic growth. *Quarterly Journal of Economics 70*, 65–94, 1956.

Solow, R. M.: Technical change and the aggregate production function. *Review of Economic Statistics 31*, 312–20, 1957.

Solow, R. M.: Investment and technical progress. In K. J. Arrow, S. Karlin & P. Suppes (eds.), *Mathematical Methods in the Social Sciences, 1959*, Stanford University Press, Stanford, 89–104, 1960.

Solow, R. M.: Intergenerational equity and exhaustible resources. *Review of Economic Studies (Symposium on the Economics of Exhaustible Resources)*, 29–45, 1974.

Solow, R. M.: Learning from "learning by doing". Third Annual Arrow Lectures, Department of Economics, Stanford University, 1993.

Stern, N.: The determinants of growth. *Economic Journal 101*, 122–33, 1991.

Stigler, G. J.: The division of labor is limited by the extent of the market. *Journal of Political Economy 59*, 185–93, 1951.

Stiglitz, J. E.: Growth with exhaustible natural resources: Efficient and optimal growth paths. *Review of Economic Studies (Symposium on the Economics of Exhaustible Resources)*, 123–37, 1974.

Stiglitz, J. E.: Explaining growth: Competition and finance. Manuscript, Department of Economics, Stanford University, 1992.

Stiglitz, J. E. & Uzawa, H.: *Readings in the Modern Theory of Economic Growth*. MIT Press, Cambridge, MA, 1969.

Stokey, N. L.: Learning by doing and the introduction of new goods. *Journal of Political Economy 96*, 701–17, 1988.

Stokey, N. L.: Human capital, product quality, and growth. *Quarterly Journal of Economics 106*, 587–616, 1991.

Swan, T. W.: Economic growth and capital accumulation. *The Economic Record 32*, 334–61, 1956.

Tobin, J.: A dynamic aggregative model. *Journal of Political Economy 53*, 103–15, 1955.

Uzawa, H.: Optimum technical change in an aggregative model of economic growth. *International Economic Review 6*, 18–31, 1965.

Verdoorn, P. J.: Fattori che regolano lo sviluppo della produttività del lavoro. *L'Industria 1*, 45–53, 1949.

Verdoorn, P. J.: Verdoorn's Law in retrospect: A comment. *Economic Journal 90*, 382–5, 1980.

von Weizsäcker, C. C.: Notes on endogenous growth on productivity. In Mirrlees and Stern, Ch. 5, 101–10, 1974.

Weitzman, M. L.: Volume, variety, and versatility in growth and trade. Manuscript, Harvard University, 1991.

Yang, X. & Borland, J.: A microeconomic mechanism for economic growth. *Journal of Political Economy 99*, 460–82, 1991.

Young, A.: Learning by doing and the dynamic effects of international trade. *Quarterly Journal of Economics 106*, 369–406, 1991.

Galton's Fallacy and Tests of the Convergence Hypothesis

Danny Quah *

London School of Economics and CEPR, London, England

Abstract

Recent tests for the convergence hypothesis derive from regressing average growth rates on initial levels: a negative initial level coefficient is interpreted as convergence. These tests turn out to be plagued by Galton's classical fallacy of regression towards the mean. Using a dynamic version of Galton's fallacy, I establish that coefficients of arbitrary signs in such regressions are consistent with an unchanging cross-section distribution of incomes. Alternative, more direct empirics used here show a tendency for divergence, rather than convergence, of cross-country incomes.

Feathers hit the ground before their weight can leave the air.

R.E.M.

I. Introduction

Do the incomes or productivity levels of different economies have a tendency to converge? Numerous researchers have recently examined this question by calculating cross-section regressions of measured growth rates on initial levels; see for instance Barro (1991), Barro and Sala-i-Martin (1991, 1992), Baumol (1986), DeLong (1988), Dowrick and Nguyen (1989), Mankiw, Romer and Weil (1992), and many others. Such regressions have, in fact, become known as "Barro regressions", and are widely used to analyze empirical growth dynamics. Evidently, in a Barro regres-

---

*This paper is substantially revised from an earlier version with the same title. I thank many colleagues, especially Milton Friedman, Marc Nerlove, and the LSE Macro Breakfast Group, for helpful comments. I also gratefully acknowledge the hospitality of the Institute for Empirical Macroeconomics at FRB Minneapolis. All data-derived graphs and calculations contained here were executed using the author's time-series, random-fields econometrics shell tsrf.

sion, a negative coefficient on initial levels is taken to indicate convergence.

This paper clarifies what such initial level regressions are able to
uncover. As used in this literature, the term convergence can mean a
number of different things:

(a) Countries originally richer than average are more likely to turn
    below average eventually, and vice-versa — the cycle repeats;
(b) Whether a country income is eventually above or below average is
    independent of that economy's original position;
(c) Income disparities between countries have neither unit roots nor
    deterministic time trends; and
(d) Each country eventually becomes as rich as all the others — the
    cross-section dispersion diminishes over time.

Cases (a) and (b) vaguely correspond to the notions of *mixing* and
ergodicity in econometrics; see e.g. White (1984). Case (c) is one formulation of persistence in income disparities: from a time-series perspective, it
is the natural way to examine dependence on initial conditions. This
particular probability model raises interesting econometric issues in the
context of unit root random fields; see Quah (1992a). It is, however, quite
different in spirit and in substance from initial level regressions. Case (d) is
closest to the notion of poorer countries eventually catching up with richer
countries.

If (a) and (b) are the cases of interest, then models for studying transitional characteristics — for example, that used in the income distribution
and earnings mobility literature — would seem appropriate. Thus, Quah
(1992b) attempts to uncover such effects in the context of heterogeneous
Markov chains. Overall, however, the work using initial levels regressions
strongly suggests case (d) as being of interest.

This paper first shows, in Section II, that the widely-used initial level
regressions described above, in fact, shed no light on convergence in the
sense of (d). It does this by developing an analogy between such regressions and Francis Galton's classical fallacy of regression towards the
mean.[1] Recall that Galton, in aristocratic manner, was concerned about the
sons of tall fathers regressing into a pool of mediocrity along with the sons
of everyone else — he inferred this from observing that taller-than-average
fathers had sons who turned out to be not as much above average as the
fathers themselves. He could not, initially, reconcile this with the population of male heights continuing to display significant cross-section disper-

---

[1] After completing the first draft of this paper, I came across Friedman (1992), which makes
much the same point as this. The discussion in Section III, however, appears nowhere else
that I have seen.

sion. I show — using exactly the same reasoning which resolves that paradox — that a negative cross-section regression coefficient on initial levels is, in fact, perfectly consistent with the absence of convergence in the sense of (d).

Barro (1991), Barro and Sala-i-Martin (1991) and Mankiw, Romer and Weil (1992) have recently shown that what they call "conditional convergence" occurs. Some of these authors further claim that this conditional convergence happens at approximately the same rate over different time periods and across different cross-sectional samples. The results described in the previous paragraph extend — in a straightforward way — to cover these cases of conditional convergence: simply apply the argument to the *residuals* of output growth, after conditioning on exogenous variables of interest.

While Galton's formulation is convenient for analyzing observations at two points in time, it offers little by way of interesting dynamics. Extending the analysis to permit such dynamics, I show, again in Section II, that a given cross-section distribution — replicating itself over time — is consistent with *arbitrary* signs on the cross-section initial levels regression coefficient. In other words, the sign of the initial levels regression coefficient says nothing about whether there is convergence or divergence.

Section III describes an alternative, more direct means for examining the convergence hypothesis, using a model of a cross-country distribution of incomes, evolving dynamically. The results here show that while one can uncover pockets of convergence, the data overall show divergence instead. The picture that emerges is one of a world where countries tend — in the long run — towards either the very rich or very poor, with the middle income classes disappearing. The disparity between the rich and poor, further, appears to be widening. Section IV briefly concludes.

II. Galton's Fallacy Dynamics

I will argue here that calculating a cross-section regression to explain time-averaged growth rates gives an example of why it is inappropriate to attempt to draw dynamic implications from cross-section evidence. The earliest example of this that I know is the famous Galton's fallacy of regression towards the mean. In this section, I make that connection explicit.

Consider Figure 1: such a graph is certainly not original. It is arguably one of the initial motivations for the entire endogenous growth literature, and has appeared in publications ranging from Paul Romer's academic papers to magazines like *The Economist*.

Figure 1 shows a wide dispersion of average growth rates for economies having low initial income levels. (The data source and a list of the different economies studied here are given in the Data Appendix.) There is little sign

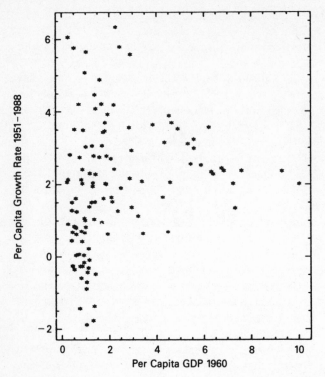

Fig. 1. Average growth (1951–88) versus initial levels (1960); 118 Summers–Heston countries.

of a negative correlation — in the cross section — between initial conditions and time-averaged growth rates. But why might one expect such a negative correlation?

Suppose that after controlling for appropriate exogenous differences — human capital, government policy, natural resources — different economies are hypothesized to have the same long-run income level, or, alternatively, the same growth path. Then in a picture like Figure 1 — again, after controlling for exogenous variables — should not there be a negative correlation in the cross section, so that countries initially starting lower catch up with or converge to those countries already ahead? Controlling for exogenous differences might be as simple as just looking at Figure 1, but using the residuals from some first-stage regression.

An alternative representation of this convergence idea is given in Figure 2: such a graph shows a collapsing of the cross-section distribution — possibly after controlling for exogenous variables — about an underlying growth path that happens to be unique across countries. It seems intuitive

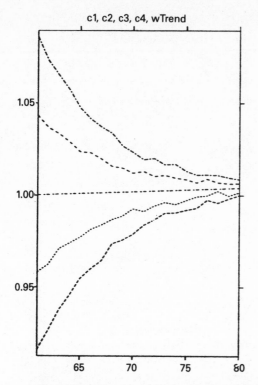

c1, c2, c3, c4, wTrend

Fig. 2. Income levels against time (time paths under hypothesized convergence).

that this dynamic characteristic should manifest in a negative correlation of time-averaged growth rates with initial conditions (such as Figure 1 ought to show).[2]

That such a negative correlation does not, in fact, imply a collapsing of the cross-section distribution is easily seem from the reasoning in Galton's fallacy. (I repeat: the argument here applies regardless of whether one takes just the raw data or the residuals from a first stage regression, i.e., controls for exogenous conditioning. Thus, the distinction between conditional and unconditional convergence is irrelevant here.) Suppose, contrary to Figure 2, that the cross-section distribution is not collapsing, but replicates itself because it happens to be the stationary distribution for

---

[2] This simple idea resurfaces in many current policy debates — among them, whether East Germany is catching up with West Germany, whether Europe is becoming a two-track system (one for the rich, another for the poor), and whether the U.S. poor are becoming poorer. See, for instance, Zimmerman (1992).

many independent and identically-distributed country incomes $Y_j(t)$. For t_1 and t_2 arbitrary points in time, the cross-section regression of $Y(t_2)$ on a constant and $Y(t_1)$ is just:

$$P[Y(t_2)|1, Y(t_1)] = E_C Y(t_2) + \lambda(Y(t_1) - E_C Y(t_1)),$$

where

$$\lambda = \text{var}_C^{-1}(Y(t_1)) \cdot \text{cov}_C(Y(t_2), Y(t_1)),$$

the subscript C denoting *cross section*. The assumption that the cross sections are in stationary state gives:

$$\text{var}_C(Y(t_1)) = \text{var}_C(Y(t_2)).$$

The Cauchy-Schwarz inequality,

$$|\text{cov}_C(Y(t_2), Y(t_1))| \leq \text{var}_C^{1/2}(Y(t_2)) \text{var}_C^{1/2}(Y(t_1)),$$

then implies that $\lambda \leq 1$, so that:

$$P[Y(t_2) - Y(t_1)|1, Y(t_1)] = \mu - (1 - \lambda) Y(t_1), \tag{†}$$

with the coefficient on $Y(t_1)$ necessarily nonpositive.

If $t_1 < t_2$ then (†) is a regression of (scaled) growth rates on an initial condition: the conclusion above then implies that the coefficient on the initial condition is always no greater than zero, even when the cross-section distribution remains invariant over time. A negative sign on the initial-condition coefficient, therefore, does not indicate a collapsing cross-section distribution. This, of course, is simply Galton's fallacy of regression towards the mean.

As formulated here, the argument takes the extreme assumption that the cross-section distribution is invariant. This makes the point particularly clear, but there is no real need for that time invariance. The coefficient in this initial-conditions regression depends only on λ, or equivalently, the relation between $\text{cov}_C(Y(t_2), Y(t_1))$ and $\text{var}_C(Y(t_2))$ and $\text{var}_C(Y(t_1))$. Therefore, the "initial-condition coefficient" can be negative — λ strictly less than 1 — even if $\text{var}_C(Y(t_2))$ exceeds $\text{var}_C(Y(t_1))$ — the cross-section distribution can diverge even when the initial conditions regression shows a negative correlation between time-averaged growth rates and initial levels! Further, nothing in the argument relies on t_2 exceeding t_1: all the same (negative) conclusions follow, even when the researcher is estimating a "final-condition" (or orrab) regression or a "middle-condition" regression. Figures 3 and 4 show that the message in Figure 1 is unchanged by replacing the initial conditions with income levels at other arbitrary dates. This kind of cross-section regression is thus completely uninformative for the dynamics of the distribution.

Average growth against:

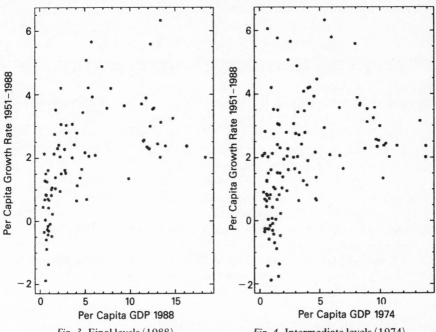

Fig. 3. Final levels (1988).   Fig. 4. Intermediate levels (1974).

Galton's fallacy reasoning, in discussing the empirics of growth, is sometimes phrased as follows: a negative initial condition provides a force for the cross-section distribution to collapse; on the other hand, ongoing disturbances provide a force in the opposite direction.[3] This phrasing is specious, however. To see why, consider starting out the cross-section distribution with all countries at the same point. Then, over time, the distribution must tend towards its stationary version. Provided that the countries are not perfectly correlated, there must be a divergence from the initial distribution. All this happens with neither a change in the underlying time-series representation for each country, nor a change in the covariance properties across countries. Thus, any regression calculated from data on these countries must remain unchanged, independent of whether the cross-section is collapsing or diverging.

If regression (†) is perturbed so that the initial condition appearing on the right is not that used to calculate the average growth rate on the left-

---

[3] These different forces underly Barro and Sala-i-Martin's (1991, 1992) distinction between β- and σ-convergence.

hand side, then we have:

$$P[Y(t_2) - Y(t_0) | 1, Y(t_1)] = \mu' - (\nu - \lambda) Y(t_1),$$

where

$$\nu = \text{var}_C^{-1}(Y(t_1)) \cdot \text{cov}_C(Y(t_0), Y(t_1)).$$

All the same observations made earlier about λ now apply equally to ν: the sign of $\lambda - \nu$ depends on $\text{cov}_C(Y(t_0), Y(t_1))$ and $\text{cov}_C(Y(t_2), Y(t_1))$ in addition to the variances of $Y(t_2)$, $Y(t_1)$, and $Y(t_0)$. No sensible inference can thus be drawn on the dynamics of the cross-section distribution by the cross-section regressions that are typically estimated. In particular, perturbing the initial condition gives no more information on the convergence properties of the distributions over time.

The strong independence and identical distribution assumption I used above plays a role only in simplifying the calculations. With heterogeneity, any time-invariant cross-section distribution is a probability mixture of the different individual time series ergodic distributions. Weak forms of dependence across countries will not affect their cross-section distribution being approached by the empirical (really just a version of the Glivenko-Cantelli law). With strong dependence or small numbers of countries, the empirical cross-section distribution is a non-degenerate random element in the space of distributions. While the calculations then become much more difficult, the flavour of the results is unaffected.

It is useful, therefore, to eschew this kind of analysis, and seek a better way to model the dynamics of this large cross-section. Figure 5 shows a three-dimensional plot of the natural logarithm of per capita country incomes, arrayed in both time and cross-sectional unit: this graphs the raw data behind the calculations previously undertaken in Figures 1, 3, and 4. While the ordering of these data along the time axis is obvious — time proceeds naturally sequentially — that along the country axis is not. Here, I have arbitrarily taken the ordering given in World Bank country codes — reported in, among other places, Summers and Heston (1991).

This graph shows the complications for dynamic inference — are countries converging over time? diverging? growing in a way depending on size ? — off of this data set. The variation in the data is as rich in the cross-section dimension as it is in the time-series. Growth rate regressions, averaging out the time dimension, are simply one — and it turns out, misleading — way to analyze such a data structure. Standard econometric methods are not well-suited to working with such data structures.

III. Direct Tests of Convergence

An alternative, more transparent way to see whether convergence occurs is to examine directly the cross-section distributions of output per worker

log GDP

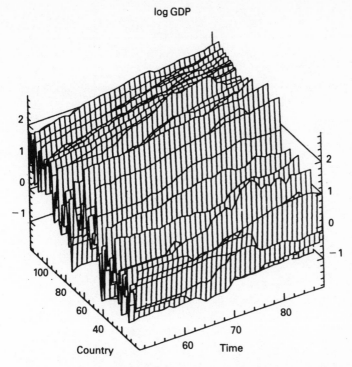

Fig. 5. Log per capita income; 118 Summers–Heston countries.

over time. Because the entire world might be growing, and because the analysis is most naturally performed abstracting from this worldwide comovement, I calculated output per worker for each country, divided by the same figure for the world. (Thus, a number like 2 below indicates twice the world average, and so on.) This normalization is an easy — but imperfect — way to abstract from world-wide growth and fluctuations; a more accurate, but also more difficult, normalization can be obtained using methods in Quah and Sargent (1993). Figures 6(a)–(d) show point-in-time (smoothed) estimates of the densities of the cross-country distribution of this normalized series: (a)–(c) are for 1962, 1974, and 1985, respectively, while (d) is taken over the entire sample 1962–85.[4]

The key message from this sequence of graphs is that the cross-section distributions do not appear to be collapsing. Instead, they seem to be

---

[4] The estimates were obtained using a Gaussian kernel with bandwidth selected automatically, as suggested in Silverman (1986). The fast Fourier transform was used to calculate the resulting kernel estimator. A reflection method took into account nonnegativity in the original data; see Silverman (1986).

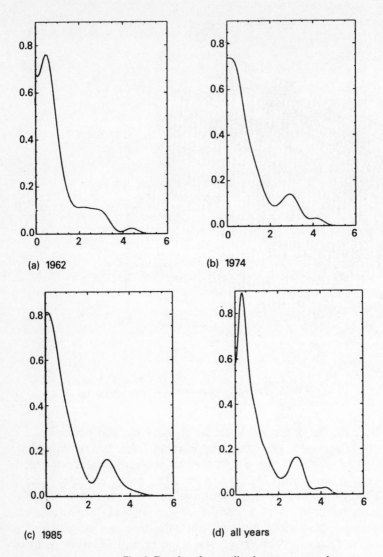

(a) 1962

(b) 1974

(c) 1985

(d) all years

Fig. 6. Density of normalized output per worker.

fluctuating over time. Filling in the gaps from 1963–73 and 1975–84 with additional graphs of the densities for each of those years would simply reinforce that idea.

Two natural questions arise here. First, recall expositions of the neoclassical growth model, as e.g. in Mankiw, Romer and Weil (1992). Those make clear that a nondegenerate distribution as in these graphs could well be consistent with that growth model in steady state — see in particular equation (6) of Mankiw, Romer and Weil (1992) and the surrounding discussion. Those models, however, cannot produce a diverging distribution over time.[5] An informative examination of this prediction therefore should examine the behavior of the cross-section distribution in steady state. But which of Figures 6 (a)–(d) is steady state?

Second, confronted with the representations of the data in Figures 6(a)–(d), a researcher is tempted to ask if the "bump" in the density between 2 and 4 in 1985 contains the same countries as that in 1974. Graphs such as these cannot tell us that.

Both questions can be answered, however, by developing a probability model of transitions — law of motion — for the distributions in Figures 6(a)–(d) that can, at the same time, be used to generate a characterization of the steady state. Quah (1993b) provides exactly such a model: discrete Markov chains are used to approximate and estimate a law of motion for the evolving distributions. While that work has not yet been able to give any measures of precision, the results suggest two interesting empirical characteristics: (1) the ergodic distribution of these cross-country incomes is one where many countries are rich and many are poor, with the middle-income countries a vanishing class; and (2) intra-distribution mobility is nontrivial — over sufficiently long periods of time, output per worker wanders outside of any fixed neighborhood. These results appear at odds with the predictions of the standard neoclassical growth model, as described in e.g. Mankiw, Romer and Weil (1992).

But those conclusions on the ergodic distribution bear an important qualification: they are conditional on the arbitrary grid that was used to discretize the point-in-time empirical distributions. From Markov chain theory, we know that a continuous first-order Markov process (otherwise well-behaved) need not even retain the Markov property when inappropriately discretized. More directly, in a discrete setting, statements to the effect that probability mass piles up in a certain part of the distribution have to be related to the choice of the discretizing grid. It is important, therefore, to check the robustness of those conclusions.

In the current work, I explore a different representation for the dynamics in the evolving distributions of Figure 6. Fix a set of increasing, nonredundant probabilities $P = \{p_1, p_2, \ldots, p_n\}$. For income distribution $\mathcal{F}_t$

---

[5] In this discussion, I have absorbed the cross-country conditioning variables of Mankiw, Romer and Weil into unobservable country-specific processes. Quah (1993a) is a study in the same spirit as the current one, but explicitly considers conditioning information. A brief discussion of the results there appears below.

in each period t, the set P determines a corresponding set of quantiles $Q(t) = \{q_1(t), q_2(t), ..., q_n(t)\}$, where, by definition, the quantiles and probabilities are related by $p_k = \mathcal{F}_t(q_k(t))$, for $k = 1, ..., n$. When P is chosen to be equally spaced on the open unit interval $(0, 1)$, each quantile-set pair $\{Q(t), Q(t+1)\}$ defines an $(n+1) \times (n+1)$ *fractile transition probability matrix* $M(t)$ of transitions from $\mathcal{F}(t)$ to $\mathcal{F}(t+1)$. (The terminology *fractile Markov chain* is from Geweke, Marshall and Zarkin (1986); it is natural also to call fractile the transition probability matrix of such a Markov chain.) Notice that given probabilities P, the fractile matrix $M(t)$ is uniquely determined even if the quantiles Q are not. If the fractile matrix M is assumed to be time-invariant, then it can be estimated by averaging across both time and countries. Further, if the quantile sets $Q(t)$ happen to be time-invariant then the representation here collapses to a version of that used by Quah (1993b).

In the subsequent analysis, I impose time-invariance in M, but leave $\{Q(t)$: integer $t\}$ as a serially correlated vector process. Therefore, the work here generalizes that in Quah (1993b), and serves as a check on the robustness of conclusions there. The dynamic evolution of the sequence of income distributions can be obtained by first forecasting Q, and then taking the convolution with M raised to the appropriate power. Because M is a fractile matrix, we immediately know that there is an ergodic distribution, and further that that ergodic distribution is uniform relative to the quantiles Q (implied by P). The corresponding ergodic distribution on the original state space is then found by combining the preceding fact with knowledge of the sequence of quantile sets $\{Q(t)$: integer $t\}$. In words, the transition matrix M parametrizes intradistribution mobility, while the vector sequence Q parametrizes movements in the entire distribution.

I have estimated four- and five-state fractile Markov chain models for the cross-country income distributions, again taken relative to world average.[6] Tables 1 and 2 give the corresponding transition probabilities M. The first striking feature is the extreme immobility over time apparent in these transition probabilities. The very richest remain so with probability at least 98 per cent; the very poorest, with probability at least 95 per cent. The interior diagonal entries in both tables are lower than the extreme diagonal endpoints: middle-income economies are less likely to remain where they are in the distribution. From the tables, we see that those middle-income economies face about equal probabilities of rising or falling. Notice that as estimated, both M's imply that the corresponding fractile Markov chains are irreducible and have all states ergodic. Thus,

---

[6] The four-state specification, of course, has $P = \{0.25, 0.50, 0.75\}$, and similarly the five-state specification, $P = \{0.2, 0.4, 0.6, 0.8\}$.

Table 1. *Cross-country output per worker, relative to world average* 4-state fractile Markov Chain, 1962–84*

	Quantile			
	[0.25]	[0.50]	[0.75]	[1.00]
(667)	0.96	0.04		
(690)	0.04	0.93	0.03	
(667)		0.03	0.95	0.02
(690)			0.02	0.98

*The states are arrayed in increasing order, thus the lower right-hand portion of the table shows transitions from the rich to the rich. The numbers in parentheses on the right are the number of country/year pairs beginning in a particular state. These numbers should be equal: they differ from each other by at most the number of years in the sample, due to rounding error. Cells showing 0 to two decimal places are left blank.

Table 2. *Cross-country output per worker, relative to world average* 5-state fractile Markov Chain, 1962–84*

	Quantile				
	[0.2]	[0.4]	[0.6]	[0.8]	[1.0]
(529)	0.95	0.05			
(552)	0.05	0.90	0.05		
(530)		0.05	0.90	0.05	
(551)			0.05	0.93	0.02
(552)				0.01	0.99

*See notes to Table 1.

the long run, steady state distributions are unique, and by the previous discussion, are also uniform (relative to Q).

To complete the description of these transition dynamics, we now consider the behavior of the quantile sets $\{Q(t)$: integer $t\}$. Over the estimation period 1962–84, these varied in quite suggestive ways. With $n = 4$, the median q_2 wandered between 0.61 in 1962 (half the world's economies had per capita incomes no greater than 61 per cent of the world average) to 0.70 in 1975, and then 0.65 in 1984. During this period, q_2 never rose above 0.76 (1978) nor fell below 0.60 (1964). By contrast, the 0.25 quantile q_1 drifted downwards from an average of 0.36 over 1962–4 to 0.27 over 1982–4; the 0.75 quantile q_3 upwards from 1.29 to 1.50. Similar behavior (naturally) manifests with $n = 5$: the 0.2 quantile q_1 drifted downwards from an average of 0.31 over 1962–4 to 0.23 over 1982–4; the 0.8 quantile q_4 upwards from 1.57 to 2.04. In words, the median roughly stays put while the upper quantiles wander upwards, and the lower quantiles downwards. These movements at the extremes are, for the most

part, monotone from year to year over 1962–84: the preceding description of time averages at the beginning and end points of the sample are
thus representative of general tendencies.[7]

Combining these observations on the dynamics of Q and the immobility
patterns in M, we come to much the same conclusions as Quah (1993b).
The cross-country income distributions evolve over time in a way that
shows a tendency for the rich remaining rich and the poor, poor, and for
the gap between rich and poor to widen. I do not present the calculations
here, but it should be clear from the structure of the transition probabilities
in Tables 1 and 2 that iterating those transition probabilities show the same
effects as uncovered in the ergodic distributions in Quah (1993b): in the
long run, there is a piling up of probability mass in the tails, and a thinning
out in the middle.

From the discussion of Section II, the usual cross-country growth
regressions shed little light on the dynamics just described in the previous
paragraph. Thus, the evidence on "convergence" that different researchers
have uncovered do not really bear on our empirical conclusions. Instead,
the empirical results here simply highlight the error in interpreting
previous findings as having demonstrated convergence.

One important aspect that other researchers have been able to investigate with cross-section regressions, and that I have not here, is the
influence of conditioning information: savings, schooling, political stability
and so on. Quah (1993a), in a different but related setting as that used
above, has studied the effects of conditioning information. That work
concludes that much the same divergence and immobility results as
obtained here remain, even after conditioning.

IV. Conclusion

The main goal of this paper was to criticize standard cross-section regression tests of the convergence hypothesis. Section II did that, in some detail.
By drawing an analogy of these regression tests with those of the classical
Galton's fallacy, and then extending the reasoning for dynamics, I have
shown why these cross-section tests are misleading for the hypothesis of
interest.

The alternative, more direct tests described in this paper provide
evidence against the convergence hypothesis. They show, instead, a world
with economies tending — in the long run — towards either the very rich or

---

[7] I have also experimented with VAR models for Q, and then forecasting from them to get an
idea of future tendencies. The time sample for estimation comprises only about 20 points,
however, so that not very much of interest was precisely estimated. The exercise nevertheless did confirm the drift tendencies in the extreme quantiles.

very poor, with the middle-income classes vanishing. The rich–poor income disparity, in addition, appears to be widening.

What are the next steps in this alternative, empirical research program, one that escapes the strictures of the classical Galton's fallacy? First, the lessons here call for theoretical growth models that generate predictions for the dynamics of the entire cross-economy distribution, not just for those of a single economy. Second, there is scope for studying time heterogeneity in these evolving distributions, in ways that are richer than simply breaks in trend or unit-root nonstationarity. (Quah (1992b) is a first step.) Third, many of the issues raised here extend naturally to empirical studies of regional and geographical dynamics and of the dynamics of large cross-sections of commodity and asset prices. Such investigations are currently under way.

Data Appendix

The data are derived from Summers and Heston (1991). Real per capita income is taken to be RGDPL (Laspeyres index); population is POP. Countries in the sample were selected by first disallowing those not having continuously available data on these two variables for the period 1960–85. I then also excluded Kuwait — a three-dimensional graph of the variables easily shows the Kuwait observation to dominate every other feature of the data. The remaining 118 countries are listed below (integers immediately before the country names are the indexes in the Summers–Heston database):

1	(1)	Algeria	2	(2)	Angola
3	(3)	Benin	4	(4)	Botswana
5	(6)	Burnundi	6	(7)	Cameroon
7	(8)	Cape Verde Is	8	(9)	Central Afr R
9	(10)	Chad	10	(12)	Congo
11	(13)	Egypt	12	(14)	Ethiopia
13	(15)	Gabon	14	(16)	Gambia
15	(17)	Ghana	16	(18)	Guinea
17	(19)	Guinea Biss	18	(20)	Ivory Coast
19	(21)	Kenya	20	(22)	Lesotho
21	(23)	Liberia	22	(24)	Madagascar
23	(25)	Malawi	24	(26)	Mali
25	(27)	Mauritania	26	(28)	Mauritius
27	(29)	Morocco	28	(30)	Mozambique
29	(31)	Niger	30	(32)	Nigeria
31	(33)	Rwanda	32	(34)	Senegal
33	(36)	Sierra Leone	34	(37)	Somalia
35	(38)	South Africa	36	(39)	Sudan
37	(40)	Swaziland	38	(41)	Tanzania

Data Appendix — *Continued*

39	(42)	Togo	40	(43)	Tunisia
41	(44)	Uganda	42	(45)	Zaire
43	(46)	Zambia	44	(47)	Zimbabwe
45	(49)	Barbados	46	(50)	Canada
47	(51)	Costa Rica	48	(53)	Dominican Rep
49	(54)	El Salvador	50	(56)	Guatemala
51	(57)	Haiti	52	(58)	Honduras
53	(59)	Jamaica	54	(60)	Mexico
55	(61)	Nicaragua	56	(62)	Panama
57	(65)	Trinidad Tobag	58	(66)	USA
59	(67)	Argentina	60	(68)	Bolivia
61	(69)	Brazil	62	(70)	Chile
63	(71)	Columbia	64	(72)	Ecuador
65	(73)	Guyana	66	(74)	Paraguay
67	(75)	Peru	68	(76)	Suriname
69	(77)	Uraguay	70	(78)	Venezuela
71	(79)	Afghanistan	72	(81)	Bangladesh
73	(82)	Burma Myanmar	74	(83)	China
75	(84)	Hong Kong	76	(85)	India
77	(87)	Iran	78	(88)	Iraq
79	(89)	Israel	80	(90)	Japan
81	(91)	Jordan	82	(92)	Korea South R
83	(94)	Malaysia	84	(95)	Nepal
85	(97)	Pakistan	86	(98)	Philippines
87	(99)	Saudi Arabia	88	(100)	Singapore
89	(101)	Sri Lanka	90	(102)	Syria
91	(103)	Taiwan	92	(104)	Thailand
93	(107)	Austria	94	(108)	Belgium
95	(109)	Cyprus	96	(110)	Denmark
97	(111)	Finland	98	(112)	France
99	(113)	Germany West	100	(114)	Greece
101	(116)	Iceland	102	(117)	Ireland
103	(118)	Italy	104	(119)	Luxembourg
105	(120)	Malta	106	(121)	Netherlands
107	(122)	Norway	108	(124)	Portugal
109	(125)	Spain	110	(126)	Sweden
111	(127)	Switzerland	112	(128)	Turkey
113	(129)	UK	114	(130)	Yugoslavia
115	(131)	Australia	116	(132)	Fiji
117	(133)	New Zealand	118	(134)	Papua N Guinea

References

Barro, R. J.: Economic growth in a cross-section of countries. *Quarterly Journal of Economics 106* (2), 407–43, 1991.

Barro, R. J. & Sala-i-Martin, X.: Convergence across states and regions. *Brookings Papers on Economic Activity 1*, 107–82, 1991.

Barro, R. J. & Sala-i-Martin, X.: Convergence. *Journal of Political Economy 100* (2), 223–51, 1992.

Baumol, W. J.: Productivity growth, convergence, and welfare. *American Economic Review 76* (5), 1072–85, 1986.

DeLong, J. B.: Productivity growth, convergence and welfare: A comment. *American Economic Review 78* (5), 1138–55, 1988.

Den Haan, W. J.: Convergence in stochastic models. WP, Department of Economics, UCSD, 1992.

Dowrick, S. & Nguyen, D.: OECD comparative economic growth 1950–85: Catch-up and convergence. *American Economic Review 79* (5), 1010–30, 1989.

Friedman, M.: Do old fallacies ever die? *Journal of Economic Literature 30* (4), 2129–32, 1992.

Geweke, J., Marshall, R. C. & Zarkin, G. A.: Mobility indices in continuous time Markov chains. *Econometrica 54* (6), 1407–23, 1986.

Mankiw, N., Romer, D. & Weil, D. N.: A contribution to the empirics of economic growth. *Quarterly Journal of Economics 107*, 407–37, 1992.

Quah, D.: International patterns of growth: I. Persistence in cross-country disparities. WP, LSE, London, 1992a.

Quah, D.: International patterns of growth: II. Persistence, path dependence, and sustained take-off in growth transition. WP, LSE, London (first draft July 1990), 1992b.

Quah, D.: Dependence in growth and fluctuations across economies with mobile capital. WP, LSE, London, 1993a.

Quah, D.: Empirical cross-section dynamics in economic growth. Forthcoming in *European Economic Review*, 1993b.

Quah, D. & Sargent, T. J.: A dynamic index model for large cross sections. In J. Stock & M. Watson (eds), *New Research on Business Cycles, Indicators, and Forecasting*, University of Chicago Press, Chicago, forthcoming, 1993.

Silverman, B. W.: *Density Estimation for Statistics and Data Analysis*. Chapman and Hall, New York, 1986.

Summers, R. & Heston, A.: The PennWorld Table (Mark 5): An expanded set of international comparisons, 1950–88. *Quarterly Journal of Economics 106* (2), 327–68, 1991.

White, H.: *Asymptotic Theory for Econometricians*. Academic Press, New York, 1984.

Zimmerman, D. J.: Regression towards mediocrity in economic stature. *American Economic Review 82* (3), 409–29, 1992.

A Dynamic Model of Investment and Endogenous Growth*

Mervyn A. King

London School of Economics and Bank of England, London, England

Mark H. Robson

KPMG Peat Marwick and London School of Economics, London, England

Abstract

Models of endogenous growth assume that private investment in either physical or human capital yields positive externalities to production possibilities as a whole. But what is the structure of such externalities? We present a model of "learning by watching" which implies a nonlinear relationship between productivity growth and the investment rate. This results in multiple steady-state growth rates in a deterministic setting, and in a rich dynamic structure that generates both growth and cycles in a stochastic model (calibrated by reference to observable shocks to tax rates in the U.K.). Economies with identical structures can experience very different growth rates for long periods. The model exhibits path-dependence and history matters.

I. Introduction

The recent literature on endogenous growth has tried to reconcile indefinite increases in incomes per head with diminishing returns to factors of production, without resort to exogenous technical progress that falls like manna from heaven. The new models generate growth endogenously by assuming positive externalities from private investment in physical or human capital to production possibilities as a whole; see Romer (1986, 1988) and Lucas (1988). The existence of a side-effect of

---

*The views expressed here are not necessarily those of the institutions to which the authors belong. We are grateful to the LSE Financial Markets Group and the Inland Revenue for financial suport, and to anonymous referees, Bill Brainard, John Campbell, David Livesey, Andrei Shleifer and Peter Whittle, and the participants in many seminars for helpful comments. We thank Victor Hung for excellent research assistance.

private embodied investment on public disembodied knowledge leads to aggregate increasing returns to scale and hence the possibility of growth.[1]

We follow the Kaldor-Arrow-Romer tradition of modelling a link from investment to productivity growth, but we argue that it is important to put some structure on the size of the externalities that are created. In particular, we argue that there are diminishing returns in the production of the externality. This assumption yields a nonlinear "technical progress function" that results in multiple steady-state growth rates and a rich dynamic structure that determines both growth and cycles. Previous papers have worked either with a linear technology for the production of knowledge, as in Uzawa (1965), Lucas (1988) King and Rebelo (1988), or at a level of generality that precludes a systematic analysis of the effects of policy variables on growth, as in Romer (1986).

Our aim is to show that economies with identical economic structures can display large dispersion of growth rates. We demonstrate that within the framework of an endogenous growth model, the historical pattern of one particular type of government intervention — tax policy — determines the level and growth rate of output. Variations in growth rates result from differing realisations of government policy, even though the underlying process generating that policy is the same in each country. Either deterministic or stochastic variations in the tax rate on capital income will generate both cyclical fluctuations around a trend growth rate and changes in the trend growth rate itself. The tax rate process is not modelled as the result of an optimisation by a benevolent government. Instead it is regarded as an exogenous stochastic process. But policy does affect both the level and growth rate of output, while as Romer (1989, p. 51) has pointed out, "in models with exogenous technological change ... it never really mattered what the government did". We use an empirically estimated stochastic process for tax rates in the results reported below. Many other types of shock could be modelled and would lead to similar results for the behaviour of the growth rate. We provide an example below in terms of stochastic depreciation.

These ideas are illustrated by extending the simplest possible neo-classical growth model to include stochastic shocks and endogenous growth in the form of a "technical progress function" that builds on the work of Kaldor (1957) and Arrow (1962). Growth and cycles are then shown to interact because the strength of the propagation mechanism depends upon agents' adjustments to shocks. Moreover, the model generates multiple steady-state growth paths and the realisation of the

---

[1] For a survey of this literature and taxonomy of these models, see King (1992) and Rebelo (1991).

stochastic shocks determines towards which growth rate the economy tends. Our work is an example of models in which there is path-dependence and history matters; see also Arthur (1989).

Two types of stochastic shocks are analysed. First, "fiscal policy shocks" to the tax wedge between the return on physical investment and the return on saving are assumed to follow an integrated stochastic process. Formally, the tax rate on comprehensive income is modelled as a Markov process. Second, the rate of economic depreciation is assumed to follow a stationary white noise process. The propagation mechanism derives from the existence of a technical progress function which relates the rate of technical progress to the investment rate — defined as the ratio of net investment to gross domestic product. This represents the effect of "learning by watching" — the demonstration effect of new ideas on the efficiency of the existing capital stock. Learning by watching is assumed to take the form of a pure Marshallian externality so that a firm does not take into account the beneficial effect of its investment on productivity in the economy. A competitive equilibrium is, therefore, feasible.

An important feature of the model is the interaction between stochastic shocks and the non-linearities that result from learning by watching. Similar economies experiencing different shocks can display different growth rates over long periods. The interaction between shocks and learning by watching makes a simple decomposition between the "cycle" and "trend" inappropriate. We have chosen to work with a particular type of stochastic shock — to tax rates. The main reason for this is that it is possible to calibrate the distribution of shocks to tax rates using observations on actual changes in particular tax rates. There is no need to rely on unobservable shocks to variables such as tastes or productivity. Given an estimated Markov process for actual tax rates on capital income in the U.K., it is possible to generate significant fluctuations in growth rates of output.

We solve for the optimal policy response function of the representative agent and hence the implied stochastic path for output and the growth rate. We construct the nonlinear stochastic difference equation that describes the evolution of capital and output over time. Closed-form solutions are not available and we use numerical methods to compute the asymptotic distributions of the growth rate of output and other variables.

A distinctive feature of the model is the existence of multiple equilibria which result from the nonlinearities — in contrast to the linear approximations studied in the real business cycle literature — so that history matters, in two ways. First, the *level* of technical knowledge depends upon the past path of output. Second, the equilibrium *growth rate* itself also depends upon historical realisations of the underlying stochastic processes. Hence two economies with identical "deep" parameters *and* initial capital stocks can not only experience different time paths for output but may also cycle around different "natural" growth rates. The stochastic path for output is such that it is impossible to decompose the variance into two parts that may be attributed to stochastic shocks to the trend growth rate, on the one hand, the transitory fluctuations on the other. An economy can experience "premature maturity", in the sense that if it starts with too high a level of capital the competitive equilibrium may lead it to cycle around a zero growth rate path.

In two respects the results of this paper have a Kaldorian flavour. First, we assume a technical progress function in which investment drives technical progress. Kaldor introduced this idea in his 1957 paper and it was taken up by Arrow (1962) in his work on learning by doing.[2] But the Kaldorian technical progress function relates the rate of growth of output per head to the rate of growth of investment per head, and so the only steady-state growth path that is feasible is given by the intersection of an exogenously given curve with the 45° line; see Kaldor (1957) and Kaldor and Mirrlees (1962). In contrast, in our model the equilibrium growth rate is endogenous. Second, Kaldor (1966) argued that "premature maturity" was responsible for the "low" (compared with other OECD countries) growth rates observed in the U.K. He attributed this to the fact that, having industrialised early, the U.K. could no longer benefit from the transfer of unproductive labour from agriculture to more productive manufacturing. No formal model was presented and it is difficult to reconcile his idea with the observation that countries with initially lower levels of productivity not only grow more rapidly but can also overtake levels of output per head in "mature" economies. In the model presented here a different explanation of the phenomenon is given by the existence of multiple steady-state growth rates.[3]

The technical progress function is motivated in Section II, and the full growth model is described in Section III. Steady-state growth paths are analysed in Section IV and the complete dynamic solution with stochastic tax rates provided in Section V. Section VI analyses stochastic depreciation, and our conclusions are presented in Section VII.

------

[2] In Arrow's model — and its various elaborations, for example, Sheshinski (1967) — the level of technical knowledge is a concave function of cumulative past investment and positive growth of output per head is impossible without population growth.

[3] In this paper we model only pure externalities arising from investment, thus retaining the ability to model outcomes as a competitive equilibrium. Kaldor (for example, 1975) would have had more sympathy with a model in which some of the increasing returns were internal to the firm, thus requiring a model of monopolistic competition; cf. Shell (1973), Canning (1988) and Romer (1988).

II. A Technical Progress Function

The idea used in this paper is that much technical progress takes the form of "learning by watching". There is a demonstration effect from observations of new ideas embodied in new investment projects to the level of output that can be produced from the existing stocks of capital and labour. Cohen and Levinthal (1989) cite a number of studies which show that many innovations in one firm or industry originated in developments from other firms and industries.[4] New investment projects in one sector of the economy have a demonstration effect on the efficiency of other sectors. Moreover, spillovers of this kind appear to be related to the ease with which innovations can be observed in closely related sectors of the economy. Jaffe, Trajtenberg and Henderson (1992) found strong evidence that geographical proximity is an important determinant of the spillover of ideas as measured by patent citations in the U.S.

Once an idea is embodied in an investment project, the spillover effect occurs up-front. Even though the project continues to operate there is no subsequent additional demonstration effect. This means that it is the investment that creates the spillover, not the capital stock, and leads to the concept of a "technical progress function". This function relates the rate of growth of productivity to the proportion of economic activity that takes the form of new investment projects, the investment rate. Its shape depends upon two opposing effects. First, the higher the rate of investment the larger the probability that existing operators will come into contact with a new idea. Second, conditional upon contact with a new idea, the addition to the growth of the productivity of existing firms declines with the number of new ideas with which contact occurs. In other words, there are decreasing returns to learning by watching. One example of this interpretation of learning by watching is the following. It captures certain aspects of the externalities of research in academic departments. Too few people doing research means little prospect of contact with the new ideas of others that may prove helpful to one's own research. But, as the number of active colleagues rises, the benefit provided by the marginal idea falls because of the opportunity cost of absorbing new ideas.

Consider an economy with a large number of individuals. The "teachers" with ideas meet randomly the "learners" who learn by watching. The relative proportions of the two types are X and $1 - X$, respectively, where X is the investment rate. As the number of agents tends to infinity

---

[4] To give one example from Cohen and Levinthal (1989, fn. 2, p. 570), "in his study of twenty-five major discoveries introduced into the United States by DuPont, Mueller (1962) indicated that, despite the company's reputation for path-breaking research, fifteen originated with work done outside the company".

the probability distribution of the number of ideas observed by a representative agent is a Poisson distribution with mean $\lambda X/(1-X)$, where λ is the average number of new ideas per investment project. The probability of contact with N ideas is

$$\text{prob}(N)=\frac{\exp[-\lambda X/(1-X)](\lambda X/(1-X))^N}{N!}. \tag{1}$$

The marginal benefit of observing an idea, the increase in productivity of existing inputs, is decreasing in N. There are decreasing returns to the activity that generates the externality. Hence the total benefit conditional upon contact with N ideas, denoted by $b(N)$, we assume to be an increasing and strictly concave function of N. The simplest function for $b(N)$ is

$$b(N)=a(1-e^{-bN}) \qquad a,b>0. \tag{2}$$

This functional form has the properties

$$b(N)\geq 0; \quad b(0)=0; \quad b'(N)>0; \quad b''(N)<0 \quad \forall N. \tag{3}$$

Combining (1) and (2) yields the unconditional benefit from learning by watching (the technical progress function, which expresses the rate of productivity growth as a function of X) as

$$\phi(X)=\sum_{N=0}^{\infty} a(1-e^{-bN})\frac{\exp[-\lambda X/(1-X)](\lambda X/(1-X))^N}{N!}. \tag{4}$$

This expression is the product of two terms. The first is simply the product of a and the sum of probabilities over all possible outcomes. The second is the moment generating function of the Poisson distribution. Hence the technical progress function may be written

$$\phi(X)=a(1-\exp[\{\lambda X/(1-X)\}\{e^{-b}-1\}]). \tag{5}$$

The technical progress function $\phi(X)$ has the following properties

$$\phi(0)=0$$
$$\phi'(X)\geq 0 \quad \forall X$$
$$\phi''(X)>0 \quad X<\bar{X}$$
$$\phi''(X)<0 \quad X>\bar{X}$$

where $\bar{X}=1-\dfrac{\lambda(1-e^{-b})}{2}$.

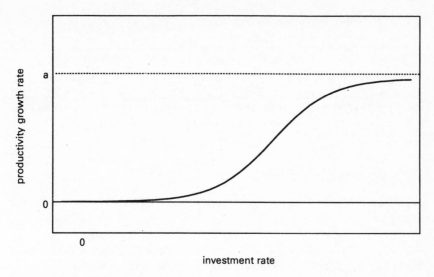

Fig. 1. The technical progress function.

Figure 1 shows the general shape of the technical progress function. It passes through the origin. The point of inflexion occurs at a positive value of X provided that $\lambda < 2$. At all non-positive levels of net investment the demonstration effect is zero, i.e., $\phi(X) = 0$ when $X < 0$. It follows naturally, therefore, that in this model negative investment does not lead to technical regress. The model does not — unlike many real business cycle models — require negative technology shocks to generate cycles. For simplicity we ignore exogenous technical progress altogether, although it is trivial to extend the model to include this. This assumption means that a stationary state is feasible in which zero net investment is accompanied by a zero rate of technical progress.[5] For expositional purposes this is convenient.

The level of output of the representative firm is given by a conventional production function which exhibits constant returns to scale in capital and labour. Output per head, y_t, as a function of capital per head, k_t, is given by

$$y_t = f(A_t, k_t). \tag{6}$$

Lower case variables refer to values at the level of the individual, upper case variables to aggregate values. The level of technical knowledge

---

[5] The technical progress function is defined here in terms of net investment so that for expositional purposes a stationary state is a feasible solution to the non-stochastic version of the model. The qualitative nature of the results is unchanged if the argument of the technical progress function is instead gross investment.

evolves over time according to

$$A_{t+1} = A_t e^{\phi(X_t)}, \tag{7}$$

where we define the aggregate net investment rate, X_t, to be gross investment, I_t, less the nonstochastic rate of depreciation δ resulting from normal wear and tear, as a proportion of total gross domestic product. In Section VI the model is extended to allow for stochastic depreciation.

III. Stochastic Growth Model

We now introduce the technical progress function into a one sector neoclassical growth model with time-varying tax rates. Investment and saving behaviour are assumed to be determined by the optimal consumption programme of an infinitely-lived "representative" individual. This is clearly a strong assumption but it enables us to compare the time path for output implied by the competitive equilibrium of an economy that permits multiple steady-state growth paths with the predictions of conventional real business cycle models. The "representative" individual is an owner–manager who maximises expected utility subject to the production constraints, assuming that he or she cannot influence the overall level of technical knowledge next period. The impact of investment on the dissemination of knowledge is a pure externality. For simplicity labour supply is fixed and the size of the population is normalised to unity. Preferences are assumed to be described by an additively separable isoelastic function of consumption per head. For individual i utility in period t is[6]

$$U_t = E_t \sum_{j=0}^{\infty} \beta^j \frac{c_{t+j}^{1-\gamma}}{1-\gamma}. \tag{8}$$

In order that steady-state growth paths are possible equilibria of the model we shall assume that technical progress is Harrod-neutral. For simplicity we assume also that the production opportunities of the representative individual are described by a Cobb–Douglas production function in which the elasticity of output with respect to capital is denoted by α. Technical progress is, therefore, both Hicks- and Harrod-neutral. Hence

$$y_t = A_t^{1-\alpha} k_t^{\alpha}. \tag{9}$$

---

[6] When $\gamma = 1$ (8) becomes the discounted sum of the natural logarithm of consumption.

The capital stock owned by the agent evolves according to the non-stochastic difference equation

$$k_{t+1} = k_t(1 - \delta) + y_t - c_t - \tau(k_t) + l_t,$$ (10)

where $\tau(\cdot)$ denotes the tax function describing the payment as a function of the capital stock and l is a lump-sum subsidy. We analyse a proportional tax on comprehensive income which implies

$$\tau(k_t) = \tau_t(y_t - \delta k_t).$$ (11)

All tax revenues are assumed to be returned to agents as a lump-sum subsidy, and so $l_t = \tau(k_t)$. Similar results to those presented below follow from the assumption that revenues are spent on government consumption. The exogenous driving force of the model will be time-varying tax rates. The tax rate τ_t is assumed to follow a Markov process described by

$$\text{prob}\{\tau_{t+1} \leq \bar{\tau} | \tau_t\} = F(\bar{\tau}, \tau_t).$$ (12)

A deterministic cycle in tax rates can be thought of as a special case of the stochastic process (12) with a degenerate Markov transition matrix. The owner–manager faces an infinite horizon stochastic programming problem that involves maximising (8) subject to (i) equations (9) and (10), (ii) the distribution of the stochastic shocks described by equations (11) and (12), and (iii) an assumption about the time path of A_t which is exogenous to the owner–manager. The assumption of rational expectations implies that technical knowledge is assumed to evolve according to (7) and the condition that $k = K$, where K is the aggregate level of capital and k is the individual level of capital.

There is one state variable, k_t, and one control variable, c_t. The necessary conditions for an optimum of this programme are the following Euler equation and transversality condition. The Euler equation is:

$$c_t^{-\gamma} = \beta E_t \{c_{t+1}^{-\gamma} \exp r_{t+1}\},$$ (13)

where the (stochastic) post-tax return to capital in period $t + 1$, denoted by r_{t+1}, is given by[7]

$$\exp r_{t+1} = 1 + (1 - \tau_{t+1})(\alpha A_{t+1}^{1-\alpha} k_{t+1}^{\alpha-1} - \delta).$$ (14)

Note that the partial derivative of output with respect to capital is taken holding A constant. The transversality condition is

$$\lim_{j \to \infty} E_t\{\beta^{t+j} u'(c_{t+j}) k_{t+j}\} = 0.$$ (15)

---

[7] We measure interest rates as continuously compounded exponential rates rather than simply one-period rates in order that when discussing the steady-state version of the model, in Section IV, the notation is both simple and consistent.

64   M. A. King and M. H. Robson

These conditions are also sufficient given that (i) the utility and production functions are concave and satisfy the Inada derivative conditions, and (ii) the stochastic process for τ_t is stationary and bounded.[8] Under these conditions there exists a unique continuous optimal policy response function; cf. Brock and Mirman (1972), Lucas and Prescott (1971) and Danthine and Donaldson (1981, Appendix 1).

To study the programming problem defined by maximising (8) subject to (9)–(12), it is helpful to transform the variables measuring output, capital and consumption into levels per efficiency unit of labour in order to arrive at a stationary system.[9] Define the transformed variables by

$$z*_t \equiv \frac{z_t}{A_t} \qquad \text{for } z = y, k, c. \tag{16}$$

The transformed system may then be defined as follows

$$y*_t = k*_t^a \tag{17}$$

$$k*_{t+1} \exp \phi(X_t) = k*_t(1 - \delta) + y*_t - c*_t, \tag{18}$$

where the government budget constraint has been used to obtain (18). The Euler equation becomes

$$\exp(\gamma\phi(X_t)) c_t^{*-\gamma} = \beta E_t \{ c_{t+1}^{*-\gamma} \exp r_{t+1} \} \tag{19}$$

$$\exp r_{t+1} = 1 + (1 - \tau_{t+1})(\alpha k_{t+1}^{*a-1} - \delta). \tag{20}$$

The solution to the infinite horizon optimisation problem for the representative agent is described by a time-invariant policy rule that maps the relevant state variables in period t — the transformed value of his capital stock, the tax rate, and the aggregate investment rate — into the agent's investment rate (and hence into the level of the transformed capital stock in period $t+1$).

$$x_t = x(k_t^*, \tau_t; X_t). \tag{21}$$

In general, as we discuss in Section V, numerical methods must be used to solve for the optimal policy response function. These involve finding a fixed point in the space of continuous functions of the mapping defined implicitly by the Euler equation.

The value of the optimal investment rate chosen by the representative agent must be consistent with the aggregate level of the investment rate that is assumed when individual decisions are made. Hence in equilibrium

$$x_t = X_t. \tag{22}$$

---

[8] In the deterministic case, conditions were provided by Mirrlees (1967).
[9] See Mirrlees (1967), Sheshinski (1967) and King, Plosser and Rebelo (1988).

With endogenous growth the competitive equilibrium investment rate is the fixed point of the mapping given by (21) and (22), and may be written as[10]

$$x_t = \underline{x}(k_t^*, \tau_t). \tag{23}$$

Equivalently, in state-space the equilibrium transformed value of the capital stock evolves according to a time-invariant function k (derived straightforwardly from the function x)

$$k_{t+1}^* = k(k_t^*, \tau_t; X_t). \tag{24}$$

From (17), (18) and (22) it also follows that

$$k_{t+1}^* = \frac{X_t k_t^{*\alpha} + k_t^*}{\exp \phi(X_t)}. \tag{25}$$

The competitive equilibrium of the economy is the intersection of these two surfaces. This may be written as

$$k_{t+1}^* = \underline{k}(k_t^*, \tau_t). \tag{26}$$

The dynamic behaviour of the economy is determined by the mapping described by equation (26). As we shall show, the optimal programme implies that a competitive equilibrium may exhibit multiple turnpikes — that is, the value of the initial capital stock determines to which of several steady-state growth paths the economy converges. The nonlinearity of the technical progress function means that the unique turnpike theorem (and the implied saddlepoint path) for the one-sector neoclassical growth model no longer holds.[11] Before providing a complete solution of the dynamic behaviour of output, it is helpful to discuss multiple equilibria by examining the existence of steady-state growth paths along which expectations are realised with perfect foresight.

IV. Deterministic Steady-state Growth Paths

In order to illustrate the existence of multiple turnpikes we consider, first, the existence of deterministic steady-state growth paths. These are

---

[10] Existence of a competitive equilibrium — the mapping described by equation (21) — is assured by the assumption that the technical progress function is bounded.

[11] Multiple turnpikes were obtained by Kurz (1968), who assumed that capital was an argument of the utility function, and by Liviatan and Samuelson (1969), who studied joint production. Our model exhibits some of the characteristics of joint production in that investment produces both capital and knowledge. Deterministic turnpike theorems in infinite horizon models are surveyed by McKenzie (1986).

characterised by the following four behavioural equations and one definitional identity. The natural growth rate — denoted by n — is given by the technical progress function

$$n = \phi(x). \tag{27}$$

If the expected growth rate of consumption is g then the Euler equation (13) becomes

$$g = \gamma^{-1}(r - \rho), \tag{28}$$

where $\rho \, (= -\ln \beta)$ is the rate of pure time preference.

The investment criterion is that the private marginal product of capital net of depreciation is equal to the cost of capital which is the post-tax rate of return grossed up by the tax rate

$$\frac{\alpha}{v} = \frac{r}{1 - \tau} + \delta, \tag{29}$$

where v denotes the steady-state capital-output ratio.

Equilibrium requires that the "warranted" — or, in modern parlance, rational expectations — growth rate g is equal to the natural rate of growth

$$g = n. \tag{30}$$

Finally, by definition

$$x = gv. \tag{31}$$

These five equations determine the steady-state equilibrium values of the five endogenous variables, n, g, v, x and r.

The solution may be illustrated diagrammatically in the growth rate–investment rate space. The natural growth rate is given by the technical progress function. The rational expectations growth rate is given by the capital market equilibrium curve given from equations (28), (29) and (31) by

$$g = \frac{x(\rho + \delta(1 - \tau))}{\alpha(1 - \tau) - \gamma x}. \tag{32}$$

Figure 2 shows the two curves, for three different values of the steady-state tax rate. Steady-state growth paths exist when the natural rate equals the rational expectations growth rate. The shape of the technical progress function was motivated above. It is clear from differentiating equation (32) that the capital market equilibrium curve is a monotone increasing and convex function of x with a vertical asymptote at $x = \alpha(1 - \tau)/\gamma$. By construction there always exists a stationary equilibrium because both

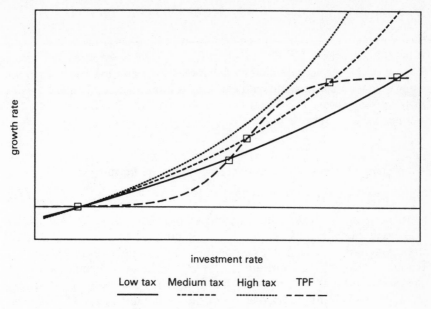

investment rate

Low tax   Medium tax   High tax   TPF

Fig. 2. Capital market equilibrium/technical progress function.

curves pass through the origin. But depending upon the parameter configuration there may also exist up to two additional equilibrium growth paths at positive growth rates.[12]

The most interesting feature of these multiple steady-state growth rates is that, for a given tax rate, the growth rate is *inversely* related to the transformed steady-state level of capital per head. The savings equation (28) shows that the growth and interest rates are positively related, and the investment equation (29) that the interest rate and capital intensity are negatively related. It is this result which will underlie some of the unusual dynamics described below. However, it can also be noted that the higher the tax rate, the lower the level of the stable high growth rate equilibrium and the higher the level of the unstable equilibrium (where these exist).

---

[12] For three non-negative growth rate equilibria to exist, a necessary condition is that the capital market equilibrium curve be steeper at the origin than the technical progress function. In the simulations reported below the parameter values used satisfy this condition. For high enough values of the tax rate only one steady-state growth-rate — namely zero — exists.

V. Growth and Cycles

The dynamic behaviour of the model is given by the nonlinear first-order difference equation for k^*, equation (26), which is given by the intersection of the surfaces defined by equations (24) and (25). Even when tax rates follow a deterministic path explicit solutions can be obtained only in very special cases. For example, when $\gamma = 1$, $\delta = 1$, and $\tau_t = 0 \forall t$, the optimal policy response function is

$$k_{t+1}^* = \exp\{-\phi(x_t)\}\alpha\beta k_t^{*\alpha}. \tag{33}$$

Combining this with (25) gives the competitive equilibrium as

$$k_{t+1}^* = \exp\{-\phi(\alpha\beta - k_t^{*1-\alpha})\}\alpha\beta k_t^{*\alpha}. \tag{34}$$

In general, however, the dynamic equilibrium must be solved by numerical methods. We search for a continuous function which is an approximation to (21) for the competitive equilibrium investment rate. On empirical grounds we constrain the tax rate to lie at percentile points on the range 0.00 to 0.99. Since (21), however, is continuous by construction, we solve initially for a discrete set of points in state space k_t^* and then interpolate using free cubic splines to estimate x_t as a continuous function of continuous $k*_t$, for the discrete τ_t. It is preferable to work with x_t rather than solving for $k*_{t+1}$ directly, since by construction x_t is much better behaved, being close to linear over most of its range with at most one point of inflexion.

Given an initial guess at the functional form, $x^0(k*_t, \tau_t)$, an improved guess x^1 is obtained by applying the Newton–Raphson method to find the required root of the Euler equation (19) and (20):

$$\exp(\gamma\phi(x_t))c_t^{*-\gamma} = \beta E_t\{c_{t+1}^{*-\gamma}(1 + (1 - \tau_{t+1})(\alpha k_{t+1}^{*\alpha-1} - \delta))\} \tag{35}$$

to a given tolerance. For a given τ_t, $k*_t$ determines x_t via the guess at the function x^0, hence also $k*_{t+1}$ from (25) and $c*_t$ from (18). But in order to solve (35) it is necessary to determine $c*_{t+1}$ too, by advancing all these equations one period. The technique employed is therefore to solve, for each discrete value of τ_t, for the value of $x^1(k*_t)$ which satisfies (35) for $k*_{t+1}$ and $c*_t$, conditional on the function $x^0(k*_{t+1})$ used, with interpolation as necessary, to determine x_{t+1}, $k*_{t+2}$ and hence $c*_{t+1}$.

Evaluating the expectation involves calculating the expression in curly brackets for every next period state of the world τ_{t+1} and multiplying by the probability of that state conditional on the current value, τ_t, since this variable is modelled as a Markov process. The derivative with respect to x_t is also required in order to use Newton's method, and its form is complicated by the fact that k_{t+1}^*, c_t^* and c_{t+1}^* are themselves functions of x_t. Two different derivatives of c^* are required because the arguments of c_t^* are

(k_t^*, x_t) whereas those of c_{t+1}^* are (k_{t+1}^*, x_{t+1}). In the first case we therefore take the derivative with respect to the second argument, and in the second case with respect to the first argument. As noted above, we need to supply a value for x_{t+1}. Although we only solve the model as discrete values of k_t^*, we can interpolate to estimate the value of x_t (equivalently k_{t+1}^*) at intermediate values for k_t^*. In order to supply a value for x_{t+1}, given the k_{t+1}^* generated by our guess at x_t, we have to interpolate because the value of k_{t+1}^* will not be constrained to coincide with a point of our arbitrarily chosen grid of values for k_t^*.

This is an approach quite distinct from that commonly used, which is to "discretise" the grid for k_t^* and so force k_{t+1}^* to take one of these discrete values on the grid too. Since one of our main interests is in investment, to obtain satisfactory results by discretisation would require an extremely fine (and hence extremely large) grid. By using our technique of interpolation (using free cubic splines) instead to approximate the true, continuous, function, we can allow the size of grid intervals to be endogenous. It is a distinct advantage of using cubic splines that in regions where we discover that the x_t function is far from linear, we can increase the number of points k_t^* at which we recompute it, so as to obtain greater accuracy. This selective technique allows the algorithm to be faster by orders of magnitude than it would be using the conventional approach.

The method is clearly equivalent to the solution of a finite horizon problem, although in this model we do not find it particularly helpful to think of it in that way. Iteration over these functions is complete when x^{N+1} differs from x^N by less than a given tolerance at every point (k_t^*, τ_t), providing an approximation to the time-invariant competitive equilibrium function for k_{t+1}^*.

For the case of a constant tax rate the difference equation for k^* is plotted in Figure 3. Its shape depends upon the number of equilibrium steady-state growth rates. Steady-state growth paths exist when $k_{t+1}^* = k_t^*$. Figure 3 is plotted for parameter values such that there are three steady-state growth equilibria. Because of the inverse relationship between the growth rate and capital intensity it can be seen that the high growth and the zero growth equilibria are stable, whereas the low growth equilibrium path is unstable.

When tax rates are stochastic — and follow a Markov process — there are as many curves as there are possible tax rates.[13] In each case the current tax rate τ_t and capital stock k_t^* jointly form a sufficient statistic for

---

[13] The same is true when tax rates follow a stationary deterministic time path — a nonlinear cycle — because, as noted above, the deterministic case corresponds to a degenerate Markov transition matrix.

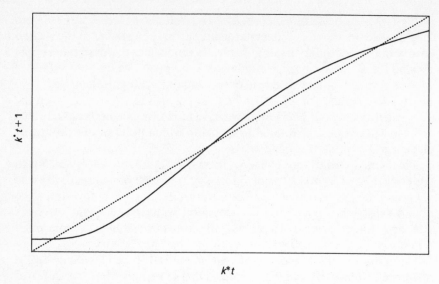

Fig. 3. Difference equation for k^*; (not to scale).

next period's capital stock k^*_{t+1}. With several curves (i.e., multiple possible tax rates) the dynamics become more interesting, and we can show the interaction between growth and cycles.

Consider, first, the simplest case in which there are only two tax rates, and hence a 2×2 transition matrix describing the stochastic process for taxes. There are two equilibrium curves relating k^*_{t+1} to k^*_t. Both can intersect the 45° line up to three times. The dynamic path for capital and output depends upon the relative positions of the two curves, which depends on the particular parameterisation of the economy and transition probabilities for the stochastic process. The number of possible configurations depends upon the number and order of the intersections with the 45° line. One possible configuration is shown in Figure 4. If the economy finds itself with a capital stock in the region AB then it will exhibit "growth cycles" around a stochastic trend which varies with the tax wedge. Similarly, in the region EF there are stable cycles around a stationary level of output. The region CD is characterised by unstable growth cycles. If the economy shifts from this region into BC then it will inevitably end up in AB and conversely if it shifts from CD into DE, it will end up in EF. In the absence of some exogenous shock to the capital stock, the economy cannot escape from regions AB or EF. Of the two, AB with the lower level of the transformed capital stock is associated with higher trend growth (recall the discussion of Section IV above).

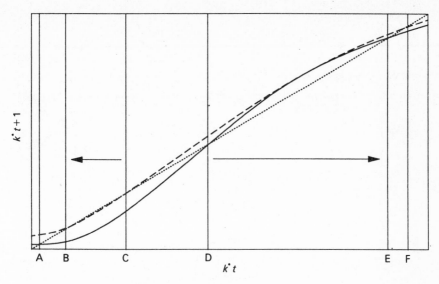

Fig. 4. Difference equation for k^* with two tax rates; (not to scale).

However, the case of two tax rates is very special. With $N > 2$ tax rates the dynamic behaviour of the economy depends upon the configuration of the possible $3N$ equilibria. With only two tax rates the ordering of the equilibria with increasing k_t^* must be S S U U S S (S for stable, U for unstable) in all cases. As the number of tax rates increases, it becomes more likely that the stable and unstable equilibria will become interspersed and therefore that the range of values of k_t^* constitutes (in the terminology of Markov theory) a single closed and irreducible set of states. This means that there are no regions, like AB and EF in Figure 4, from which the economy cannot escape, so that it is not necessary to posit exogenous shocks to enable the economy to move from high trend growth to zero trend growth or vice versa. This phenomenon is directly comparable to the concept of a "stable" set introduced in Brock and Mirman (1972) to which, since the possible ordering of S and U equilibria is there discussed at length, the interested reader is referred. However, whether the pheno-menon of a single irreducible set of states for the feasible values of k_t^* occurs in our model depends on the calibration in any particular case, the number of feasible tax rates (because they are taken to be discrete), their range and the transition probabilities.

If the range of values of k_t^* does constitute such a closed and irreducible set of states, the initial value of the capital stock in simulations will be irrelevant. That is to say, two economies which have the same parameters

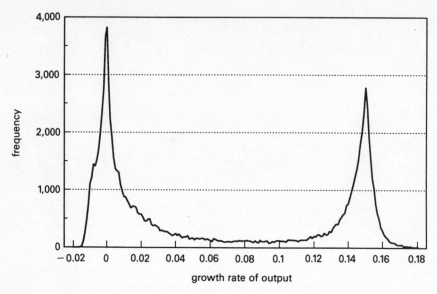

Fig. 5. Stationary distribution of growth rates, 100,000 observations.

and transition matrices, but different initial conditions and realisations of the stochastic variable, must have the same long run probability distribution of the *transformed* values of all relevant variables, such as the capital stock and output.

The frequency distribution of growth rates in such a case may be computed by simulation. Figure 5 shows the frequency distribution of the growth rate for the following plausible set of parameter values: $\alpha = 0.45$, $\beta = 0.98$, $\gamma = 1.0$, $\delta = 0.085$, and the Markov transition matrix for the tax rate on income from capital was estimated using observed changes in tax rates in the U.K. over the period 1913 to 1987. Similar results were obtained using U.S. data — further discussion of the data on tax rates may be found in King and Robson (1990). For these parameter values the $\{k_t^*\}$ constitute a closed and irreducible set of states. The distribution of growth rates shown in Figure 5 is bimodal, around the zero and high steady-state growth rates. The *actual* levels of output and consumption depend upon the entire past history of shocks. by contrast when there is more than one such closed and irreducible set (typically two, corresponding to zero and high growth rate cycles) then there are multiple asymptotic distributions for the transformed variables which depend on the initial conditions. The economy will be driven to either a zero or a high growth rate stochastic cycle and once there can never re-emerge. In this case history determines not only the current level of output but also the asymptotic distribution of growth rates. With additional sources of shocks, however, it is possible that the economy may jump from the zero growth to the high growth rate path, or vice versa. To illustrate this possibility we now introduce stochastic depreciation.

VI. Stochastic Depreciation

In the model of Section V, a sequence of low tax rates can take the economy from a path of stochastic cycles around a zero trend growth rate to a region of high growth cycles. Other sources of stochastic shocks may achieve the same effect. In particular we show in this section that a partial destruction of the capital stock, such as that resulting from a major war, for example, may move the economy onto a high growth path. Suppose that at the beginning of each period there is a stochastic depreciation rate, denoted by ε_t, over and above the normal depreciation rate δ. The stochastic difference equation for k^* (formerly equation 18)) becomes

$$k_{t+1}^* \exp \phi(X_t) = (1 - \varepsilon_{t+1})(k_t^*(1 - \delta) + y_t^* - c_t^*). \tag{36}$$

The idea of infrequent war destruction could be captured by a simple two-point distribution in which there was a very high probability that ε was zero, and a correspondingly small probability that ε was large. Solving for the competitive equilibrium in this case yields the result that two economies that are *completely* identical in all respects — the same values of the "deep" preference and technology parameters and the same initial capital stock — can experience very different paths for output and growth. Suppose both economies start with identical initial capital stocks. Then if one economy suffers the "high" depreciation rate and the other does not, but from then on only the normal depreciation rate occurs, the economy that "suffered" the high rate may shift from zero growth cycles to the regime of cycles around the high growth rate and the other undamaged economy will stagnate, cycling around the stationary state. For some parameter configurations the first economy can be better off — as measured by the expected utility of the representative agent — from the effects of a "war"; for others worse off. Of course, if the high depreciation state recurs then the loss of capital could offset the benefits of shifting to a high growth regime.

Examples of the time path of output for these two economies are shown in Figure 6. The economy that experiences the adverse shock to depreciation (country A) not only catches up the country (B) that does not, but actually overtakes it. This is the sort of phenomenon that commentators seem to have in mind when they refer to the advantages that Japan and Germany experienced from losing the war.

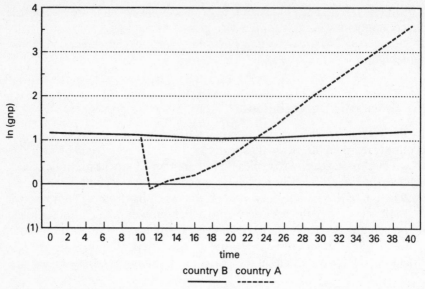

Fig. 6. Effect of exceptional depreciation on output.

VII. Conclusions

In the model of endogenous growth with stochastic fiscal policy and depreciation shocks, it is clear that shocks of either type can alter both the trend growth rate and the transitory adjustment path. Innovations to the trend and autoregressive components of output are correlated. It is, therefore, impossible to decompose the variance of output into proportions that can be attributed to a random walk component on the one hand and stationary shocks on the other. A much richer nonlinear stochastic time series process for output, investment and growth rates emerges.

The existence of multiple steady-state growth means that, even with identical structures and starting points, economies can experience very different growth patterns that have permanent effects on both the level and rate of growth of output. Within this simple framework, it would make no sense to explain observed international differences in growth rate and levels of output per head without an examination of the historical experience of the countries concerned, turning on its head Hahn's (1971) phrase "The theory of growth is not a theory of economic history".

References

Arrow, K. J.: The economic implications of learning by doing. *Review of Economic Studies 29*, 155-73, 1962.

Arthur, W. B.: Competing technologies, increasing returns and lock-in by historical events. *Economic Journal 99*, 116-31, 1989.

Bizer, D. S. & Judd, K. L.: Taxation and uncertainty. *American Economic Review, Papers and Proceedings 79*, 331-6, 1989.

Brock, W. A. & Mirman, L. J.: Optimal economic growth and uncertainty: The discounted case. *Journal of Economic Theory 4*, 497-513, 1972.

Canning, D.: Increasing returns in industry and the role of agriculture in growth, *Oxford Economic Papers 40*, 463-76, 1988.

Cohen, W. M. & Levinthal, D. A.: Innovation and learning: The two faces of R&D. *Economic Journal 49*, 569-96, 1989.

Danthine, J.-P. & Donaldson, J. B.: Stochastic properties of fast vs. slow growing economies. *Econometrica 49*, 1007-33, 1981.

Hahn, F. H.: Introduction. In F. H. Hahn, (ed.), *Readings in the Theory of Growth*, Macmillan, London, 1971.

Jaffe, A. B., Trajtenberg, M. & Henderson, R.: Geographic localization of knowledge spillovers as evidenced by patent citations. NBER WP 3993, Cambridge, MA, 1992.

Kaldor, N.: A model of economic growth. *Economic Journal 68*, 591-624, 1957.

Kaldor, N.: *Causes of the Slow Rate of Economic Growth of the United Kingdom.* Cambridge University Press, 1966.

Kaldor, N.: What is wrong with economic theory? *Quarterly Journal of Economics 89*, 347-57, 1975.

Kaldor, N. & Mirrlees, J. A.: A new model of economic growth. *Review of Economic Studies 29*, 174-90, 1962.

King, M. A.: Growth and distribution. *European Economic Review 36*, 585-92, 1992.

King, M. A. & Robson, M. H.: On tax rate dynamics. Mimeo, LSE Financial Markets Group, London, 1990.

King, R. G., Plosser, C. I. & Rebelo, S. T.: Production, growth and business cycles. *Journal of Monetary Economics 21*, Part I, 195-232; Part II, 309-41, 1988.

King, R. G. & Rebelo, S. T.: Business cycles with endogenous growth. Mimeo, University of Rochester, 1988.

Kurz, M.: Optimal economic growth and wealth effects. *International Economic Review 9*, 348-57, 1968.

Liviatan, N. & Samuelson, P. A.: Notes on turnpikes: Stable and unstable. *Journal of Economic Theory 1* (4), 454-75, 1969.

Lucas, R. E.: On the mechanics of economic development. *Journal of Monetary Economics 22*, 3-42, 1988.

Lucas, R. E. & Prescott, E. C.: Investment under uncertainty. *Econometrica 39*, 659-81, 1971.

McKenzie, L. W.: Optimal economic growth, turnpike theorems and comparative dynamics. In K. J. Arrow & M. D. Intriligator (eds.), *Handbook of Mathematical Economics, Volume III*, North-Holland, Amsterdam, 1986.

Mirrlees, J. A.: Optimum growth when technology is changing. *Review of Economic Studies 34*, 95-124, 1967.

Mueller, W. F.: The origins of the basic inventions underlying DuPont's major product and process innovations 1920 to 1950. In R. R. Nelson (ed.), *The Rate and Direction of Inventive Activity*, Princeton University Press, 1962.

Rebelo, S. T.: Long run policy analysis and long run economic growth. *Journal of Political Economy 99*, 500-21, 1991.

Romer, P. M.: Increasing returns and long-run growth. *Journal of Political Economy 94*, 1002–37, 1986.

Romer, P. M.: Endogenous technological change. Mimeo, University of Rochester, 1988.

Romer, P. M.: Capital accumulation in the theory of long-run growth. Chapter 2 in R. J. Barro (ed.), *Modern Business Cycle Theory*, Basil Blackwell, Oxford, 1989.

Shell, K.: Inventive activity, industrial organisation and economic growth. In J. A. Mirrlees & N. H. Stern (eds.), *Models of Economic Growth*, Macmillan, London, 1973.

Sheshinski, E.: Optimal accumulation with learning by doing. In K. Shell (ed.), *Essays on the Theory of Optimal Economic Growth*, MIT Press, 1967.

Uzawa, H.: Optimum technical change in an aggregative model of economic growth. *International Economic Review 6*, 18–31, 1965.

Permanent International Productivity Growth Differentials in an Integrated Global Economy*

Willem H. Buiter

Yale University, New Haven, CT and NBER, Cambridge MA, USA

Kenneth M. Kletzer

University of California, Santa Cruz, CA, USA

Abstract

The paper analyzes the role of differences in household behavior as a source of persistent and even permanent differences between national or regional productivity growth rates when there are constant static returns to scale in production, free international capital mobility and costless international diffusion of technology. The non-tradedness of an essential input, such as human capital, in the growth process can account for permanent international productivity growth differentials. Differences in national policies affecting private saving, whether through lump-sum intergenerational redistribution or through the taxation of financial asset income, can influence the long-run growth differentials. So do the subsidization of private sector inputs and the free provision of public sector inputs in the human capital formation process.

I. Introduction

Much of the rapidly growing literature on endogenous growth has emphasized increasing returns to scale and/or differences in technology, factor endowments, initial conditions and industrial structure as explana-

---

*We would like to thank, for helpful comments, the participants at the Conference on Fiscal Policies in Open Macro Economies organized by the National Bureau of Economic Research Inc., the Centre for Economic Policy Research and the Tokyo Center of Economic Research in Tokyo in January 1991, at which the first version of this paper was presented. Special thanks are due to our discussants, Akihisa Shibata and Tohru Inoue, and to Takatoshi Ito, George Alogoskoufis, Charles Bean, Allan Drazen, Assaf Razin, Paul Romer, Rick van der Ploeg and Xavier Sala-i-Martin. Two anonymous referees provided very helpful comments on an earlier version of this paper.

tions for persistent and permanent differences in productivity growth rates between nations and regions.[1] Where a two- or multi-country approach is adopted, the richness of the specification of technology and firm behavior stands in stark contrast to the sparseness of the specification of the household sector, which seldom ventures beyond the identical representative consumer.

When differences in technology and industrial structure are not present, as in some of the work of Barro (1989a, b) and in Barro and Sala-i-Martin (1990b), differences in tastes and in other determinants of household behavior can yet account for permanent productivity growth differentials, as long as international or interregional factor mobility is restricted.[2]

The first objective of this paper is to restate and develop the role of differences in household behavior as a source of persistent and permanent differences between national or regional productivity growth rates, in a world with perfect international mobility of financial capital. We present our argument about the importance of household tastes and of policies influencing household behavior when there are constant returns to scale with common technologies and industrial structures between nations or regions. We do not deny that increasing returns or asymmetries in technology and industrial structure may be an important part of the story of unequal growth and development. For expository reasons, however, we abstract from these possible sources of permanent productivity growth differentials.

Under the assumptions of free international technology transfer, constant returns to scale, perfect international financial capital mobility and no non-traded essential growth inputs, most existing growth models (of both the exogenous and the endogenous variety) would imply global convergence of output per worker. Differences in national savings rates would not account for differences in national rates of accumulation of augmentable factors of production. In the simplest version of the model (absent adjustment costs) convergence would be immediate.

The implication that levels and growth rates of output per worker should be equalized across the globe is a source of empirical embarrass-

---

[1] See e.g. Romer (1986, 1987, 1989, 1990a,b,c), Lucas (1988), Grossman and Helpman (1989a,b,c,d; 1990; 1991), Young (1989), Azariadis and Drazen (1990), Feenstra (1990) and Quah and Rauch (1990).

[2] In the macroeconomic literature, Lucas (1988, pp. 14–7) recognizes and emphasizes the importance of factor mobility assumptions for the predictions of neo-classical growth theory. It is equally important for endogenous growth theory with constant returns (of which our paper is an example) and for endogenous growth theory with increasing returns.

ment.[3] This remains true even if its sharp edges are dulled somewhat by allowing for political and administrative restrictions on the international mobility of financial capital and for adjustment costs in the accumulation of augmentable factors of production. Our approach starts from the recognition that there are important "local" or national essential complementary inputs into the production process that cannot be imported but have to be "homegrown". We are thinking of the social, political, cultural, legal and educational infrastructure without which modes of production and economic organization conducive to high productivity cannot be realized.

In our formal model, we try to capture some of the essence of these "homegrown" inputs by including in the production function a non-traded capital good ("human capital") whose production requires a non-traded input (efficiency units of labor time devoted to education and training) that has an alternative use in consumption as intrinsically valued leisure. Our model makes the analytically convenient simplifying assumption that human capital cannot be traded at all. The key non-convergence result goes through even if human capital can be traded, as long as the importable human capital goods are not perfect substitutes for the domestically produced ones.

We realize that our non-traded human capital good whose production requires a non-traded current input that has alternative uses as a consumption good, captures very partially our notion of "homegrown" infrastructure. Some elements of the homegrown infrastructure (the rule of law, the

---

[3] Recent examples of studies that investigate national differences in per capita output levels and growth rates using as (one of) the technological maintained hypotheses the constant or decreasing returns to augmentable factors of production model and the common global technology of production include the empirical studies of Barro (1989a,b), King and Rebelo (1989), Benhabib and Jovanovic (1989) and Cohen (1990). For more on the facts regarding convergence, see Baumol (1986) and Baumol, Blackman and Wolff (1987). Easterly (1989) has a technology that can exhibit increasing returns to scale but focuses on the case of constant returns to reproducible factors and either a constant value for the irreproducible factor or independence of output from the irreproducible factor in steady state. In Easterly (1990) the model is simplified to exhibit constant returns to reproducible factors. Irreproducible factors play no role. Edwards (1989) develops and tests a simple model of growth in developing countries in which the assumption of access to a common global technology is abandoned. It is replaced by one of gradual catching up by a technologically backward nation to the higher external level of technology. The rate at which a country catches up is postulated to be an increasing function of the degree of external orientation in the country's international trade relations.

Barro and Sala-i-Martin (1990b) use a model without factor mobility to analyze convergence of growth rates among regions within a nation state (the states of the U.S.). They recognize that this framework is unrealistic for countries and especially for the U.S. states and note that extensions of the neoclassical growth model that allow for features of an open economy tend to speed up the predicted rate of convergence.

clear definition and defense of property rights, the enforcement of contracts and general popular attitudes towards entrepreneurship, business and private profit) possess aspects of "zero-one" dummy variables (or of variables with a bounded range of variation) rather than of capital-like augmentable inputs whose quantity can be varied (given time and effort) without upper bound. Other "homegrown" inputs such as a skilled and educated labor force fit quite easily into our formal straight-jacket. It is true that countries can send their citizens abroad to advance their education and that the processes of education and training within a country can make use of imported inputs. This, however, is — and has been historically — of second-order importance.

An alternative model of household behavior that leads to similar implications for international productivity growth differences is presented in Buiter and Kletzer (1992a). That model makes the assumption that income from future human capital cannot be used as collateral for borrowing to finance education and training when young.

The second objective of our paper is to analyze the role of policies that affect human capital formation and private financial saving. Among the policies we consider are those that effect direct lump-sum intergenerational redistribution, either in balanced-budget fashion or through the issuing of public debt. A two-country OLG model is the natural vehicle for investigating these issues.[4] We show that intergenerational redistribution policies that cause "financial crowding out" and reduce conventionally measured private saving are likely to boost human capital formation.

In addition to considering the effects of direct intergenerational redistribution on growth differentials, we also consider the effects of residence-based taxes on savings, of subsidies to borrowing for human capital formation and of the free provision of public sector inputs into the education and learning process.[5]

---

[4] Two-country exogenous growth models with a Samuelson (1958) — Diamond (1965) OLG household sector include Buiter (1981) and Buiter and Kletzer (1990, 1991a). Two-country exogenous growth models with a Yaari–Blanchard uncertain lifetimes OLG household sector include Frenkel and Razin (1987) and Buiter (1989). A very simple two-country endogenous growth model with the Samuelson–Diamond OLG household sector is developed in Buiter and Kletzer (1991b). A two-country endogenous growth model with the Yaari-Blanchard OLG household sector is studied by Alogoskoufis and van der Ploeg (1991). Closed economy endogenous growth models with a Samuelson–Diamond OLG household sector have been developed by Azariadis and Drazen (1990) and Jones and Manuelli (1990b); the Yaari–Blanchard version has been studied by Alogoskoufis and van der Ploeg (1990a,b).

[5] Other papers analyzing the consequences of the use of distortionary taxes in (closed) endogenous growth models with a representative agent household sector are Rebelo (1990), King and Rebelo (1990) and Barro and Sala-i-Martin (1990a). The latter also consider productive public spending. Jones and Manuelli (1990a) analyze an infinite-lived representative agent version of the open economy endogenous growth model with distortionary taxes.

The outline of the rest of the paper is as follows. Section II develops the model. Section III contains the main results concerning the effects of international differences in household tastes and in budgetary policies on international productivity growth differentials. Section IV concludes and briefly discusses the relationship between intergenerational redistribution policies, conventional financial crowding out and human capital formation.

II. The Model

Household Behavior

The decisions concerning consumption, labor supply, human capital formation and financial portfolio allocation are taken by households. The household sector in each country is modeled through a three period overlapping generations model. We only derive the household decision rules for the home country. The corresponding decision rules for the foreign households are obtained by attaching the superscript * to foreign taste parameters and household choice variables. The same notational convention is followed for firms and governments. While there are many identical consumers in each generation, we only use an additional subscript to designate individual consumers where this is required to avoid ambiguity.

In the first period of her life ("youth"), a consumer born in period t has an endowment of time, h_t^0 when measured in efficiency units, which she can either choose to consume as leisure ℓ_t in period t or to allocate to an alternative use, which we call education, e_t. This education process during the first period of the household's life adds to the endowment of labor time in efficiency units h_t^1 during the second period ("middle age"), i.e., during period $t + 1$ for a household born in period t.

While young the household can also choose to spend private resources other than time on human capital formation. Such private spending on education m_t will have to be financed by borrowing, since the household is born without financial endowment and does not earn any income in the first period of its life. Public spending on the education of an individual young household, g_t also boosts h_t^1. For simplicity, the young are assumed not to pay any taxes or to receive any transfer payments other than the benefits from the "transfer in kind" g_t, which cannot be resold by the recipient.

Endogenous growth is permitted in our model because of two features of the technology. First, the production function of traded output is constant returns to scale in two inputs that can be accumulated, human and physical capital. Second, the production of the two augmentable inputs is itself subject to constant returns to scale in the traded good and the augmentable inputs.[6]

Human capital lives on after death. We model this formally by assuming that h_{jt}^0, the amount of time measured in efficiency units (human capital) which the jth household of generation t is endowed with at birth, is given by the average amount of human capital achieved by the previous generation during middle age, that is, letting N_t denote the number of households–consumers in period t,

$$h_{jt}^0 = \frac{1}{N_{t-1}} \sum_{i=1}^{N_{t-1}} h_{it-1}^1 .$$

Each member of a new generations stands, as regards its starting level of human capital (knowledge, education), on the shoulders of the average member of the previous generation. We also assume, although this is not essential to obtain endogenous growth, that there is an externality in the human capital formation process. From the definition of h_{jt}^0, it is clear that h_{jt-1}^1 is *non-rival* with respect to the levels of human capital achieved in period t by members of generation t. If generation t is larger, more members of generation t will benefit from the higher average level of education achieved by the previous generation.

The externality and source of inefficiency occur because we also assume that the effect of h_{jt-1}^2 on h_{it}^1, is *non-excludable*. Those in generation t who benefit from the knowledge accumulated by generation $t-1$ cannot be made to pay for these benefits. By permitting the use of purchased inputs in the human capital accumulation process, our human capital accumulation mechanism extends the one developed by Lucas (1988), following Razin (1972) and Uzawa (1965). Azariadis and Drazen (1990) developed a very general specification of the intergenerational transmission of human capital, which encompasses ours.[7] Borjas (1992) presents empirical

---

[6] In general, non-decreasing returns in both production processes is necessary for endogenous growth.

[7] We were not aware of the contribution of Azariadis and Drazen (1990) (henceworth A&D) when the first version of this paper was written. The focus of the A&D paper is quite different from ours. Using a model of a closed economy, they emphasize nonconvexities in the production and accumulation of human capital as a source of possible multiple locally stable stationary equilibria. When there are no traded inputs in the human capital production technology, our specification of the human capital accumulation technology can be written as follows:

$$h_t^1 / h_{t-1}^1 = 1 + \eta e_t / h_{t-1}^1 , \eta > 0.$$

evidence for human capital externalities by showing that the average level of human capital of an individual's ethnic group for the previous generation positively affects the individual's productivity level.[8]

The per capita stock of human capital used in employment by generation t during period $t+1$, h_t^1, is assumed to be a constant returns to scale function of the current inputs e_t, m_t and g_t and the inherited per capita stock of human capital h_t^0, which equals the per capita level of human capital achieved by the previous generation h_{t-1}^1.

We believe our assumption of an intergenerational externality in human capital accumulation to be realistic. It also solves the technical problem, first highlighted by Jones and Manuelli (1990b), of endowing new generations in an OLG model with an asset whose value will grow at the endogenously determined growth rate.

During middle age, the only household choice concerns how much to consume, c_t^1. The entire endowment of labor time services in efficiency units h_t^1 is supplied inelastically in the labor market. Lump-sum taxes (transfers if negative) τ_t^1 are paid.

In the last period of life ("old age" or "retirement") households do not work or educate themselves. The old consume c_t^2, which equals the value of the resources they carried into old age through saving in the first two periods of their lives, minus any lump-sum taxes τ_t^2 paid in their last period.

A special but informative case of the human capital accumulation technology of A&D — given in their equation (13b) — can, using our notation, be written as

$$h_t^1/h_{t-1}^1 = 1 + \gamma(h_{t-1}^1)e_t,$$

where γ is an increasing function of h_{t-1}^1 with a finite upper bound. The non-convexity in the human capital production function of A&D can generate "threshold externalities" (radical differences in dynamic behavior arising from local variations in social returns to scale). Multiple steady states with significantly different levels of education and training can be associated with small differences in initial conditions, giving rise to "development traps".

Our constant returns to scale production function of human capital rules out this particular source of multiplicity of steady states. Like any Diamond OLG mode, however, our model may well possess multiple stationary equilibria for the global economy. We do not study the behavior of the aggregate global economy but instead focus on permanent *differences* between the growth rates of labor productivity of the two countries that make up the global economy. These can occur, in or out of steady state, despite the assumption of identical, constant returns technologies and despite the equalization of the ratio of physical to human capital brought about by perfect international mobility of financial capital and the absence of source-based capital income taxation.

[8] Note that unless, through vigorous intermarriage *à la* Bernheim and Bagwell (1988), all of society effectively constitutes one big happy family, the human capital formation externality, whose domain is both intergenerational and across families or dynasties, will not be fully internalized even if universal operative intergenerational gift motives were assumed.

Formally, each competitive[9] household of generation t $(t \geq 0)$ maximizes its lifetime utility function U_t, given in (1) with respect to ℓ_t, e_t, m_t, h_t^1, c_t^1 and c_t^2, subject to (2), (3) and (4) and the usual non-negativity constraints:

$$U_t = \beta^2 u(c_t^2) + \beta u(c_t^1) + v(\ell_t)^{10} \tag{1}$$

$$(1 + r_{t+1} - \theta_{t+1} - \varphi_{t+1}) m_t - h_t^1 w_{t+1} + c_t^1 + \tau_t^1$$
$$+ (1 + r_{t+2} - \theta_{t+2})^{-1}(c_t^2 + \tau_t^2) \leq 0 \tag{2}$$

$$\ell_t = h_t^0 - e_t \tag{3}$$

$$h_t^1 = h_t^0 \left[1 + \psi \left(\frac{e_t}{h_t^0}, \frac{m_t + g_t}{h_t^0} \right) \right] \tag{4}$$

$c_t^1, c_t^2, m_t \geq 0$; $0 \leq \ell_t, e_t \leq h_t^0$. At the initial date, $t = 0$, $h_0^0 > 0$.

Equation 2 is the lifetime budget constraint of a representative member of generation t. w_{t+1} is the wage paid per unit of efficiency labor in period $t+1$. The before-tax interest factor on loans from period t to period $t+1$ is $1 + r_{t+1}$. θ_t is the period t residence-based tax rate on all non-human asset income in the home country. It is therefore also the subsidy rate to all domestic borrowing, including borrowing by the young. We also consider the subsidization of "student loans" (borrowing by the young to finance expenditures on traded goods used in human capital formation) as a policy instrument. φ is the subsidy rate on these loans. We assume that τ_t^1 and τ_t^2 are such that (2) can be satisifed for non-negative values of c_t^1, c_t^2 and m_t.

$\psi(.,.)$, the constant returns to scale production function for the growth of the household's human capital stock, is positive when both its arguments assume positive values, has positive but diminishing marginal products to both inputs and is strictly concave and twice continuously differentiable.

Our assumption of perfect substitutability of public and private traded inputs into the human capital formation process has two virtues. The first is analytical simplicity. The second is that it avoids an all too easy (and not very convincing) way of creating a role for government in the human capital formation process: assuming m and g to be imperfect substitutes.[11]

---

[9] Each household of each generation t takes w_{t+1}, r_{t+1}, r_{t+2}, h_t^0, τ_t^1, τ_t^2, θ_{t+1}, θ_{t+2}, φ_{t+1}, and g_t as given.

[10] $u(\cdot)$ and $v(\cdot)$ are increasing, strictly quasi-concave, twice continuously differentiable and satisfy the Inada conditions

$$\lim_{x \to \infty} u'(x) = \lim_{x \to \infty} v'(x) = 1/\lim_{x \to 0} u'(x) = 1/\lim_{x \to 0} v'(x) = 0; \quad \beta > 0.$$

[11] Assuming imperfect substitutability between m and g would result in additional tedious algebra, but would not qualitatively change the effects of g on human capital formation and private financial saving, as long as an increase in g does not reduce the marginal products of education and private traded inputs.

Note that there is no externality in the ψ process: public expenditure on education benefiting the ith individual can only be enjoyed by the ith individual: it is excludable and rival. It also cannot be resold by the recipient.

Equation (5) gives the intergenerational transmission of human capital:

$$h_t^0 = h_{t-1}^1. \tag{5}$$

Population grows at a constant proportional rate:

$$N_t = (1+n)N_{t-1} \qquad n > -1; \quad N_0 > 0. \tag{6}$$

The solution to the household optimization problem is given by equations (2)–(5) and the first-order conditions:

$$u'(c_t^1) = (1 + r_{t+2} - \theta_{t+2})\beta u'(c_t^2) \tag{7}$$

$$v'(\ell_t) = \beta u'(c_t^1) w_{t+1} \psi_1 \left(\frac{e_t}{h_t^0}, \frac{m_t + g_t}{h_t^0} \right) \tag{8}$$

$$1 + r_{t+1} - \theta_{t+1} - \varphi_{t+1} = w_{t+1} \psi_2 \left(\frac{e_t}{h_t^0}, \frac{m_t + g_t}{h_t^0} \right). \tag{9}$$

Equation (7) is the familiar martingale condition for the discounted marginal utility of consumption. Equation (8) equates the marginal utility of leisure in period t to the discounted marginal utility of the extra consumption permitted in period $t+1$ by allocating an additional unit of time to education in period t. Equation (9) equates the marginal cost of borrowing to finance additional traded inputs into the education process to the value of the marginal product of the traded education input.

With perfect international integration of financial markets, the use of traded productive inputs alone will therefore not result in taste differences generating permanent differences in human capital accumulation rates and in productivity growth rates. It is equation (8) that accounts for the dependence of the optimal value of the non-traded human capital accumulation input on the parameters of the utility function and thus for the possibility of permanent productivity growth differentials.

The household decision rules for the foreign country are completely analogous to those for the home country and will not be reproduced here. Parameters, variables and functions with the superscript * will characterize the foreign country. Note that while all taste and policy parameters can differ between the two countries, the human capital accumulation technology (η, α, ρ and δ) is the same in both countries.

Firm Behavior

Firms face competitive output and input markets and maximize profits. Non-negative quantities of the two factors of production, human capital (or efficiency units of labor) and physical capital, can be varied costlessly. All firms are identical. The representative firm's production function is linear homogeneous in the two factors of production, increasing in both its arguments, strictly concave, twice continuously differentiable and satisfies the Inada conditions. Capital depreciation is ignored.

The aggregate production function for the home country is given in equation (10). It exhibits constant returns to scale in the two inputs, human and physical capital, is increasing, strictly concave and satisfies the Inada conditions. The representative domestic firm's first-order conditions equating the real interest rate to the marginal product of capital and the real wage to the marginal product of efficiency labor are given in equations (11) and (12), respectively. Y denotes aggregate output, K the aggregate physical capital stock, H the aggregate stock of human capital and $k \equiv K/H$:

$$Y_t = H_t f(k_t) \tag{10}$$

$$r_t = f'(k_t) \tag{11}$$

$$w_t = f(k_t) - k_t f'(k_t) = \omega(k_t), \qquad \omega' = -k_t f''(k_t) > 0. \tag{12}$$

The derivation of foreign country output, interest rate and wage rate is analogous. Note that the two countries also have identical production technologies for traded output $f(\cdot)$. At the initial date, $t = 0$, $K_0 + K_0^* > 0$.

Government

In both countries the government spends on the education of its young, levies lump-sum taxes on the middle-aged and the old, taxes all asset income of its residents at a proportional rate θ, subsidizes education loans at a proportion rate φ, pays interest on its debt and borrows to finance any excess of current outlays over current revenues. Government debt is single-period debt denominated in the traded output. The stock of home country government debt outstanding is B_t. The home country government single-period budget identity is given in equation (13). The conventional solvency constraints, given in (14a) is assumed to apply.[12] The foreign country counterparts are obvious and have been omitted:

---

[12] See Buiter and Kletzer (1992b) for an analysis of the conditions under which the conventional government solvency constraint (22a) is implied by more robust notions of feasibility of goverment tax, spending and financing plans.

$$B_{t+1} = (1+r_t)B_t + g_t N_t - \tau^1_{t-1} N_{t-1} - \tau^2_{t-2} N_{t-2}$$

$$- \theta_t \left\{ \left[\frac{c^2_{t-2} + \tau^2_{t-2}}{1+r_t - \theta_t} \right] N_{t-2} - m_{t-1} N_{t-1} \right\} + \varphi_t m_{t-1} N_{t-1} \qquad (13)$$

$$\lim_{T \to \infty} \prod_{i=0}^{T} (1+r_{t+i})^{-1} B_{t+1+T} = 0 \qquad (14a)$$

B_0 and B_0^* are given.

The budget identity and the solvency constraint of the home government together imply the present value budget constraint:

$$B_t = \sum_{i=0}^{\infty} \Delta_{t+i} \left[\tau^1_{t+i-1} N_{t+i-1} + \tau^2_{t+i-2} N_{t+i-2} + \theta_{t+i} \left(\frac{c^2_{t+i-2} + \tau^2_{t+i-2}}{1 + r_{t+i} - \theta_{t+i}} \right) \right.$$

$$\left. \times N_{t+i-2} - (\theta_{t+i} + \varphi_{t+i}) m_{t+i-1} N_{t+i-1} - g_{t+i} N_{t+i} \right] \qquad (14b)$$

$$\Delta_{t+i} \equiv \prod_{j=0}^{i} (1 + r_{t+j})^{-1}.$$

This says that the outstanding value of the public debt should be equal to the present discounted value of the future primary (non-interest) public sector budget surpluses.

For future use, we introduce the following notation:

$$T_t \equiv \tau^1_t + \frac{\tau^2_t}{1 + r_{t+2} - \theta_{t+2}} \qquad (15)$$

$- T_t$ is the present value (discounted to period $t+1$) of the net lifetime lump-sum fiscal transfer to a member of generation t. Note that while $(1 + r_{t+1} - \theta_{t+1} - \varphi_{t+1})g_t$, the period $t = 1$ value of the public educational inputs spent on a member of generation t, can be viewed as income-in-kind, it is not a lump-sum transfer.

Market Equilibrium

There is perfect international mobility of financial capital. In the absence of distortionary source-based taxes on capital income, the domestic and foreign before-tax interest rates and rates of return on fixed capital will be equalized:

$$r_t = r_t^* = f'(k_t) = f'(k_t^*). \qquad (16)$$

The after-tax rates of return to private saving, $1 + r_t - \theta_t$ in the home country and $1 + r_t - \theta_t^*$ in the foreign country, however, can differ.

From the production function, equalization of capital–human capital ratios in the two economies implies that the wage rates (of efficiency labor) in the two countries are also equalized, although labor itself is not traded internationally and workers are not internationally mobile:

$$w_t = w_t^*. \tag{17}$$

The fact that both countries' labor markets clear each period means that

$$H_t = h_{t-1}^1 N_{t-1} \tag{18a}$$

$$H_t^* = h_{t-1}^{*1} N_{t-1}^*. \tag{18b}$$

Home country private financial wealth at the beginning of period $t + 1$, A_{t+1}, is given by (19a). F_{t+1} denotes the net foreign assets of the home country at the beginning of period $t + 1$. Note that $F = -F^*$.

$$A_{t+1} \equiv [w_t h_{t-1}^1 - c_{t-1}^1 - \tau_{t-1}^1 - (1 + r_t - \theta_t - \varphi_t)m_{t-1}]N_{t-1} - m_t N_t \tag{19a}$$

$$F_{t+1} \equiv A_{t+1} - K_{t+1} - B_{t+1}. \tag{19b}$$

The old (those born in period $t - 2$) will not be holding any assets: they have at the end of period t just exhausted the last of their lifetime savings. The savings of the middle-aged (those born in period $t - 1$) will be the sum of their primary (non-interest) current surpluses during middle age $(w_t h_{t-1}^1 - c_{t-1}^1 - \tau_{t-1}^1$ per person of generation $t - 1$) and their compounded primary current surpluses from their youth $(-(1 + r_t - \theta_t - \varphi_t)m_{t-1}$ per member of generation $t - 1$). The young at the end of period t will have negative per capita savings equal to $-m_t$, the value of their borrowing to finance their education (student loans).

The condition for equilibrium in the world capital market, where equalization of domestic and foreign interest rates and wage rates has already been imposed, is

$$K_{t+1} + K_{t+1}^* + B_{t+1} + B_{t+1}^* = A_{t+1} + A_{t+1}^*. \tag{20}$$

Equation (20) states that the total stock of non-human assets at the beginning of period $t + 1$, $K_{t+1} + K_{t+1}^* + B_{t+1} + B_{t+1}^*$, has to be willingly held by the private sectors of the two countries.

We define

$$b \equiv B/H, \ b^* \equiv B^*/H^* \text{ and } \sigma_t^* \equiv \frac{h_t^{*1} N_0^*}{h_t^1 N_0}\left(\frac{1 + n^*}{1 + n}\right)^t.$$

σ^* is a measure of the relative size of the foreign country. Equation (20) can now be rewritten as:

$$(1 + \sigma_t^*) k_{t+1} + b_{t+1} + \sigma_t^* b_{t+1}^* = \frac{(c_{t-1}^2 + \tau_{t-1}^2)}{1 + f'(k_{t+1}) - \theta_{t+1}} [(1+n) h_t^1]^{-1} - \frac{m_t}{h_t^1}$$

$$+ \sigma_t^* \left(\frac{(c_{t-1}^{*2} + \tau_{t-1}^{*2})}{1 + f'(k_{t+1}) - \theta_{t-1}^*} [(1+n^*) h_t^{*1}]^{-1} - \frac{m_t^*}{h_t^{*1}} \right). \tag{21}$$

When an equilibrium converges to a steady state, the limiting share of the global capital stock employed in both of the countries may be positive or may be zero in one country. The relative size of one of the countries will converge toward zero if the long run growth rate of human capital differs between the two countries. For model parameters and policies such that the long run growth rates are the same, a steady state can exist in which σ^* is positive and finite.

In general, infinite-horizon OLG models may possess indeterminant or unstable equilibria. Proving existence of an equilibrium or of a steady state is not a simple matter for this model and is well beyond the scope of this paper. Note that while saving by generation $t-1$ at date t depends on the interest rate for $t+1$, capital accumulation at date t depends on these savings minus the borrowing for education by generation t which depends on the interest rates for dates $t+1$ and $t+2$ under perfect foresight. However, we can assure that the set of economies for our model for which equilibria exist, are stable and converge to steady states is non-empty with an example. If $u(c)$ and $v(\ell)$ and logarithmic, then m_t, e_t and c_t^1 do not depend on r_{t+2} so that a standard fixed point argument proves existence of an equilibrium. In the analysis that follows, we assume that an equilibrium exists and is stable.

III. International Productivity Growth Differentials

With perfect financial capital mobility leading to equalization of physical capital intensities and of wage rates per unit of efficiency labor, it is easily seen that international differences in the growth rate of output per worker are due solely to differences in the growth rate of human capital per worker. Noting that $Y_t = H_t f(k_t) = h_{t-1}^1 N_{t-1} f(k_t)$, output per worker Π in the home country is given by

$$\Pi_t \equiv Y_t / N_{t-1} = h_{t-1}^1 f(k_t).$$

The rate of growth of home country output per worker, π is given by

$$\pi_t \equiv \frac{\Pi_{t+1}}{\Pi_t} - 1.$$

Similarly, with a common technology and free capital mobility, we have for the foreign country:

$$\Pi_t^* \equiv Y_t^*/N_{t-1}^* = h_{t-1}^{*1} f(k_t)$$

$$\pi_t^* \equiv \frac{\Pi_{t+1}^*}{\Pi_t^*} - 1.$$

It follows that the differences in the growth rate of output per worker are given by:

$$\pi_t - \pi_t^* = \left(\frac{h_t^1}{h_{t-1}^1} - \frac{h_t^{*1}}{h_{t-1}^{*1}} \right) \frac{f(k_{t+1})}{f(k_t)}. \tag{22}$$

In steady state,[13] the labor productivity growth differential is given by:

$$\pi - \pi^* = \frac{h_t^1}{h_{t-1}^1} - \frac{h_t^{*1}}{h_{t-1}^{*1}}.$$

Equations (4) and (22) imply that the productivity growth differential is given by

$$\pi_t - \pi_t^* = \left[\psi \left(\frac{e_t}{h_{t-1}^1}, \frac{m_t + g_t}{h_{t-1}^1} \right) - \psi \left(\frac{e_t^*}{h_{t-1}^{1*}}, \frac{m_t^* + g_t^*}{h_{t-1}^{1*}} \right) \right] \frac{f(k_{t+1})}{f(k_t)}. \tag{23}$$

When the constraint $m_t \geq 0$ is not binding, the optimal program of the home country generation t household and the factor market equilibrium conditions yield equations (24) through to (27). These can be solved for c_t^1, c_t^2, e_t and m_t as functions of k_{t+1}, k_{t+2}, h_{t-1}^1, the home country fiscal policy parameters θ_{t+1}, $\theta_{\tau+2}$, φ_{t+1}, τ_t^1, τ_t^2 and g_t, and the home country subjective discount factor β:[14]

$$u'(c_t^1) = [1 + f'(k_{t+2}) - \theta_{t+2}] \beta u'(c_t^2) \tag{24}$$

$$v'(h_{t-1}^1 - e_t) = \beta u'(c_t^1) \omega(k_{t+1}) \psi_1 \left(\frac{e_t}{h_{t-1}^1}, \frac{m_g + g_t}{h_{t-1}^1} \right) \tag{25}$$

---

[13] For a steady state to exist, preferences must be homothetic.

[14] When the constraint $m_t \geq 0$ binds, the value of the marginal product of traded inputs in the human capital accumulation process is below the after-tax rate of interest $(1 + f'(k_{t+1}) - \theta_{t+1} - \varphi_{t+1} > w_{t+1} \psi_2)$. Equation (36) is dropped and $m_t = 0$ in this case.

$$1 + f'(k_{t+1}) - \theta_{t+1} - \varphi_{t+1} = \omega(k_{t+1}) \psi_2 \left(\frac{e_t}{h_{t-1}^1}, \frac{m_t + g_t}{h_{t-1}^1} \right) \tag{26}$$

$$[1 + f'(k_{t+1}) - \theta_{t+1} - \varphi_{t+1}]^{-1} m_t - h_{t-1}^1 \left[1 + \psi \left(\frac{e_t}{h_{t-1}^1}, \frac{m_t + g_t}{h_{t-1}^1} \right) \right] \omega(k_{t+1})$$

$$+ c_t^1 + \tau_t^1 + (1 + f'(k_{t+2}) - \theta_{t+2})(c_t^2 + \tau_t^2) = 0. \tag{27}$$

An analogous set of equations for the foreign country allows us to solve for c_t^{1*}, c_t^{2*}, e_t^* and m_t^* as functions of k_{t+1}, k_{t+2}, h_{t-1}^{1*}, the foreign fiscal policy parameters θ_{t+1}^*, θ_{t+2}^*, φ_{t+1}^*, τ_t^{1*}, τ_t^{2*} and g_t^* and the foreign subjective discount factor β^*.

We restrict our attention to the effects of small changes in these parameters on the productivity growth differential starting in *symmetric* equilibria (that is, equilibria characterized by identical values of all parameters and identical initial conditions across the two countries). Because we analyze the effects of small perturbations of these parameters on the productivity growth differential, rather than on the separate growth rates themselves, we do not need to consider how the perturbations affect k_{t+1} and k_{t+2}.[15] We also assume that our equilibrium is stable. The effect of changes in taste and policy parameters and in initial conditions on the international productivity growth *differential* can then be found by considering the effect on the domestic productivity growth *level* of changes in domestic taste and policy parameters and in domestic initial conditions, at given values of k_{t+1} and k_{t+2}. These effects are found from total differentiation of equations (24)–(27). The Appendix provides the resulting set of equations simplified to allow straightforward derivation of the effects reported below. We know what happens to domestic productivity growth when we know what happens to e_t and to $m_t + g_t$. To conserve space, we only report the results for the case where the constraint $m_t \geq 0$ is binding when the effects of variations in g_t are discussed.

A Reduction in the Time Preference Rate

The signs of the effects of an increase in β are the following:

$$\frac{dm_t}{d\beta} > 0; \ \frac{de_t}{d\beta} > 0; \ \frac{d(\pi_t - \pi_t^*)}{d\beta} > 0; \ \frac{dc_t^1}{d\beta} \ \text{is ambiguous}; \ \frac{dc_t^2}{d\beta} > 0 \ .$$

---

[15] Whether k_{t+1} and k_{t+2} rise or fall will matter for the effects of perturbations on the separate growth rates, but not for the impact on the differences between these growth rates in a symmetric equilibrium when the perturbations are small.

The intuition is clear. Reduced impatience lowers the demand for early consumption of leisure, ℓ_t, and therefore increases the amount of time spent in education while young, e_t. Since the two inputs in the human capital growth function are complements $(\psi_{12} > 0)$, the use of the traded input, m_t, also increases. The productivity growth differential therefore moves in favor of the country with the lower rate of time preference. A higher value of β also increases the demand for consumption when old, c_t^2, while the effect on consumption when middle-aged, c_t^1, is ambiguous.

Note that with borrowing by the young to finance the purchase of traded inputs into the human capital accumulation process, the effect of a lower rate of time preference on home country relative private financial wealth is ambiguous. This is true even if there is no government debt and the government budget is balanced continuously. While a higher value of β will cause the middle-aged to save more, it will also cause the young to dissave more by taking out more "student loans" (m_t increases). Since the increased value of the human capital assets acquired by the young is not counted in conventionally measured saving, the net effect of an increase in β on conventionally measured private financial wealth is ambiguous.

An Increase in the Present Value of Lifetime Lump-sum Taxes

Note that an increase in lump-sum taxes paid when middle-aged had the same effects as an increase in the discounted lump-sum taxes paid when old. We therefore only discuss the impact of changes in $T_t = \tau_t^1 + (1 + r_{t+2} - \theta_{t+2})^{-1} \tau_t^2$, which are as follows:

$$\frac{dm_t}{dT_t} > 0; \ \frac{de_t}{dT_t} > 0; \ \frac{d(\pi_t - \pi_t^*)}{dT_t} > 0; \ \frac{dc_t^1}{dT_t} < 0; \ \frac{dc_t^2}{dT_t} < 0 \ .$$

Any change in the government's policy concerning borrowing and lump-sum taxes and transfers that increases the net lifetime lump-sum tax burden on generation t, will raise human capital formation by that generation. The negative effect of an increase in T_t on lifetime income will reduce consumption of leisure while young and consumption of traded goods during middle and old age. The increase in e_t induces (because e and m are complementary inputs, $\psi_{12} > 0$) an increase in m_t. Human capital formation and productivity growth in the home country are boosted relative to their foreign counterparts. Clearly, these results may not apply when (distortionary) labor income taxes, rather than lump-sum taxes, are increased.

Increasing T_t will have effects on the dynamics of government debt that must be taken into account unless we also change the lump-sum taxes imposed on future generations. However, we can assure that any increase in T_t has a one-time effect on outstanding government debt by adjusting τ_{t+i}^1 and τ_{t+i}^2 for each $i > 0$, such that T_{t+i} is unchanged and total tax revenues decline by the required interest on the change in the debt every future period.[16]

The productivity growth differential can be increased forever by choosing a balanced-budget intergenerational redistribution that raises the discounted present value of lifetime taxes for all generations. Consider, for instance, a permanent balanced-budget tax increase imposed on the middle-aged with the proceeds used to finance a tax cut for the old, that is, a permanent increase in the scale of an unfunded social security retirement scheme.[17] For simplicity, let the stock of public debt B_t equal zero for all t. During middle age each person pays a tax increase worth μ and during old age she receives a tax reduction worth $(1 + n)\mu$. That is:

$$d\tau_{t+i}^1 = -(1 + n)^{-1} d\tau_{t+i-1}^2 = \mu > 0 \text{ for all } i \geq -2.$$

The present discounted value of lifetime taxes falling on generation $t + i$ changes by

$$\mu \left(\frac{r_{t+2+i} - n}{1 + r_{t+2+i}} \right)$$

which is positive if, as we assume, the interest rate exceeds the rate of growth of population.[18] With leisure a normal good, this policy therefore

---

[16] This is a consequence of the fact that public debt is redundant when lump-sum taxes and transfers are unrestricted. We can decrease the outstanding debt at every date without changing the real equilibrium for the economy; see Buiter and Kletzer (1992b).

[17] In period t the government can only change τ_{t-1}^1, the tax on the middle-aged, and τ_{t-2}^2, the tax on the old. Period t human capital formation is performed by the young in that period, that is by generation t. Human capital formation in period t will only be a function of expectations at time t concerning τ_t^1 and τ_t^2. The behavior of members of generation t during period t is therefore only affected by tax changes in period t to the extent that such changes in τ_{t-1}^1 and τ_{t-2}^2 carry *announcement effects* concerning τ_t^1 and τ_t^2, the taxes they will pay when middle-aged and old. Of course, if the changes in τ_{t-1}^1 and τ_{t-2}^2 are news with respect to the information set of period $t - 1$, then the saving behavior of the middle-aged in period t will be affected. The scope for time-inconsistent policy behavior in a model like ours is clearly considerable. For reasons of space these issues will not be considered further.

[18] While the competitive equilibria of OLG models such as the one we are considering may be dynamically inefficient, we consider the consequences of a cut in lump-sum taxes during period t when the interest rate is above the growth rate of physical capital in each period, which is sufficient for dynamic efficiency in our non-stochastic model. Any government, acting unilaterally, could issue debt or vary lump-sum taxation to achieve a national Pareto improvement if dynamic inefficiency prevailed; see Buiter and Kletzer (1990a, 1990b). In steady state, the growth rate of physical capital equals the growth rate of population, n, plus the growth rate of per capita human capital. The latter is non-negative in our model. If the interest rate exceeds the steady-state growth rate of aggregate human capital it therefore also exceeds n.

increases forever more the home country allocation of time to education and thus the rate of growth of the stock of human capital relative to that in the rest of the world.

This example also illustrates the point that intergenerational redistribution that favors human capital formation will tend to reduce conventionally measured financial saving (and vice versa). As noted before, the increase in T_t (for all t in our example) will increase m_t together with e_t. This increase in financial dissaving by the young is reinforced by a reduction in saving by the middle-aged, for familiar life-cycle reasons. The increase in the scale of the home-country unfunded social security retirement scheme reduces saving by the middle-aged and therefore reduces further the total national stock of non-human assets held by domestic residents.[19]

Higher Public Spending on the Traded Human Capital Accumulation Input

When the constraint $m_t \geq 0$ is not binding, the effects of an increase in public education expenditure are the following:

$$\frac{d(m_t + g_t)}{dg_t} < 0; \ \frac{de_t}{dg_t} < 0; \ \frac{d(\pi_t - \pi_t^*)}{dg_t} < 0; \ \frac{dc_t^1}{dg_t} > 0; \ \frac{dc_t^2}{dg_t} > 0 \ .$$

As long as the non-negativity constraint on private spending on education is not binding, an increse in g_t, public spending on education will lead to a *reduction* in $m_t + g_t$, the total amount spent on education by the private and public sectors combined. Time spent on education, e_t, will also be reduced and the relative growth rate of home country human capital will decline unambiguously. Consumption when middle-aged and when old increase, despite the reduction in h_t^1, because of the smaller amount of educational debt carried into middle age.

As a profit maximizing *firm* facing a given wage and interest rate, the young worker would respond to the in-kind free gift of g_t by reducing his private input of m_t one for one. The free gift of g_t, however, also has an income effect on the young worker as a consumer the same as would a decrease in T_t by $(1 + r_{t+1} - \theta_{t+1} - \varphi_{t+1})g_t$. The net result is the more than 100 per cent crowding out of private education spending by public spending on education.

If the increase in public spending on the education of a member of generation t, g_t, is matched by a corresponding increase in the present discounted value of the life-time lump-sum taxes paid by generation t, T_t,

---

[19] This does not require the interest rate to be above the population growth rate.

so as to be distributionally neutral between generations, there is no income effect associated with the increase in public spending on education, and the "direct crowding out" of private by public spending is exactly one-for-one; see Buiter (1977).

If an aim of policy is to boost human capital formation, this model suggests that increasing public spending on education while the private sector still engages in private spending on education, would not be very effective. An obviously superior policy is one pursued (up to a point) by most governments: the removal of the education decision from the realm of private decision making. Compulsory school attendance up to a certain age is indeed the rule in most societies. It can be checked easily that with administrative assignment of e and of g and access to non-distortionary taxes, Pareto-efficient equilibria can be supported.[20]

When the $m_t \geq 0$ constraint is binding, the effect of an increase in public spending on education, g_t, on private time spent on education is ambiguous. The increase in the quantity of the complementary factor of production g_t raises the marginal return to another hour spent in education. The income effect, however, goes the other way and suggests an increase in the demand for leisure. Even when e_t declines, however, the net effect on the growth rate of human capital is positive. The intuition for this is that the positive income effect of the increase in public spending also raises the demand for c_t^1 and c_t^2. The net effect of an increase in g_t on h_t^1 and on the home country productivity growth rate is therefore positive when the non-negativity constraint on m_t is binding.

---

[20] To achieve an equilibrium for this 2-country economy that is Pareto efficient, the two governments are required to subsidize human capital formation in order to internalize the externality and to forswear the use of distortionary taxes. They also should refrain from choosing values of their human capital accumulation inputs g and g^* that make the constraints $m \geq 0$ or $m^* \geq 0$ binding. In addition one of the governments may have to use lump-sum taxes and transfers to ensure dynamic efficiency. The first-best policy to internalize the externality is to subsidize time spent by the young in education, e_t. In our model such an education subsidy is equivalent either to a subsidy on the wage earned by the middle-aged or to a tax on leisure.

If in our model we also permitted the young to work (in addition to choosing between leisure and education), and if work did not produce a human capital externality, then the equivalence between a subsidy to education, a tax on leisure and a wage subsidy to the middle-aged would break down. Efficiency would then require a subsidy to education or a tax both on leisure and on time spent working while young. The equivalence between an education subsidy and a tax on leisure would also break down when the middle-aged can choose leisure, unless age discrimination can be built into the leisure tax. A subsidy to borrowing by the young for educational expenditures is not needed in the first best. If a tax on leisure or a wage subsidy are not feasible, then subsidizing student loans will be a second-best policy. Subsidizing private borrowing in general will be next best.

An Increase in the Student Loan Subsidy Rate

The analysis of the effects of a change in φ_{t+1}, the subsidy rate on student loans taken out in period t, is straightforward. Note that the effect on generation t of a change in φ_{t+1} is the same as the effect on generation t of a change in θ_{t+1}, the general subsidy to borrowing (tax on lending) undertaken in period t. In addition, a change in θ_{t+1} will affect the marginal cost of borrowing or lending in period t by generation $t-1$. We consider this below, when we report the effects of a change in θ_{t+2} on generation t.

An increase in φ_{t+1} or θ_{t+1} reduces the marginal cost of borrowing to finance the purchase of traded inputs in the accumulation of human capital. The substitution effect of an increase in the subsidy rate on student loans works to increase m_t, e_t, c_t^1 and c_t^2. When m_t is positive, the positive income effect of an increase in φ_{t+1} or θ_{t+1} will reinforce the substitution effects as regards c_t^1 and c_t^2. Since leisure is a normal good, however, the income effect will tend to reduce e_t. If the net effect on e_t is negative, it is possible, since e_t and m_t are complementary inputs, that m_t also declines, despite the reduction is the marginal cost of borrowing. The household as consumer of leisure overwhelms the household as producer in this case. If both m_t and e_t fall, the home country productivity growth rate declines. Even in this case, the total amount of resources carried into middle age will be larger as a result of the increase in φ_{t+1} or θ_{t+1}, because of the increased subsidy. If income effects are small, the productivity growth differential will increase.

If we compensate for the increased educational subsidy with an increase of equal value in T_t (the present discounted value of lifetime lump-sum taxes paid by generation t) in a way that is distributionally neutral between generations, only the marginal incentive effects will be present and m_t, e_t and $\pi_t - \pi_t^*$ will increase unambiguously.

An Increase in the Tax on Saving during Middle Age

The effects of an increase in θ_{t+2} by one unit on the behavior of generation t are the same as the effects of an increase in T_t of magnitude

$$\hat{T}_t = \frac{\tau_{t+2} + c_{t+2} + u'(c_t^2)/u''(c_t^2)}{(1 + r_{t+2} - \theta_{t+2})^2}.$$

which has an ambiguous sign. This is the sum of a real income effect from the reduction in the marginal return to saving during middle age (changing the present value of $c_{t+2} + \tau_{t+2}$) and an intertemporal substitution effect.

Steady-state Productivity Growth Differentials

When the preference ordering generating U_t in equation (1) is homothetic,[21] the steady state verison of equations (24)–(27) can be written as:

$$u'(c^1/h_{-1}^1) = (1 + f'(k) - \theta)\beta u'(c^2/h_{-1}^1) \tag{28}$$

$$v'(1 - (e/h_{-1}^1)) = \beta u'(c^1/h_{-1}^1)\omega(k)\psi_1\left(\frac{e}{h_{-1}^1}, \frac{m+g}{h_{-1}^1}\right) \tag{29}$$

$$1 + f'(k) - \theta - \varphi = \omega(k)\psi_2\left(\frac{e}{h_{-1}^1}, \frac{m+g}{h_{-1}^1}\right) \tag{30}$$

$$(1 + f'(k) - \theta - \varphi)m/h_{-1}^1 - \left[1 + \psi\left(\frac{e}{h_{-1}^1}, \frac{m+g}{h_{-1}^1}\right)\right]\omega(k)$$

$$+ (c^1 + \tau^1)/h_{-1}^1 + (1 + f'(k) - \theta)(c^2 + \tau^2)/h_{-1}^1 = 0. \tag{31}$$

For a steady state to exist, each exogenous flow variable must be constant when expressed as a fraction of human capital per member of the young generation, that is, g/h_{-1}^1, τ^1/h_{-1}^1 and τ^2/h_{-1}^1 must be constant. Equations (28)–(31) then determine the steady-state values of m/h_{-1}^1, e/h_{-1}^1, c^1/h_{-1}^1 and c^2/h_{-1}^1 as functions of β, θ, φ, g/h_{-1}^1, τ^1/h_{-1}^1, τ^2/h_{-1}^1 and k. An analogous set of equations applies to the foreign country. If we restrict ourselves again to perturbations of a *symmetric* stationary equilibrium (identical values of all parameters in the two countries), we can analyze the effects of changes in taste and policy parameters without having to work out the effect of these parameter changes on the steady-state ratio of physical to human capital, k. Furthermore, the steady state effects of β, θ, φ, g/h_{-1}^1, τ^1/h_{-1}^1 and τ^2/h_{-1}^1 on m/h_{-1}^1, e/h_{-1}^1, c^1/h_{-1}^1 and c^2/h_{-1}^1 (and therefore on the steady state productivity growth differential), are exactly the same as the impact effects of β, θ_t,[22] φ_t, g_t, τ_t^1 and τ_t^2 on m_t, e_t, c_t^1 and c_t^2, given h_{t-1}^1, derived in the previous subsections.

---

[21] If the preference ordering generating U_t defined in equation (1) is homothetic, it follows that

$$\beta^2 u(c_t^2) + \beta u(c_t^1) + v(\ell_t) = \lambda[\beta^2 u(c_t^2/\lambda) + \beta u(c_t^1/\lambda) + v(\ell_t/\lambda)]$$

for all $\lambda > 0$.

[22] The steady-state effects of a change in θ are the same as the impact effects of equal changes in θ_{t+1} and θ_{t+2}.

Only Traded Inputs into Human Capital Accumulation

Inter-country differences in productivity growth rates disappear in our model when all inputs into human capital accumulation are tradable. This effectively is the case analyzed in Alogoskoufis and van der Ploeg (1991). Consider, for example, the following human capital accumulation function in which only traded inputs enter:

$$h_t^1 = h_t^0\{1 + \eta[(m_t + g_t)/h_t^0]^\lambda\} \quad 0 < \lambda < 1.$$

With this strictly concave accumulation function, the first-order condition for m_t becomes, when the non-negativity constraint on m_t is not binding

$$1 + r_{t+1} - \theta_{t+1} - \varphi_{t+1} = \eta\lambda[(m_t + g_t)/h_t^0]^{\lambda-1}w_{t+1}.$$

With perfect international mobility of financial capital and no differential source-based taxes on capital rentals, the before-tax interest rate will be equalized in the world economy. With a common production function the wage rate (per unit of efficiency labor) will also be equalized throughout the world economy. With a common human capital accumulation technology (common values of η and λ in this example) and common distortionary tax rates, the equilibrium value of $(m_t + g_t)/h_t^0$ is equalized throughout the world economy. Taste parameters (such as β and β^*) therefore no longer matter for differences in productivity growth rates. Neither do redistributive lump-sum taxation or public sector deficits. The only aspect of fiscal policy in our model that matters for growth differentials are the tax rates on non-human asset income and student loan subsidy rates (θ, θ^*, φ and φ^*). Different source-based capital rental tax rates would *cet. par.* cause different wages to be generated in the parts of the world where they apply. By raising the return to human capital accumulation a higher home country relative real wage would *cet. par.* increase m_t and thus the relative growth rate of home country human capital.

Note that a permanently higher value of φ will *cet. par.* be associated with a permanently higher home country relative growth rate of human capital and a permanently higher relative rate of growth of output per worker. An increase in θ will have the same effects.

Also, higher public spending on education would *cet. par.* (i.e., without allowing for possible consequences for the world rate of interest and the wage rate of the financing decisions associated with higher public spending) crowd out private spending on education one-for-one:

$d(m_t + g_t) = 0.$[23] If m and g were imperfect substitutes, crowding out would be less than one-for-one.

If the non-negativity constraint $m_t \geq 0$ on private expenditure on education is binding, the government can of course boost the growth rate of human capital simply by raising g_t, its own expenditure on education.

IV. Conclusion

The conventional system of national income, expenditure and product accounts fails to register most of a key input into the human capital formation process: time spent in education and training. In addition, it fails to record altogether the output of that process: the increase in the stock of human capital. It does register (correctly) as negative household saving the borrowing by households in order to finance purchases of marketed inputs into human capital formation. The purchase of these traded inputs is, however, erroneously classified as consumption rather than as household investment. This has the important implication that it is not necessarily true that any policy which reduces conventionally measured domestic saving is growth unfriendly. Even in the real world, loans taken out by younger households need not be consumption loans, but may instead be used to finance growth-enhancing unrecorded human capital formation.

In our model, the non-tradedness of an essential input into the accumulation of human capital implies that any policy that redistributes in lump-sum fashion between generations can have opposite effects on human capital formation and conventionally measured financial saving. An increase in the present discounted value of the lifetime lump-sum taxes paid by generation t raises human capital formation and reduces financial saving by that generation when the interest rate exceeds the growth rate of population.

A higher public debt burden will, to the extent that it represents a net intergenerational redistribution towards the old, increase a country's growth rate of human capital and output relative to the rest of the world. More generally, deficit financing policies and lump-sum intergenerational redistribution policies that boost conventionally measured financial saving will reduce human capital accumulation. The level of the growth rate of the

---

[23] In our framework here, any consequences of lump-sum financing of, say, increased home country public spending on education would affect domestic and foreign interest rates and wage rates equally. This would therefore not alter productivity growth differentials.

country that raises its public debt burden could of course decline, since a higher public debt burden also lowers financial saving and physical capital formation.

For example, suppose that a tax is levied on the old in period t and that the revenues from this one-time levy are used to retire public debt. Following the wealth levy, the present discounted value of net future tax receipts is therefore reduced by the same amount. This "present value tax dividend" can be distributed across generations in such a manner that the present discounted value of lifetime taxes for all current and future generations (except the unfortunate current old) is lower. For instance, the same size tax cut could be given to the middle-aged each period.

This policy would raise the permanent income (at given wages and interest rates) of all generations born in period $t-1$ or later. It would therefore reduce the expenditure of time and traded goods on human capital formation (and the associated borrowing) during youth by all generations born in period t or later. Current and future middle-aged all increase their saving for life-cycle purposes. Human capital formation and financial saving move in opposite directions.

The essential implications of this paper do not depend on the specific details of the human capital accumulation mechanism we assume, which relies heavily on education–leisure choice. Buiter and Kletzer (1992a) present an alternative (or complementary) mechanism giving rise to the same qualitative conclusions based on the plausible assumption that human capital may be inferior to physical capital as collateral for borrowing to finance educational expenditures.[24] The qualitative properties of our model are the same whether we assume a non-traded essential growth input or invoke a binding self-financing constraint for a traded growth input. In this alternative model, it is a labor–leisure choice rather than an education–leisure choice that causes the growth rate of human capital to depend on household preferences and on policies affecting household behavior. Both mechanisms may well be operative in practice.

---

[24] Barro, Mankiw and Sala-i-Martin (1992) also discuss the importance of self-financing constraints for convergence of growth rates under international capital mobility.

Appendix

This appendix provides the information necessary to derive the effects of taste and policy parameter perturbations on household choices of e_t, m_t, c_t^1 and c_t^2 reported in the text. Totally differentiating equations (24)–(27) and substituting out the result for (24) to eliminate dc_t^2 yields the following equation system:

$$
\begin{bmatrix}
-\omega\psi_1\beta u''(c_t^1) & -(v''(\ell_t)+\omega\psi_{11}\beta u'(c_t^1)) & -\omega\psi_{12}\beta u'(c_t^1) \\
0 & \omega\psi_{12} & \omega\psi_{22} \\
-\left(1+\dfrac{u''(c_t^1)}{(1+r_{t+2}-\theta_{t+2})^2\beta u''(c_t^2)}\right) & \omega\psi_1 & 0
\end{bmatrix}
\begin{bmatrix}
dc_t^1 \\
de_t \\
dm_t
\end{bmatrix}
$$

$$
=
\begin{bmatrix}
0 \\
0 \\
1
\end{bmatrix} dT_t
+
\begin{bmatrix}
\omega\psi_1 u'(c_t^1) \\
0 \\
\dfrac{-u'(c_t^2)}{(1+r_{t+2}-\theta_{t+2})\beta u''(c_t^2)}
\end{bmatrix} d\beta
+
\begin{bmatrix}
\omega\psi_{12}\beta u'(c_t^1) \\
-\omega\psi_{22} \\
-\omega\psi_2
\end{bmatrix} dg_t
$$

$$
+
\begin{bmatrix}
0 \\
-1 \\
-m
\end{bmatrix}(d\theta_{t+1}+d\varphi_{t+1})
+
\begin{bmatrix}
0 \\
0 \\
(1+r_{t+2}-\theta_{t+2})^{-2}\left[c_t^2+\tau_t^2+\dfrac{u'(c_t^2)}{u''(c_t^2)}\right]
\end{bmatrix} d\theta_{t+2}.
$$

We assume that $u(c)$ and $v(\ell)$ are strictly concave and that ψ satisfies ψ_1, $\psi_2 > 0$, ψ_{11}, $\psi_{22} < 0$, $\psi_{12} > 0$ and $\psi_{11}\psi_{22}-\psi_{12}\psi_{12} \geq 0$. It is straightforward to invert the first matrix.

References

Alogoskoufis, George S. & van der Ploeg, Frederick: Endogenous growth and overlapping generations. DP in Economics 26/90, Birkbeck College, University of London, Nov. 1990a.

Alogoskoufis, George S. & van der Ploeg, Frederik: On budgetary policies and economic growth. CEPR DP 496, Dec. 1990b.

Agoloskoufis, George S. & van der Ploeg, Frederik: On budgetary policies, growth and external deficits in an interdependent world. Paper presented at the NBER/CEPR/TCER Conference on Fiscal Policies in Open Macro Economies, Tokyo, Jan. 7-8, 1991.

Azariadis, Costas & Drazen, Allan: Threshold externalities in economic development. *Quarterly Journal of Economics 105*, 501–26, May 1990.

Barro, Robert J.: A cross-country study of growth, saving and government. NBER WP 2855, 1989a.

Barro, Robert J.: Economic growth in a cross section of countries, NBER WP 3120, Sept. 1989b.

Barrow, Robet J. & Sala-i-Martin, Xavier: Public finance in models of economic growth. NBER WP 3362, May 1990a.

Barro, Robert J. & Sala-i-Martin, Xavier: Economic growth and convergence across the United States. NBER WP 3419, Aug. 1990b.

Barro, Robert J., Mankiw, N. Gregory & Sala-i-Martin, Xavier: Capital mobility in neoclassical models of growth. Mimeo, Harvard University, June 1992.

Baumol, William J.: Productivity growth, convergence and welfare. *American Economic Review 76*, 1072–85, Dec. 1986.

Baumol, William J., Blackman, Sue Anne Batey, Wolff, Edward: *Productivity Growth: The Long View*, Cambridge, MA MIT Press, 1989.

Benhabib, Jess & Jovanovic, Boyan: Externalities and growth accounting. NBER WP 3190, 1989.

Bernheim, B. Douglas & Bagwell, Kyle: Is everything neutral? *Journal of Political Economy 96*, 308–38, Apr. 1988.

Borjas, George J.: Ethnic capital and intergenerational mobility. *Quarterly Journal of Economics 107*, 123–50, Feb. 1992.

Buiter, Willem H.: "Crowding out" and the effectiveness of fiscal policy. *Journal of Public Economies 7*, 309–28, 1977.

Buiter, Willem H.: Time preference and international lending and borrowing in an overlapping-generations model. *Journal of Political Economy 89*, 769–97, Aug. 1981.

Buiter, Willem H.: *Budgetary Policy, International and Intertemporal Trade in the Global Economy*, North-Holland, Amsterdam, 1989.

Buiter, Willem H. & Kletzer, Kenneth M.: Fiscal policy, interdependence and efficiency, NBER WP 3328, Apr. 1990.

Buiter, Willem H. & Kletzer, Kenneth M.: The welfare economics of cooperative and non-cooperative fiscal policy. *Journal of Economic Dynamics and Control 15*, 215–44, 1991a.

Buiter, Willem H. & Kletzer, Kennth M.: Persistent differences in national productivity growth rates with a common technology and free capital mobility; the roles of public debt, capital taxation and policy towards human capital formation. *Journal of the Japanese and International Economies 5*, 325–53, Dec. 1991b.

Buiter, Willem H. & Kletzer, Kenneth M.: Permanent international productivity growth differentials in an integrated global economy. NBER WP 4220, Nov. 1992a.

Buiter, Willem H. & Kletzer, Kenneth M.: Government solvency, Ponzi finance and the redundancy and usefulness of public debt. NBER WP 4076, May, 1992b.

Cohen, Daniel: Slow growth and LDC debt in the eighties: An update. Mimeo, CEPREMAP, Paris, Oct. 1990.

Diamond, Peter A.: National debt in a neo-classical growth model. *American Economic Review 55*, 1126–50, 1965.

Easterly, William: Policy distortions, size of government, and growth. NBER WP 3214, Dec. 1989.

Easterly, William: Endogenous growth in developing countries with government-induced distortions. Mimeo, World Bank, Aug. 1990.

Edwards, Sebastian: Openness, outward orientation, trade liberalization and economic performance in developing countries. NBER WP 2908, Mar. 1989.

Feenstra, Robert: Trade and uneven growth. NBER WP 3276, Mar. 1990.

Frenkel, Jacob A. & Razin, Assaf: *Fiscal Policies and the World Economy*. MIT Press, Cambridge, MA, 1987.

Grossman, Gene M. & Helpman, Elhanan: Product development and international trade. *Journal of Political Economy 97*, 1261–83, 1989a.

Grossman, Gene M. & Helpman, Elhanan: Endogenous product cycles. NBER WP 2913, Mar. 1989b.

Grossman, Gene M. & Helpman, Elhanan: Quality ladders in the theory of growth. NBER WP 3099, Sept. 1989c.

Grossman, Gene M. & Helpman, Elhanan: Quality ladders and product cycles. NBER WP 3201, Dec. 1989d.

Grossman, Gene M. & Helpman, Elhanan: Comparative advantage and long-run growth. *American Economic Review 80*, 796–815, 1990.

Grossman, Gene M. & Helpman, Elhanan: *Innovation and Growth in the Global Economy.* MIT Press, Cambridge, MA, 1991.

Jones, Larry E. & Manuelli, Rodolfo: A convex model of equilibrium growth: Theory and policy implications. *Journal of Political Economy 98*, 1008–38, Oct. 1990a.

Jones, Larry E. & Manuelli, Rodolfo: Finite lifetimes and growth. NBER WP 3469, 1990b.

King, Robert G. & Rebelo, Sergio: Transitional dynamics and economic growth in the neoclassical model. NBER WP 3185, Nov. 1989.

King, Robert G. & Rebelo, Sergio: Public policy and economic growth: Developing neoclassical implications. NBER WP 3338, Apr. 1990.

Lucas, Robert E. Jr.: On the mechanics of economic development. *Journal of Monetary Economics 22*, 3–42, 1988.

Quah, Danny & Rauch, James E.: Openness and the rate of economic growth. Mimeo, M.I.T., Cambridge, MA, Oct. 1990.

Razin, Assaf: Investment in human capital and economic growth. *Metroeconomica 24*, 101–16, May–Aug. 1972.

Rebelo, Sergio: Long run policy analysis and long run growth. NBER WP 3325, Apr. 1990.

Romer, Paul. M.: Increasing returns and long-run growth. *Journal of Political Economy 94*, 1002–37, Oct. 1986.

Romer, Paul. M.: Growth based on increasing returns due to specialization. *American Economic Review, Papers and Proceedings 77*, 56–62, May 1987.

Romer, Paul M.: Human capital and growth: Theory and evidence. NBER WP 3173, Nov. 1989.

Romer, Paul M.: Capital, labor, and productivity. *Brookings Papers on Economic Activity, Microeconomics*, 337–67, 1990a.

Romer, Paul M.: Endogenous technical change. *Journal of Political Economy 98*, 5, Pt. 2, S71–S102, 1990b.

Romer, Paul M.: Are nonconvexities important for understanding growth? NBER WP 3271, Feb. 1990c.

Samuelson, Paul A.: An exact consumption-loan model of interest, with or without the social contrivance of money. *Journal of Political Economy 66*, 467–82, 1958.

Uzawa, Hirofumi: Optimum technical change in an aggregate model of economic growth. *International Economic Review 6*, 18–31, 1965.

Young, Alwyn: Learning by doing and the dynamic effects of international trade. Mimeo, Columbia University, Nov. 1989.

Growth, Human Capital Spillovers and International Policy Coordination*

Keith Blackburn

University of Southampton, England

Morten Overgaard Ravn

University of Aarhus, Denmark and European University Institute, San Domenico di Fiesole, Italy

Abstract

The paper is concerned with public policy and economic development in a world of inter-dependent economies. Its objective is to show how the international coordination of economic policy is a means of promoting growth across countries. The analysis is based on a two-country endogenous growth model in which the production of human capital depends on country-specific tax-financed public expenditure and worldwide previously accumulated knowledge. We consider optimal policy as the outcome of a dynamic game between benevolent governments. We show that both growth (which itself has no normative significance) and welfare are, indeed, higher under cooperation than under non-cooperation.

I. Introduction

Neoclassical growth theory explained how an economy could be in a balanced growth equilibrium when the marginal productivity of its accumulable factor is strictly decreasing. But because of this property the theory had little or nothing to say about growth itself, which was determined exogenously at some arbitrary rate of labour-augmenting (Harrod-neutral) technological process. Romer (1986), in his seminal contribution to new growth theory, described the conditions under which an economy could be in a balanced growth equilibrium when its production technology

---

*We are grateful for the comments of an anonymous referee and the editors of this Journal. We also wish to thank seminar participants at the University of Aarhus, the University of Southampton, the European University Institute and the 1993 Winter Symposium of the Econometric Society. The usual disclaimer applies.

is homogeneous of degree one, or greater than one, in the accumulable factor. Under such circumstances, growth occurs endogenously, being determined by the deep parameters of the economy, including those describing government policy. There is now overwhelming evidence that government policy does, indeed, matter for economic growth.[1] By altering the fiscal and monetary, financial and trade, regimes of economies, governments have considerable potential to affect growth performance. In this paper we seek to study the link between policy and growth from a new angle. Our interest is in the international growth repercussions of national policies in a world of interdependent economies. Our objective is to show how the international coordination of economic policies is a means of promoting growth.

The paper draws together the literatures on endogenous growth and international policy coordination. As indicated above, the key to generating sustainable growth is a production technology with constant or increasing returns to inputs that can be accumulated. Existing models differ in the way they motivate this technology and the optimality properties of the balanced growth equilibrium.[2] Established growth mechanisms include human capital accumulation, cf. King and Rebelo (1990), Lucas (1988) and Rebelo (1991), private externalities, cf. Romer (1986), public externalities, cf. Barro (1990) and Barro and Sala-i-Martin (1992), and research and development, cf. Grossman and Helpman (1990, 1991) and Romer (1987, 1990). There is little in this literature by way of rigorous analysis of macroeconomic policy. What analysis there is tends to involve numerical simulations of arbitrary changes in tax rates or comparative equilibrium exercises of alternative trade regimes. It would be interesting to know what optimal policies might look like. In our view, the literature would benefit from a more systematic treatment of policy which respects the equilibrium behaviour of both the private and public sectors.

The literature on international policy coordination is concerned with the potential inefficiencies of non-cooperative behaviour on the part of governments of interdependent economies; see Canzoneri and Henderson (1988), Hughes-Hallett (1986, 1987), Levine and Currie (1987), Miller and Salmon (1985), Oudiz and Sachs (1984) and Sachs (1983).[3] These inefficiencies reflect a failure to take account of cross-country externalities. By internalizing these externalities, cooperation between governments is a

---

[1] For surveys of this evidence, see Easterly and Rebelo (1992), Fischer (1991, 1993) and Roubini and Sala-i-Martin (1991).

[2] For a survey of these models, see Sala-i-Martin (1990).

[3] Other contributions can be found in Buiter and Marston (1985). Fischer (1987) provides a survey of the literature.

means of improving policy outcomes. There are circumstances under which policy cooperation can be counterproductive. One of these is when governments strategically interact with not only themselves but also private agents; see Kehoe (1989), Rogoff (1985) and Jensen (1993).[4] Notwithstanding this, however, it can be argued that by considering only stationary economies, the literature has understated the potential gains from cooperation. An important unexplored issue is whether cooperation is a means of promoting growth across countries.[5]

We believe that a cross-fertilization of ideas from the literature on endogenous growth and international policy coordination offers a potentially rewarding avenue for further research. Accordingly, this paper is concerned with the design of public policy and the implications for growth in a world of interdependent economies. Our analysis is based on a two-country endogenous growth model in which there are national and international externalities associated with the accumulation of human capital. The technology for producing new knowledge depends on country-specific tax-financed public expenditure and worldwide existing knowledge. Decentralized choices lead to an inefficient competitive balanced growth equilibrium in which growth rates converge regardless of the distributions of taxes and initial human capital stocks. Convergence of per capita income levels requires tax to be the same across countries. We study equilibrium tax policy as the outcome of a dynamic game between benevolent governments. We show that growth and welfare are higher under cooperation than under non-cooperation. The orders of magnitude of these gains are indicated by results from numerical simulations.

The model is described in Section II. In Section III we compute the balanced growth equilibrium for given tax rates. Equilibrium policy under different "rules of the game" is studied in Section IV. Section V concludes.

II. A Framework

The analysis is based on a model developed by Tamura (1991) in which growth occurs from international externalities in the production of knowledge. We reinterpret that model as an artificial world of two inter-

---

[4] In the absence of a commitment technology, the time inconsistency of optimal policy invites credibility problems. Non-cooperative behaviour acts as a discipline on governments, tempering each one's individual incentive to create policy surprises. Cooperation weakens this by removing the competition between governments. For a survey of the literature on credibility, see Blackburn and Christensen (1989).

[5] Since writing this paper, we have discovered an analysis of the issue in Devereux and Mansoorian (1992). That analysis differs from ours, being based on a different model with possibly different implications.

dependent economies and extend it to include tax-financed public policy. Unlike the approach taken so far in the new growth literature, we endogenize policy by regarding it as the solution to a well-defined dynamic optimization problem of a government. This problem is to maximize welfare which is not the same as maximizing growth: growth itself has no normative significance in our framework.

We consider two symmetric artificial economies indexed by $i, j \in \{1, 2\}$. Each economy is populated by a constant large number of identical, infinitely-lived agents endowed with perfect foresight.[6] Each agent produces and consumes a single perishable commodity and allocates a fixed time endowment between leisure and investment in human capital. The decision problem for each agent is

$$\max_{\{c_{it}, \lambda_{it}, h_{it+1}\}_{t=0}^{\infty}} \quad W_i = \sum_{t=0}^{\infty} \beta^t [\log(c_{it}) + \nu \log(1 - \lambda_{it})] \tag{1}$$

$$\text{s.t.} \quad c_{it} = (1 - \tau_{it}) h_{it} \tag{2}$$

$$h_{it+1} = A(h_{it} \lambda_{it})^\alpha g_{it}^\gamma H_{it}^\psi H_{jt}^{1-\alpha-\gamma-\psi} \tag{3}$$

for $i, j \in \{1, 2\}$. We have chosen the technologies describing atemporal preferences, production of output and production of knowledge which give the greatest clarity of exposition.

Equation (1) is the intertemporal utility function, where $\nu > 0$ and $\beta \in (0, 1)$ is a discount factor. Utility depends on consumption, c_{it}, and the time spent on investing in human capital, λ_{it}.[7]

Equation (2) is the budget constraint, where τ_{it} is a flat-rate income tax and h_{it} is human capital. To generate perpetual growth, we assume constant returns to scale so that the production function is linearly homogeneous in h_{it}.

Equation (3) describes human capital accumulation, where $\alpha, \gamma, \psi \in (0, 1)$, $\alpha + \gamma + \psi \in (0, 1)$ and $A > 0$ is a technological shift or learning parameter. The quantity g_{it} is public expenditure which we prefer to think of as representing more than just spending on social infrastructure and the provision of law and order. We also have in mind the provision of information through such means as government publications, public libraries and national museums. Barro (1990) considers the case in which public expenditure is an input to the production of output. The quantity H_{it} is the

---

[6] Allowing for population growth would be a straightforward extension of no significance.
[7] Total time has been normalized to unity. Introducing a time allocation to the production of output is a trivial extension of the model which does not alter the results that follow. Since utility is logarithmic and $\beta \in (0, 1)$, utility is bounded under constant geometric growth.

(average) aggregate stock of human capital at home and captures spillover effects within the same country. The appearance of H_{jt}, the aggregate stock of human capital abroad, is motivated by Tamura (1991) as reflecting a system of imperfect property rights in the acquisition and transmission of knowledge across countries. The human capital production function displays decreasing returns to each input separately and constant returns to all inputs jointly. The inclusion of g_{it}, H_{it} and H_{jt} in this function implies that there are national and international externalities in the production of human capital. These variables depend on aggregate private equilibrium behaviour which the representative agent treats rationally as exogenous uncontrollable sequences.

A special feature of our model is that the two countries are connected through cross-country spillovers in the accumulation of human capital but not through trade in goods and capital markets. Devereux and Mansoorian (1992) construct a two country model with trade in goods but no direct cross-country knowledge spillovers. It is an empirical question as to which type of international linkage is more important. Our disregard of other linkages is intended as a simplification.

The government in each economy has a monopoly in taxing domestic income and faces the budget constraint

$$g_{it} = \tau_{it} H_{it}. \tag{4}$$

If the tax rate is constant, as we show it is in equilibrium, the government maintains a constant share of output along the balanced growth path.[8] The objective of each government is to choose a sequence of tax rates which maximizes the welfare of the representative agent subject to private equilibrium behaviour and the "rules of the game". The "rules of the game" dictate whether governments behave cooperatively or non-cooperatively.

III. Balanced Growth Equilibrium

The decision problem for each agent, denoted P_i, may be written in terms of the functional equation

$$P_i \colon V(h_{it}, g_{it}, \tau_{it}, H_{it}, H_{jt}) = \max_{\{\lambda_{it}, h_{it+1}\}} \{\log((1 - \tau_{it})h_{it}) + \nu \log(1 - \lambda_{it})$$

$$+ \beta V(h_{it+1}, g_{it+1}, \tau_{it+1}, H_{it+1}, H_{jt+1})\} \tag{5}$$

---

[8] Combining equations (4) and (2) delivers the resource constraint for the economy as a whole which may be ignored. We have deliberately constrained the government to run a balanced budget so as to sharpen the analysis. An important issue to be explored is the relationship between debt, deficits and growth.

subject to equation (3) and given h_{i0}. The value function, $V(\cdot)$, exists and satisfies the usual conditions (uniqueness, concavity and differentiability) for the dynamic program to have a well-defined solution. In obtaining this solution, each agent forecasts the time paths of τ_{it}, g_{it}, H_{it} and H_{jt}, denoted by the sequences $\{\tau_{it}\}_{t=0}^{\infty}$, $\{g_{it}\}_{t=0}^{\infty}$, $\{H_{it}\}_{t=0}^{\infty}$ and $\{H_{jt}\}_{t=0}^{\infty}$, assuming that his or her actions have no effect on these variables. In the balanced growth perfect foresight equilibrium, conjectures are realized and all variables grow at the same constant rate.

The problem in equation (5) produces the following relationships:

$$\frac{v}{1-\lambda_{it}} = \frac{\alpha\beta V'(h_{it+1}|g_{it+1}, \tau_{it+1}, H_{it+1}, H_{jt+1})h_{it+1}}{\lambda_{it}} \tag{6}$$

$$V'(h_{it+1}|g_{it+1}, \tau_{it+1}, H_{it+1}, H_{jt+1}) = \frac{1}{h_{it+1}}$$

$$+ \frac{\alpha\beta V'(h_{it+2}|g_{it+2}, \tau_{it+2}, H_{it+2}, H_{jt+2})h_{it+2}}{h_{it+1}}, \tag{7}$$

where $V'(h_{it+s}|\cdot) = \partial V(h_{it+s}, \cdot)/\partial h_{it+s}$. Combining these relationships delivers

$$\frac{\lambda_{it}}{1-\lambda_{it}} = \frac{\alpha\beta}{v}\left(1 + \frac{v\lambda_{it+1}}{1-\lambda_{it+1}}\right) \tag{8}$$

which establishes that $\lambda_{it} = \lambda_{jt} = \lambda \in (0, 1)$: agents in each country invest the same constant amount of time in human capital production and the investment is independent of growth and policy.[9] In particular,

$$\lambda = \frac{\alpha\beta}{\alpha\beta + v(1-\alpha\beta)}. \tag{9}$$

The growth rate in each economy for any given tax rate follows from equations (3), (4) and (9) as

$$\frac{H_{it+1}}{H_{it}} = \Delta_{it} = A\left(\frac{H_{jt}}{H_{it}}\right)^{1-\alpha-\gamma-\psi} \tau_{it}^{\gamma}\lambda^{\alpha}. \tag{10}$$

---

[9] The independence is specific to the logarithmic utility function, which is why we have chosen that function for convenience. Our results are not substantially altered under a more general CES preference structure.

A key implication of equation (10) is that, if taxes are constant, there is cross-country convergence in growth rates regardless of the distributions of taxes and initial human capital stocks. The irrelevance of initial human capital for convergence is due to the international spillover effect of knowledge. Because of this spillover, the economy with the least human capital has the highest rate of return to human capital investment. This is the basic insight of Tamura (1991). But unlike the model in that paper, the framework developed here does not predict automatic convergence in per capita income levels. For this to occur, tax rates must be the same across countries.[10]

It is a feature of the model that taxes have a positive but diminishing effect on growth. On the other hand, higher taxes are not costless since they reduce consumption. One might wish to modify the model so that higher taxes eventually reduce growth as well. Doing this would introduce only minor additional considerations without changing the basic message of the paper. We prefer to keep the analysis tightly focused by abstracting from these considerations.

Henceforth, we assume that agents of each country are endowed with the same initial human capital, $h_{i0} = h_{j0} = h_0$. Then if taxes are identical (and constant) also, $\tau_i = \tau_j = \tau$, each country experiences the common rate of growth, $H_{it+1}/H_{it} = H_{jt+1}/H_{jt} = H_{t+1}/H_t$, where

$$\frac{H_{t+1}}{H_t} = \Delta = A\tau^\gamma\lambda^\alpha. \tag{11}$$

---

[10] These results may be established as follows. Define $X_t = \log(H_{it}) - \log(H_{jt})$ and $\xi_t = \log(\tau_{it}) - \log(\tau_{jt})$. From equation (10), we have $X_{t+1} = (2(\alpha + \gamma + \psi) - 1)X_t + \gamma\xi$. Since α, γ, $\psi \in (0, 1)$ and $\alpha + \gamma + \psi \in (0, 1)$, we know that $|2(\alpha + \gamma + \psi) - 1| \in (0, 1)$ so that this difference equation is stable, generating monotonic convergence if $\alpha + \gamma + \psi > 1/2$ and cyclical convergence if $\alpha + \gamma + \psi < 1/2$. If tax rates are constant, the solution is $X_t = (2(\alpha + \gamma + \psi) - 1)^t X_0 + \gamma\xi/2(1 - \alpha - \gamma - \psi)$.

Hence $X_{t+1} - X_t = (2(\alpha + \gamma + \psi) - 1)^t X_0 2(\alpha + \gamma + \psi - 1)$ so that

$$\lim_{t \to \infty} (X_{t+1} - X_t) = 0,$$

implying convergence in growth rates. If taxes are the same across countries, $\xi = 0$ so that

$$\lim_{t \to \infty} X_t = 0,$$

implying convergence in per-capita income levels.

The value of welfare in each country is $W_i = W_j = W$ and follows straight-forwardly as

$$W = \frac{1}{1-\beta} \left[\log(1-\tau) + \frac{\beta(\log(A) + \gamma \log(\tau) + \alpha \log(\lambda))}{1-\beta} \right.$$
$$\left. + \log(H_0) + \nu \log(1-\lambda) \right]. \tag{12}$$

Equations (11) and (12) are useful for future reference.[11] Observe that there are no transitional dynamics: both economies are always on the balanced growth path and all variables are determined once initial human capital is known. The externalities in the model mean that the decentralized balanced growth equilibrium is inefficient.

IV. Equilibrium Policy

Each government is a benevolent maximizer of social welfare. It should be stressed that this is not the same as maximizing growth. The problem is to choose a sequence of tax rates which optimizes an intertemporal trade-off between current and future consumption. This problem is made interesting by the interdependence between countries associated with the human capital spillover effect. Growth and welfare in each country are determined by the tax policies in both countries.

We think of the solution to the problem as the equilibrium of a dynamic game between governments. This game is different from the types of game normally considered in the policy cooperation literature. There are no conflicts in our game, only positive externalities from government policy. The issue is whether governments take account of these externalities. The game may be either cooperative or non-cooperative and, in the case of the latter, either "isolationist" or "strategic". Cooperation involves both governments choosing tax strategies so as to maximize a joint welfare function taking account of the policy and human capital externalities. Non-cooperation involves each government choosing its own tax strategy, taking as given the tax strategy of the other government, so as to maximize its own welfare function. By "isolationist" we mean a situation in which the government of each country takes as given, as well, the production of human capital in the other country. This would be the case of an irrational government or a government of a small economy. By "strategic" we mean the case in which the government of each country takes account of the effect of its own policy on the production of human capital abroad. In all cases, each government optimizes subject to private equilibrium behaviour.

---

[11] Equation (12) establishes that W is bounded, so that the problem is well-defined as we claimed earlier.

Analytical Solutions

Let P_1^{NC1}, P_1^{NC2} and P_1^C be the problems solved by each government under "isolationist" non-cooperation, "strategic" non-cooperation and cooperation, respectively. These problems are defined as follows:

$$P_1^{NC1}: V(H_{it}, H_{jt}) = \max_{|\tau_{it}, H_{it+1}|} \{\log((1 - \tau_{it})H_{it}) + \beta V(H_{it+1}, H_{jt+1})\}, \quad (13)$$

$$P_1^{NC1}: V(H_{it}, H_{jt}) = \max_{|\tau_{it}, H_{it+1}, H_{jt+1}|} \{\log((1 - \tau_{it})H_{it}) + \beta V(H_{it+1}, H_{jt+1})\}, \quad (14)$$

$$P_1^C: V(H_{it}, H_{jt}) = \max_{|\tau_{it}, \tau_{jt}, H_{it+1}, H_{jt+1}|} \{\mu \log((1 - \tau_{it})H_{it})$$

$$+ (1 - \mu) \log((1 - \tau_{jt})H_{jt}) + \beta V(H_{it+1}, H_{jt+1})\} \quad (15)$$

subject to equation (10), where $V(\cdot)$ is the value function of the government and $\mu \in (0, 1)$ is the welfare weight under cooperation. In P_1^{NC1} the government of country i chooses the sequence$\{\tau_{it}\}_{t=0}^{\infty}$ and $\{H_{it+1}\}_{t=0}^{\infty}$ so as to maximize country i's welfare, ignoring the positive effect of H_{it+1} on H_{jt+2} and then the positive effect of H_{jt+2} on H_{it+3}. In P_1^{NC2} the government solves the same problem but, this time, takes account of the human capital spillovers. In P_1^C the sequences for both countries' tax rates and human capital are chosen so as to maximize a joint welfare function, taking full account of the spillover effects. The problems are solved in an Appendix where it is shown that the optimal tax rate in each case is constant and the same for both countries, $\tau_{it} = \tau_{jt} = \tau \in (0, 1)$. The precise expressions are

$$\tau^{NC1} = \frac{\gamma\beta}{1 - \beta(\alpha + \psi)} \quad (16)$$

$$\tau^{NC2} = \frac{\gamma\beta[1 - \beta(\alpha + \gamma + \psi)]}{\gamma\beta[1 - \beta(\alpha + \gamma + \psi)] + (1 - \beta)[1 + \beta - 2\beta(\alpha + \gamma + \psi)]} \quad (17)$$

$$\tau^c = \frac{\gamma\beta}{1 - \beta(1 - \gamma)}, \quad (18)$$

where we have set $\mu = 1/2$ in the case of cooperation.[12] Thus, equilibrium growth and welfare in each case follow from appropriate substitutions in equations (11) and (12).

---

[12] Since we model the two countries symmetrically it seems most natural to set the welfare weight, μ, equal to a half. If the weight is different from a half, the country with the lowest weight would be taxed more heavily since the planner assigns more weight to utility in the other country. There is relatively little work on the effects of asymmetries in policy coordination games; one exception is Jensen (1992).

It is straightforward to establish that $\tau^{NC1} < \tau^{NC2} < \tau^c$ (hence, $\Delta^{NC1} < \Delta^{NC2} < \Delta^C$) unambiguously: a non-cooperative "isolationist" government, which makes lower public expenditures than a non-cooperative "strategic" government, which makes lower public expenditures than a cooperative government. The intuition is well-known: non-cooperative decision making fails to take full account of the international spillovers of growth-generating public policy. The impact of higher taxes on domestic consumption assumes greater importance than if the spillovers were respected. This is most acute in the "isolationist" case. Cooperation is a means of achieving higher growth by internalizing the externalities. This is the main result of the paper.

Numerical Simulations

We have simulated the model under a range of parameter values around a benchmark set of $\{\beta = 0.966, \ \alpha = 0.9, \ \gamma = 0.019, \ \psi = 0.041\}$. These parameter values were chosen as follows.[13] First, a benchmark case refers to the "isolationist" non-cooperative case (setting the time unit equal to a year). We set the rate of growth equal to 1.6 per cent per year and assumed a tax rate of 20 per cent (implying a government share of output of 20 per cent). β was chosen to replicate a before tax real interest rate of 6.4 per cent per year. The value of α was chosen so that externalities of government expenditure and the human capital stocks were small. Next, we assumed that the parameters of domestic and foreign average human capital stocks were small. We then assumed that the parameters of domestic and foreign average human capital stocks in the production of new human capital were identical, i.e., $\psi = (1 - \alpha - \gamma)/2$. Given this and the value of α, we computed the implied value of γ from equation (16) consistent with the tax rate of 20 per cent. The share of agents' time devoted to market activities was assumed to be equal to 0.2, which in turn implied a value of ν. Given these values, we computed the value of the technology parameter, A, consistent with the growth rate of 1.6 per cent using equation (11).

We conduct two types of welfare comparison. The first involves a straightforward comparison of utilities across cases. The second, proposed by Lucas (1987), is based on the parameters π^1 and π^2 which satisfies either of the following two relationships $\sum_{t=0}^{\infty} \beta^t U(c_t^C(1 - \pi^1), \ 1 - \lambda) = \sum_{t=0}^{\infty} \beta^t U(c_t^{NC2}, \ 1 - \lambda)$, where $U(\cdot)$ is the momentary utility function, c^C is consumption under cooperation and c^{NC2} is consumption under strategic non-cooperation, or $\sum_{t=0}^{\infty} \beta^t U(c_t^{NC2}(1 - \pi^2), \ 1 - \lambda) = \sum_{t=0}^{\infty}$

---

[13] The reasoning behind these parameter choices can be found in King, Plosser and Rebelo (1988) and King and Rebelo (1990).

$\beta' U(c_t^{NC1}, 1 - \lambda)$ where c^{NC1} is consumption under "isolationist" non-cooperation. Thus, π is a measure of the welfare loss associated with moving from one policy environment to another. Since consumption grows at a constant rate, π is determined such that agents are indifferent between (1) the tax rate in one environment and (2) the tax rate in another with a $100 \times \pi$ per cent reduction in consumption each period. The convenient formula for computing π in each case turns out to be $\pi^1 = 1 - [(1 - \tau^{NC2})/(1 - \tau^C)][\tau^{NC2}/\tau^C]^{\beta\gamma/(1-\beta)}$ and $\pi^2 = 1 - [(1 - \tau^{NC1})/(1 - \tau^{NC2})][\tau^{NC1}/\tau^{NC2}]^{\beta\gamma/(1-\beta)}$. The results of the simulations are summarized in Table 1 and Figures 1–5.

For the benchmark case, we observe non-trivial growth and welfare gains from cooperation. There is a 22 per cent reduction in growth and an 11.5 per cent reduction in welfare on moving from cooperation to "strategic" non-cooperation. The reduction in growth is associated with a 14 per cent increase in initial consumption and the reduction in welfare corresponds to a 3 per cent fall in consumption each period. The costs become greater still on moving to the "isolationist" environment. Growth and welfare decline by a further 24 per cent and 26.5 per cent, respectively. The additional welfare loss is equivalent to a further 6 per cent reduction in consumption each period.

The sensitivity analysis involves varying each parameter in turn, holding all other parameters constant. The results continue to indicate substantial gains from respecting the international spillover of policies. There is no noticeable reduction in the differences between growth rates for any of the parameter variations. Welfare losses are increasing in γ and decreasing in β, α and ψ. The rates of these changes are always greater on moving between the non-cooperative cases than on departing from the cooperative case. Nevertheless, even for high values of β, α and ψ, the costs of non-cooperation remain non-trivial.

The relatively large welfare gains (and increases in growth rates associated with these) of moving to optimal policies are consistent with other types of findings in the literature. Jones, Manuelli and Rossi (1991) look at the effects of optimal taxation in an endogenous growth model. In situations with exogenously given paths of government expenditures, these authors find that replacing the current U.S. tax structure with an optimal Ramsey taxation scheme can have large positive growth and welfare effects.[14] Jones, Manuelli and Rossi (1991) also analyze the additional

---

[14] Such experiments have also been carried out by others, e.g. by Lucas (1990) who found results similar to those of Jones, Manuelli and Rossi (1991). The questions associated with Ramsey taxation analyzed in those papers are different, however, from those analyzed here since we include only one tax rate and also model optimal government spending. In the Ramsey problem, the tax structure is sought that maximizes consumers' utility given a path of government spending and market determination of equilibrium prices and quantities.

Table 1. *Simulation results for benchmark parameter values*

	Cooperation	"Strategic"	Non-cooperation	"Isolationist"
Optimal tax	0.349	0.259		0.200
Growth rate	0.027	0.021		0.016
Welfare	7.695	6.808		5.000
% decrease in growth rate	21.632		23.788	
% increase in initial consumption	13.812		7.954	
% decrease in welfare	11.527		26.553	
$\pi \times 100\%$	2.990		5.998	

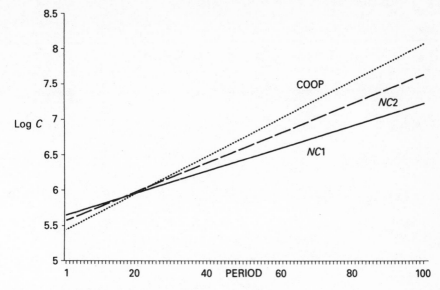

Fig. 1. Equilibrium paths of consumption

effect of endogenizing government spending and find substantial welfare and growth gains.

V. Concluding Remarks

The method of policy analysis in this paper contrasts sharply with the rudimentary approach taken so far in the new growth literature. We have endogenized policy in an endogenous growth model by considering it as the solution to a well-defined optimization problem of a government. Our primary intention has been to construct a simple example of how inter-national coordination of economic policy is a means of promoting growth across countries. Ignoring this possibility, as conventional models of policy coordination have done, means that one runs the risk of understating the costs of sovereign decision making.

We hope to address other issues in policy and growth in future research. Two issues of immediate interest are the long-run effects of government borrowing and the political economy of growth. Studying these will form part of a more general research program on debt, deficits, democracy and development. The beginnings of this research can be found in contribu-

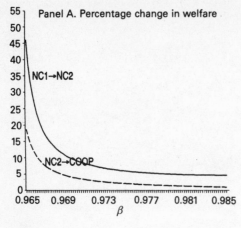

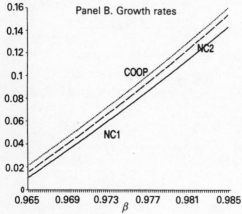

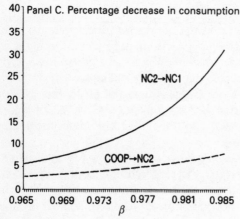

Fig. 2. Varying β.

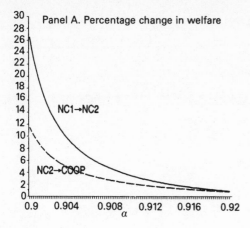

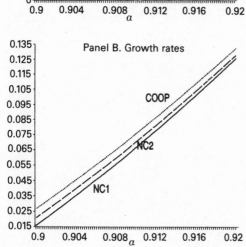

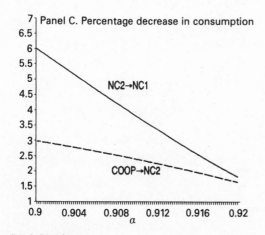

Fig. 3. Varying α.

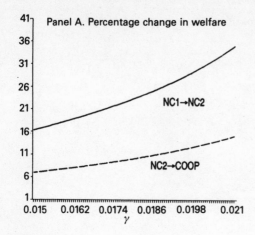

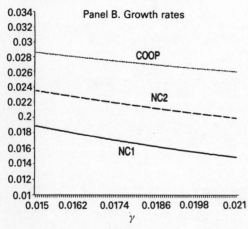

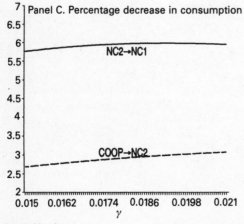

Fig. 4. Varying γ.

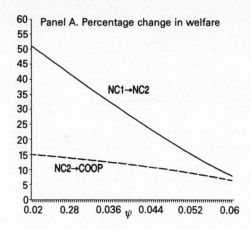

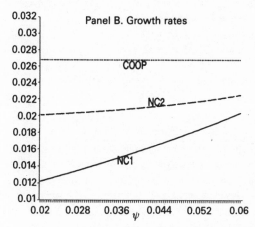

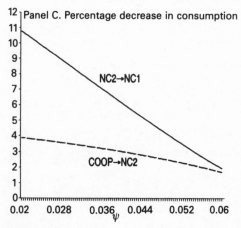

Fig. 5. Varying ψ.

tions of other authors such as Alesina and Rodrik (1991), Parente and Prescott (1991) and Persson and Tabellini (1991).

Appendix

The problems P_1^{NC1}, P_1^{NC2}, P_1^C are solved in the following manner. First, observe problem P_1^{NC1}. In this problem each government maximizes utility of its own agents and neglects (irrationally) the cross country spillovers associated with human capital accumulation. The first-order condition for taxes in this case reads,

$$\frac{\partial V(H_{it}, H_{jt})}{\partial \tau_{it}} = -\frac{1}{1 - \tau_{it}} + \beta \frac{\partial V(H_{it+1}, H_{jt+1})}{\partial H_{it+1}} \frac{\partial H_{it+1}}{\partial \tau_{it}},$$

where the first term on the r.h.s. is the effect of taxes on current utility and the second term gives the effect of taxes on future welfare (which works through human capital accumulation). Using (10) this can be rewritten as,

$$T_{it} = \gamma \beta V_i'(H_{it+1}, H_{jt+1}) H_{it+1}, \tag{A1}$$

where $T_{kt} = \tau_{kt}/(1 - \tau_{kt})$ and $V_k'(H_{it+s}, H_{jt+s}) = \partial V(H_{it+s}, H_{jt+s})/\partial H_{kt+s}$ for $k \in \{i, j\}$. Optimizing with respect to human capital accumulation gives us,

$$\frac{\partial V(H_{it+1}, H_{jt+1})}{\partial H_{it+1}} = \frac{1}{H_{it+1}} + \beta \frac{\partial V(H_{it+2}, H_{jt+2})}{\partial H_{it+2}} \frac{\partial H_{it+2}}{\partial H_{it+1}},$$

where the first term on the r.h.s. gives the effect of human capital on domestic momentary utility and the second term the effect on future welfare through the effect on H_{it+2}. Notice, as mentioned above, that the effect on future welfare through spillovers to the other country are neglected. By using (10), again, we obtain:

$$V_i'(H_{it+1}, H_{jt+1}) H_{it+1} = 1 + \beta(\alpha + \gamma + \psi) V_i'(H_{it+2}, H_{jt+2}) H_{it+2}. \tag{A2}$$

Next, we insert equation (A1) in (A2):

$$\beta(\alpha + \gamma + \psi) T_{it+1} - T_{it} = -\gamma \beta. \tag{A3}$$

The solution to this difference equation is immediately clear as:

$$T_{it} = T_i = \frac{\gamma \beta}{1 - \beta(\alpha + \gamma + \psi)} \tag{A4}$$

which yields the solution for τ^{NC1} in equation (16). Problems P_1^{NC2} and P_1^C are solved analogously. For these problems we obtain the following optimality conditions:

$$P_i^{NC2}: \quad T_{it} = \gamma \beta V_i'(H_{it+1}, H_{jt+1}) H_{it+1} \tag{A5}$$

$$V_i'(H_{it+1}, H_{jt+1}) H_{it+1} = 1 + \beta(\alpha + \gamma + \psi) V_i'(H_{it+2}, H_{jt+2}) H_{it+2}$$
$$+ \beta(1 - \alpha - \gamma - \psi) V_j'(H_{it+2}, H_{jt+2}) H_{jt+2} \tag{A6}$$

$$V'_j(H_{it+2}, H_{jt+2})H_{jt+2} = \beta(1 - \alpha - \gamma - \psi)V'_i(H_{it+3}, H_{jt+3})H_{it+3}$$
$$+ \beta(\alpha + \gamma + \psi)V'_j(H_{it+3}, H_{jt+3})H_{jt+3} \tag{A7}$$

$$P_i^C: \quad \mu T_{it} = \gamma\beta V'_i(H_{it+1}, H_{jt+1})H_{it+1} \tag{A8}$$

$$(1 - \mu)T_{jt} = \gamma\beta V'_j(H_{it+1}, H_{jt+1})H_{jt+1} \tag{A9}$$

$$V'_i(H_{it+1}, H_{jt+1})H_{it+1} = \mu + \beta(\alpha + \gamma + \psi)V'_i(H_{it+2}, H_{jt+2})H_{it+2}$$
$$+ \beta(1 - \alpha - \gamma - \psi)V'_j(H_{it+2}, H_{jt+2})H_{jt+2} \tag{A10}$$

$$V_j(H_{it+1}, H_{jt+1})H_{jt+1} = (1 - \mu) + \beta(1 - \alpha - \gamma - \psi)V'_i(H_{it+2}, H_{jt+2})H_{it+2}$$
$$+ \beta(\alpha + \gamma + \psi)V'_j(H_{it+2}, H_{jt+2})H_{jt+2}. \tag{A11}$$

Notice the difference between these and (A1)–(A2). For problem P_1^{NC2} the condition for taxes is identical to that for problem P_1^{NC1} since each government is maximizing utility of only its own agents. In contrast, the sum of utilities, weighted by μ, is maximized in P_1^C; one therefore obtains the additional condition given by (A9); note also that μ enters into the conditions.

The cross country externality associated with human capital accumulation is now rationally taken into account by the third term on the r.h.s. of (A6), which is the effect of H_{it+1} on future welfare through the effects on H_{jt+2} (which in turn affects H_{it+3}). Equation (A7) internalizes this latter effect. The first term on the r.h.s. giving the effect on future welfare through the effect on H_{it+3} and the second term giving the additional effect through H_{jt+3}. Equations (A10) and (A11) are identical to (A6) and (A7) except from the welfare weight replacing the unit effect (the first term on the r.h.s. of equation (A10)) and from the fact that it is now realized that country j's welfare is affected by changes in country j's human capital (this is the first term on the r.h.s. of equation (A11)).

From these equations we want to obtain expressions parallel to (A3). For problem P_1^{NC2} this is done by rewriting (A5) as:

$$V'_j(H_{it+2}, H_{jt+2})H_{jt+2}(\beta(\alpha + \gamma + \psi) - L)$$
$$= -\beta(1 - \alpha - \gamma - \psi)V'_i(H_{it+2}, H_{jt+2})H_{it+2},$$

where L is the lag operator. From this expression we substitute $V'_j(H_{it+2}, H_{jt+2})H_{jt+2}$ into equation (A6) and make use of equation (A5). Doing this (and performing the same manipulations for the cooperative case) delivers the following two difference equations,

$$P_i^{NC2}: \quad \beta^2(1 - 2(\alpha + \gamma + \psi))T_{it+2} + 2\beta(\alpha + \gamma + \psi)T_{it+1} - T_{it}$$
$$= -\gamma\beta(1 - \beta(\alpha + \gamma + \psi)) \tag{A12}$$

$$P_i^C: \quad \beta^2(1 - 2(\alpha + \gamma + \psi))T_{it+2} + 2\beta(\alpha + \gamma + \psi)T_{it+1} - T_{it}$$
$$= -\gamma\beta(1 + \beta - 2\beta(\alpha + \gamma + \psi)), \tag{A13}$$

where we have set $\mu = 1/2$ in order to get (A13).

The solutions to equations (A12) and (A13) are obtained as follows. Observe that the homogeneous parts of these relationships are the same. Write them as:

$$(\Omega_2 L^{-2} + \Omega_1 L^{-1} - 1)T_{it} = -(1 - \xi_1 L^{-1})(1 - \xi_2 L^{-1})T_{it}, \tag{A14}$$

where $\Omega_2 = \beta^2(1 - 2(\alpha + \gamma + \psi))$, $\Omega_1 = 2\beta(\alpha + \gamma + \psi)$, L is the lag operator and $\xi_1 = 1/\varepsilon_i$ for the characteristic roots ε_i $(i = 1, 2)$. The roots are $\varepsilon_1 = 1/\beta$ and $\varepsilon_2 = 1/\beta(2(\alpha + \gamma + \psi) - 1)$. Hence,

$$P_i^{NC2}: \quad T_{it} = \frac{\gamma\beta(1 - \beta(\alpha + \gamma + \psi))}{(1 - \beta)(1 + \beta - 2\beta(\alpha + \gamma + \psi))} \tag{A15}$$

$$P_i^{C}: \quad T_{it} = \frac{\gamma\beta}{1 - \beta} \tag{A16}$$

which deliver the expressions for τ^{NC2} and τ^C in equations (17) and (18).

References

Alesina, A. & Rodrik, D.: Distributive politics and economic growth. CEPR DP 565, 1991.

Barro, R. J.: Government spending in a simple model of endogenous growth. *Journal of Political Economy 98*, 103–25, 1990.

Barro, R. J. & Sala-i-Martin, X.: Public finance in models of economic growth. *Review of Economic Studies 59*, 645–61, 1992.

Blackburn, K. & Christensen, M.: Monetary policy and policy credibility — Theories and evidence. *Journal of Economic Literature 27*, 1–45, 1989.

Buiter, W. H. & Marston, R. C. (eds.): *International Economic Policy Coordination.* Cambridge University Press, 1985.

Canzoneri, M. B. & Henderson, D.: Is sovereign policy making bad? *Carnegie-Rochester Conference Series on Public Policy 28*, 93–140, 1988.

Devereux, M. B. & Mansoorian, A.: International Fiscal Policy Coordination and Economic Growth. *International Economic Review 33* (2), 249–68, 1992.

Easterly, W. & Rebelo, S.: Fiscal policy and economic growth: An empirical investigation. Paper presented at the Conference on How Do National Policies Affect Long Run Growth?, Lisbon, Jan. 14–16, 1993.

Fischer, S.: International macroeconomic policy coordination. NBER WP 2244, 1986.

Fischer, S.: Growth, macroeconomics and development. NBER WP 3702, 1991.

Fischer, S.: The role of macroeconomic factors in growth. Paper presented at the Conference on How Do National Policies Affect Long Run Growth?, Lisbon, January 14–16, 1993.

Grossman, G. M. & Helpman, E.: Comparative advantage and long-run growth. *American Economic Review 80*, 796–815, 1990.

Grossman, G. M. & Helpman, E.: Quality ladders and product cycles. *Quarterly Journal of Economics 106*, 557–86, 1991.

Hughes-Hallett, A. J.: International policy design and the sustainability of policy bargains. *Journal of Economic Dynamics and Control 10*, 469–94, 1986.

Hughes-Hallett, A. J.: The impact of interdependence on economic policy design: The case of the US, EEC and Japan. *Economic Modelling 4*, 377–96, 1987.

Jensen, H.: Sustaining policy cooperation between economies of different size. Memo 1992–17, Institute of Economics, University of Aarhus, 1992.

Jensen, H.: International monetary cooperation in economies with centralized wage setting. Forthcoming in *Open Economies Review 4* (3), 1993.

Jones, L. E., Manuelli, R. E. & Rossi, P. E.: Optimal taxation in models of endogenous growth. Unpublished manuscript, Northwestern University, 1991.

Kehoe, P., Policy coordination among benevolent governments may be undesirable. *Review of Economic Studies 56*, 289–96, 1989.

King, R. G., Plosser, C. I. & Rebelo, S.: Production, growth, and business cycles I. The basic neo-classical model. *Journal of Monetary Economics 21*, 195–232, 1988.

King, R. G. & Rebelo, S.: Public policy and economic growth: developing neo-classical implications. *Journal of Political Economy 98*, 126–50, 1990.

Levine, P. & Currie, D. A.: Does international macroeconomic policy coordination pay and is it sustainable? *Oxford Economic Papers 39*, 38–74, 1987.

Lucas, R. E.: *Models of Business Cycles*, Blackwell, Oxford, 1987.

Lucas, R. E.: On the mechanics of economic development. *Journal of Monetary Economics 22*, 3–42, 1988.

Lucas, R. E.: Supply-side economics: An analytical review. *Oxford Economic Papers 42*, 293–316, 1990.

Miller, M. & Salmon, M.: Policy coordination and the time inconsistency of optimal policy in open economies. *Economic Journal 95* (Supplement), 124–35, 1985.

Oudiz, G. & Sachs, J.: Policy coordination among the industrial countries. *Brookings Papers on Economic Activity*, 1–77, 1984.

Parente, S. L. & Prescott, E. C.: Technology adoption and growth. Federal Reserve Bank of Minneapolis Staff Report 136, 1991.

Persson, T. & Tabellini, G.: Is inequality harmful for growth: theory and evidence. UCLA Berkely WP, 1991.

Rebelo, S.: Long-run policy analysis and long-run growth. *Journal of Political Economy 99*, 500–21, 1991.

Rogoff, K.: Can international monetary policy cooperation be counter-productive? *Journal of International Economics 18*, 199–217, 1985.

Romer, P.: Increasing returns and long-run growth. *Journal of Political Economy 94*, 1002–37, 1986.

Romer, P.: Growth based on increasing returns due to specialization. *American Economic Review 77*, 56–62, 1987.

Romer, P.: Endogenous technological change. *Journal of Political Economy 98*, 71–102, 1990.

Sachs, J.: International policy coordination in a dynamic macroeconomic model. NBER WP 1166, 1983.

Sala-i-Martin, X.: Lecture notes on economic growth (II): Five prototype models of endogenous growth. NBER WP 3564, 1990.

Tamura, R.: Income convergence in an endogenous growth model. *Journal of Political Economy 99*, 522–40, 1991.

Optimal Saving, Interest Rates, and Endogenous Growth

Thorvaldur Gylfason*

University of Iceland, Reykjavik, Iceland and Institute for International Economic Studies, Stockholm, Sweden

Abstract

The apparent failure of economists thus far to establish a positive empirical link between interest rates and saving does not, by itself, discredit the hypothesis of a direct structural relationship between the two, *ceteris paribus*. This structural relationship may be shifting about in response to changes in exogenous variables such as tastes and technology in a way that is consistent with *any* type of reduced-form correlation between interest rates, and saving in the data. This point is demonstrated within a simple model of optimal saving, interest rates and economic growth. The different implications of endogenous *versus* exogenous growth are explored in this context.

I. Introduction

Econometric research is widely viewed by economists as having failed to establish a clear empirical relationship between interest rates and the saving behavior of households. Many studies, it is true, have reported significantly positive effects of interest rates on saving propensities in several countries. Others have concluded that no such evidence can be distilled from the data. Still others have indicated an inverse relationship between saving propensities and interest rates. Table 1 provides a glimpse of the variety of results that have been reported in twenty-four empirical studies over the past quarter of a century. Summarizing the evidence,

*I am grateful for the thoughtful comments provided by the editors and referees of this Journal and by Ragnar Arnason, Fridrik M. Baldursson, Sheetal Chand, Már Gudmundsson, Henrik Horn, Thórarinn G. Pétursson, Peter Svedberg, and other seminar participants at the University of Iceland, the Institute for International Economic Studies at the University of Stockholm, and the Fiscal Affairs Department of the International Monetary Fund. Even so, I am solely responsible for the views expressed in the paper.

Professor Alan S. Blinder of Princeton University, a member of President Clinton's Council of Economic Advisers, has recently said that "... there is *zero* evidence that tax incentives that enhance the rate of return on saving actually boost the national saving rate. *None. No* evidence. Economists now accept that as a consensus view." (Interview in *Challenge* September–October 1992, p. 16).

The representative estimates shown in Table 1 can be interpreted in at least three different ways. First, the fact that half of the studies, or 12 out of 24, failed to corroborate a significantly positive relationship between interest rates and saving may be regarded as an indication that this relationship, if it exists at all, can hardly be strong. This impression may be strengthened by five studies, i.e., Houthakker and Taylor (1970), Weber (1970, 1975) and Springer (1975, 1977), that have reported a significantly *negative* relationship between interest rates and saving in the United States — without, however, quantifying the relationship (which is why these five studies are not included in Table 1). On the other hand, the remaining 12 studies included in the table seem to indicate a fairly strong positive link between interest rates and saving: the average estimate of $\delta s/\delta r$ in the 24 studies is 0.7. This estimate is consistent with a long-run elasticity of saving rates with respect to real interest rates of about 0.3. The equations estimated in almost all the studies reviewed above were derived explicitly or implicitly from the theory of intertemporal choice. A useful and detailed survey of empirical work on saving behavior is provided by Smith (1991).

The third interpretation, which I find the most plausible, is that saving rates and interest rates are jointly determined endogenous variables in macroeconomic analysis. As virtually any other pair of (stationary) endogenous macroeconomic variables, saving rates and interest rates can move in the same direction or in opposite directions depending on the movements of the exogenous variables that affect both of them. Therefore, the observation that saving rates and interest rates can move all over the map in principle and in practice does *not* by itself constitute a legitimate refutation of the hypothesis that the optimal propensity to save is stimulated by an increase in interest rates, *other things being equal.* For example, Hall's (1988, p. 365) conclusion that "... periods of high expected real interest rates have not been periods of rapid growth of consumption" is not *per se* inconsistent with a positive partial or causal relationship between saving and interest rates.

This, however, has not been the prevalent interpretation of the literature thus far. Rather, the apparent absence of a strong empirical link between interest rates and saving according to a half of the studies summarized above has generally not been considered surprising in view of the neoclassical theory of intertemporal choice developed by Fisher (1907, 1930) and formalized by Ramsey (1928). This view is expressed by

Table 1. *Overview of empirical results*

Study	$\delta s/\delta r$	Country	Period
Wright (1967, 1969)	0.5	U.S.A.	1897–1959
Taylor (1971)	2.0	U.S.A.	1953–69
Heien (1972)	4.4	U.S.A.	1948–65
Juster & Wachtel (1972)	0.7	U.S.A.	1954–72
Blinder (1975)	0.0	U.S.A.	1949–72
Boskin (1978)	0.7	U.S.A.	1929–69
Fry (1978)	0.2	7 LDCs	1962–72
Howrey & Hymans (1978)	0.0	U.S.A.	1951–74
Blinder (1981)	0.0	U.S.A.	1953–77
Gylfason (1981)	0.7	U.S.A.	1952–78
Mankiw (1981)	0.0	U.S.A.	1948–80
Summers (1981)	4.5	Calibrated	
Carlino (1982)	0.0	U.S.A.	1957–78
Evans (1983)	1.0	Calibrated	
Friend & Hasbrouck (1983)	0.0	U.S.A.	1932–80
Giovannini (1983)	0.0	7 LDCs	1964–80
Blinder & Deaton (1985)	0.0	U.S.A.	1954–84
Mankiw *et al.* (1985)	0.5	U.S.A.	1950–81
Montgomery (1986)	0.0	U.S.A.	1953–82
Baum (1988)	0.0	U.S.A.	1952–82
Campbell & Mankiw (1989)	0.0	U.S.A.	1953–85
Campbell & Mankiw (1991)	0.0	5 MDCs	1957–88
Barro (1992)	0.6	10 MDCs	1957–90

Note: $\delta s/\delta r$ denotes the effect on the saving rate s (i.e., aggregate saving as a proportion of gross national product) of an increase in the interest rate r by one percentage point. The values of $\delta s/\delta r$ shown above where computed from estimates of elasticities by assuming $s = 0.1$ and $r = 0.04$ when representative values of s and r were not presented or could not be deduced from the study in question.

Deaton (1992, p. 61), among others. According to this theory, the optimal *rate of growth* of consumption is positively and unambiguously related to the real rate of interest by the Ramsey rule. In one simple formulation, this rule implies that

$$\frac{\Delta C_t}{C_t} = (r - \rho)\,\sigma, \tag{1}$$

where Δ is the first-difference operator in discrete or continuous time; C_t is real consumption at time t; r is the real rate of interest (and is exogenously determined from the representative consumer's point of view); ρ is the subjective rate of time preference, a constant; and σ is the elasticity of intertemporal substitution, also a constant by assumption. Thus, an increase in interest rates stimulates saving unambiguously as long as $\sigma > 0$ in the sense that it induces the individual to postpone consumption. The extent of the postponement depends solely on the elasticity of substitution. Hansen and Singleton (1983) and others (including several of the studies reviewed in Table 1) have reported positive and in some cases quite high estimates of σ, while Hall's (1988) empirical conclusion is that σ is close to zero. On the other hand, Campbell and Mankiw (1989) and Deaton (1992) consider the simple Ramsey equation (1) and extensions thereof too simple to serve as reliable guides to the extent of intertemporal substitution.

In the above simple formulation of the solution of the Fisher–Ramsey problem, the *level* of consumption at a point in time is

$$C_t = C_0 e^{(r-\rho)\sigma t}. \tag{2}$$

Initial consumption C_0 is determined from boundary conditions:

$$C_0 = [\sigma\rho + (1-\sigma)r] W_0. \tag{3}$$

Here W_0 denotes initial wealth, that is, the present discounted value of current and future income from labor and interest.

Equations (2) and (3) together imply that consumption (and hence also saving) at any given time bears an ambiguous relation to the interest rate for given initial consumption or wealth, depending on the elasticity of substitution:

$$\frac{dC_t}{dr} = [(1-\sigma)(1+\sigma rt) + \sigma^2 \rho t] e^{(r-\rho)\sigma t} W_0. \tag{4}$$

Specifically, an elasticity of substitution above unity ($\sigma > 1$) is necessary (but not enough) to derive a negative relationship between consumption and interest in this case. On the other hand, an elasticity of substitution below unity ($\sigma < 1$) implies a positive relationship between the two for given W_0. This well-known result has generally been regarded as a dynamic confirmation of the view that static substitution effects and income effects of interest rate changes on consumption and saving may conflict because lenders may react to higher interest rates by spending more and saving less out of given income. In a wide class of models, substitution effects outweigh income effects only when the elasticity of intertemporal substitution exceeds one; see, for example, Hall (1978), Summers (1981), Mankiw, Rotemberg and Summers (1985) and Deaton (1992). This interpretation is not without problems, however, for it can be shown that, with certain commonly assumed forms of utility functions, income effects cancel out on aggregation across individuals, leaving only substitution effects of changes in interest rates on aggregate consumption and saving.

Even so, the apparent failure of economists thus far to establish a positive empirical link between interest rates and saving does not, by itself, discredit the hypothesis of a direct structural relationship between the two, *ceteris paribus*, because this structural relationship may be shifting about in a way that is consistent with *any* type of reduced-form correlation between interest rates and saving in the data.

To set the stage for a further exploration of this issue, a simple model of optimal saving, interest rates and economic growth is presented in Section II. The model features an unambiguously positive structural relationship between the propensity to save and the interest rate, but it does not preclude the possibility of a negative reduced-form correlation between the two in response to changes in exogenous variables that reflect tastes and technology. The same applies to saving and growth: they can be either positively and negatively correlated when growth is endogenous. The results are summarized in Section III, which concludes with a brief discussion of their relevance for public policy.

II. Analytical Framework

In this section, a simple model is developed for the purpose of exploring the interaction of saving behavior, interest rates and economic growth under different assumptions about the nature of the growth process.

Consumption and Saving

Consider an economy where infinitely lived households choose a path of consumption C_t and of real and financial assets A_t, including money, so as to maximize their utility over time:

$$\int_0^\infty \left[\frac{1}{1 - \frac{1}{\sigma}} \right] (C_t^\lambda A_t^{1-\lambda})^{1-\frac{1}{\sigma}} e^{-\rho t} dt. \tag{5}$$

Utility depends on current consumption and accumulated saving, i.e., assets, so that an increase in income that increases both current consumption and asset holdings intended for future consumption increases utility through *both* channels as long as $\lambda < 1$. The elasticity of substitution of consumption for assets is set equal to 1 for simplicity by assuming the inner function within the second pair of parentheses to have a Cobb–Douglas form, while σ is the elasticity of intertemporal substitution of the composite Cobb–Douglas bundle of consumption and assets and ρ is the rate of time preference as before. All the parameters (σ, λ, $1 - \lambda$, and ρ) are positive and constant by assumption. Labor supply is left out of the utility function to avoid complexity.

The maximization of the integral in (5) takes place subject to the constraint that the accumulation of assets (saving, in other words) equal total income less consumption:

$$\Delta A_t = Y_t + rA_t - C_t, \tag{6}$$

where Y_t is real labor income and rA_t is real interest income. The steady-state solution to this dynamic maximization problem involves

$$\frac{C_t}{A_t} = \left(\frac{\lambda}{1-\lambda}\right)\left[\left(\frac{1}{\sigma}\right)g + \rho - r\right] \equiv f(g, r). \tag{7}$$

Here g is the optimal rate of growth of consumption and asset holdings along the steady-state equilibrium path. Consumption is thus proportional to asset holdings in long-run equilibrium. The ratio of consumption to assets is *inversely* related to the interest rate (i.e., $\delta f/\delta r < 0$) as long as $0 < \lambda < 1$. Moreover, this ratio is *directly* related to the rate of growth (i.e., $\delta f/\delta g > 0$) if $0 < \lambda < 1$ and $\sigma > 0$ as we have assumed. Without assets in the utility function (i.e., with $\lambda = 1$), the equilibrium solution to the above problem simplifies to the familiar Ramsey rule, $g = (r - \rho)\sigma$.

Equations (6) and (7) enable us to describe the long-run relationships among consumption, saving, asset holdings, the interest rate, and the rate of growth in a particularly simple way:

$$c = \frac{C_t}{Y_t} = \frac{f(g, r)}{f(g, r) + g - r}, \tag{8}$$

$$s = \frac{S_t}{Y_t} = \frac{g}{f(g, r) + g - r}, \tag{9}$$

$$a = \frac{A_t}{Y_t} = \frac{1}{f(g, r) + g - r}. \tag{10}$$

These equations are obtained as follows. First, because $s = S_t/Y_t = \Delta A_t/Y_t = (\Delta A_t/A_t)(A_t/Y_t)$ we have $s = ga$ in the steady state by definition. Moreover, we also have $s = 1 + ra - c$ by equation (6). But $c = C_t/Y_t = (C_t/A_t)(A_t/Y_t)$ which equals $f(g, r)a$ in the steady state by equation (7). Thus we can see that $s = ga = 1 + ra - f(g, r)a$ which, when we solve for a, gives equation (10). It follows directly that $c = f(g, r)a$ gives equation (8) and that $s = ga$ gives equation (9). These equations — (8), (9), and (10) — could also be derived from a utility function with a nonunitary elasticity of substitution between consumption and assets, that is, one in which the inner Cobb–Douglas function in (5) was replaced by a CES function; in that case, the middle term in equation (7) would become slightly more complicated, but the qualitative properties of $f(g, r)$ would remain unchanged.

Because $\delta f/\delta r < 0$ for given growth by equation (7), both the saving rate (s) and the asset ratio (a) are unambiguously positively related to the interest rate (r) for given growth (g) by equations (9) and (10). These relationships are independent of the intertemporal elasticity of substitution (σ). On the other hand, the direction of the effect of an increase in the interest rate on the propensity to consume (c) is indeterminate by equation (8). An increase in the rate of interest can conceivably increase both the propensities to consume and to save because $c + s = 1 + ra$ by equation (6).

The optimal saving rate can now be expressed in terms of the structural parameters of the intertemporal utility function (λ, σ, and ρ) as well as the interest rate (r) and the rate of growth (g) by substituting equation (7) into equation (9). This yields

$$s = \frac{(1-\lambda)g}{\left[1 - \lambda\left(1 - \frac{1}{\sigma}\right)\right]g + \lambda\rho - r}. \tag{11}$$

Here again we have an unambiguously positive nonlinear relationship between the saving rate and the interest rate, regardless of the value of σ. Specifically, if $\sigma = 1$, the expression for the saving rate simplifies to $s = (1 - \lambda)g/(g + \lambda\rho - r)$. This means that $\delta s/\delta r = s/(g + \lambda\rho - r)$. The corresponding interest elasticity of the saving rate is $\varepsilon = (\delta s/\delta r)(r/s) = r/(g + \lambda\rho - r)$; this elasticity is positive as long as $g > r - \lambda\rho$. Also, we now see that increased flexibility of consumption over time (i.e., an increase in σ) and increased patience (i.e., a decrease in ρ) both lead to increased saving, other things being equal. Moreover, increased growth lifts the saving rate as long as $r > \lambda\rho$ (to see this, divide through equation (11) by g). Lastly, if assets are removed from the utility function (i.e., if we set $\lambda = 1$), equation (7) boils down to the Ramsey rule, $g = (r - \rho)\sigma$, and the expression for the optimal saving rate simplifies to $s = (r - \rho)\sigma a$ by equations (9) and (11).

The upward-sloping saving function (the SS schedule) in Figure 1 shows the pairs of saving rates (s) and interest rates (r) that satisfy equation (9) or, equivalently, equation (11). This schedule describes the representative household's optimal consumption plan over time given the exogenous or endogenous rate of growth (g) and the taste parameters λ, σ, and ρ.

Production and Investment

In order to close the model, we now need to specify the mechanism by which the rate of growth and the rate of interest are determined. Let us assume a Cobb–Douglas production function for simplicity:

$$Q_t = B_t N_t^{1-\beta} A_t^{\beta}, \tag{12}$$

where $Q_t (= Y_t + rA_t)$ is total output, B_t is a technological shift parameter, N_t is labor, and $0 < \beta \le 1$. Money and other financial assets are included as factors of production in addition to capital on the grounds that they enable firms to economize on the use of other inputs; cf. Fischer (1974). Firms maximize profits by equating the marginal product of their real and financial capital $\beta(Q_t/A_t) = \beta(Q_t/Y_t)(Y_t/A_t) = \beta[(Y_t + rA_t)/Y_t](Y_t/A_t) = \beta(1 + ra)/a$ to the exogenously given interest rate r. Because $s = ga$ and $a = [\beta/(1 - \beta)]/r$, we now obtain

$$s = \left(\frac{\beta}{1-\beta}\right)\left(\frac{g}{r}\right). \tag{13}$$

Thus, the rate of saving (and investment) is inversely related to the interest rate for given productivity, by which is meant the contribution of capital to output as measured by the output elasticity β in the production function (12), and for given growth on the supply side of the economy. An essentially similar negative relationship between investment and interest can also be derived from an explicitly intertemporal model where firms maximize their present discounted value and where new capital is costly to install; see e.g. Kouri (1982).

This relationship is illustrated by the downward-sloping investment function (the II schedule) in Figure 1. Just as the SS schedule traces the combinations of interest rates (r) and saving rates (s) that maximize the utility of consumers over time for given tastes (i.e., λ, σ, and ρ) and growth (g), as we have seen, the II schedule shows the pairs of r and s that earn firms maximum profit from their investment for given productivity (β) and growth (g). This suffices to close the model: optimal saving and the interest rate can now be determined through the interplay of consumers and producers for given values of the exogenous parameters of the system, with or without endogenous growth.

Equilibrium with Exogenous Growth

Let us begin by assuming constant returns to scale in production and decreasing returns to capital, as in Solow (1956). Then the rate of growth of output and of capital equals the exogenously determined rate of growth of the labor force $n = \Delta N_t/N_t$, adjusted for efficiency. In this case, equations (11) and (13) form a closed system in which the saving rate and the interest rate are determined in reduced form by the underlying taste and technology parameters of the model:

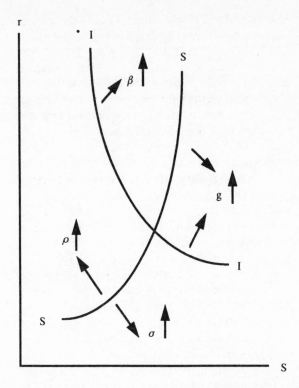

Fig. 1. Saving and interest.

$$s = \frac{1 - \lambda + \left(\dfrac{\beta}{1-\beta}\right)}{1 - \lambda \left(1 - \dfrac{1}{\sigma} - \dfrac{\rho}{n}\right)}, \tag{14}$$

$$r = \frac{\lambda\rho + \left[1 - \lambda\left(1 - \dfrac{1}{\sigma}\right)\right] n}{1 + (1-\lambda)\left(\dfrac{1-\beta}{\beta}\right)}. \tag{15}$$

A quick glance at this pair of reduced-form equations and the under-lying structural equations (11) and (13), and at the corresponding inter-section of the two familiar-looking schedules in Figure 1, suggests why interest rates and optimal saving can move all over the map in principle and in practice, and why it must therefore be difficult to identify the structural relationship between saving and interest rates in econo-metric work. Specifically, supply shocks tend to make the interest rate and the saving rate move in the same direction. For example, equation (15) shows that the interest rate rises with increased growth (because $1 - \lambda[1 - (1/\sigma)] > 0$) or productivity, and the saving rate also rises by equation (14). This explains the plus signs in the first two columns of Table 2 that summarizes the effects of changes in the exogenous parameters of the model on the interest rate and the saving rate. On the demand side, an increase in the elasticity of intertemporal substitution σ and in patience (i.e., a decrease in ρ) increases saving and reduces the rate of interest. This explains the mixed sign pattern shown in the last two columns of Table 2.

In sum, then, the table shows why interest rates and saving sometimes move in the same direction and sometimes not, depending on the source of the exogenous shocks to the system. Even so, growth, interest, and saving remain fundamentally positively correlated for given technology (β) and tastes (σ and ρ). Put differently, the rates of growth, interest, and saving cannot move in opposite directions in this model unless at least one of the two key taste parameters (σ or ρ) changes. The model thus preserves, through optimal saving, the fundamental positive link between interest and growth associated with the Golden Rule; see Phelps (1961).

A special case. Before proceeding to the case of endogenous growth, it may be instructive to consider a special version of the exogenous-growth model above in which assets do not enter the intertemporal utility function so that $\lambda = 1$ in expression (5). In this case, the dynamic utility maximiza-tion by the representative household leads to the Ramsey rule, $g = (r - \rho)\sigma$. This is confirmed by substituting $\lambda = 1$ into equations (14) and (15), for thus we get

$$r = \rho + \frac{n}{\sigma}, \tag{16}$$

$$s = \frac{\left(\dfrac{\beta}{1 - \beta}\right)}{\left(\dfrac{\rho}{n} + \dfrac{1}{\sigma}\right)}. \tag{17}$$

These reduced-form equations have all the same comparative-statics properties as the preceding pair of equations (cf. Table 2) except increased productivity now leaves the rate of interest unaffected.

Endogenous Growth

We now turn to the case where the rate of growth is modeled as an endogenous variable. Suppose technology is embodied in capital so that $B_t = A_t^{1-\beta}$ in equation (12) at the macroeconomic level. Aggregate production is then characterized by increasing returns to scale and constant returns to capital, broadly defined; see Romer (1986):

$$Q_t = N_t^{1-\beta} A_t. \tag{18}$$

Profit maximization by each individual firm requires equality between the interest rate and the marginal product of capital at the microeconomic level as before, compare equation (12). This now implies that

$$r = \beta N_t^{1-\beta} \tag{19}$$

by equation (18). Thus, the representative firm does not reckon with technological spill-over effects reflected in the macroeconomic production function (18) by assumption. A stationary interest rate requires N_t to be held constant because of the scale effects of employment on growth and interest in this version of the model. Output grows at the same endogenously determined rate as consumption and asset holdings, so that the propensities to consume to save and the asset ratio (c, s, and a) are constant in equilibrium as before. Notice also that now the ratio of asset holdings to output is given by $A_t/Q_t = N_t^{\beta-1}$ by equation (18), so that $s = ga = g(A_t/Q_t)(Q_t/Y_t) = gN_t^{\beta-1}(1+ra) = gN_t^{\beta-1}[1+r(s/g)] = gN_t^{\beta-1}/[1-rN_t^{\beta-1}]$. Therefore, $\delta s/\delta r > 0$ as before.

When the labor force is exogenously determined and growth is endogenous, the roles of the interest rate and growth are interchanged in the model. In the *Solow version* of the model, the rate of growth was determined solely by the exogenous rate of growth of the efficiency-adjusted labor force, and the interest rate and the saving rate adjusted as

Table 2. *The interest rate, saving, and exogenous growth: comparative statics*

	n	β	σ	ρ
r	+	+	−	+
s	+	+	+	−

shown in Figure 1. In the *Romer version* of the model, on the other hand, the interest rate depends solely on productivity and employment both of which are exogenously given by assumption. Thus, the interest rate now becomes an exogenous variable instead of growth. In Figure 1, the interest rate is now represented by a horizontal line (not shown) as implied by equation (19) and the rate of growth adjusts to ensure that the SS and II schedules intersect at that exogenously determined rate of interest. Now, for example, an increase in intertemporal substitution (σ) will shift the SS schedule to the right as before and thus trigger an increase in growth that will shift the SS schedule back to the left and the II schedule to the right until the two schedules intersect on the horizontal interest-rate line that has not moved by assumption. The outcome of the experiment is thus that saving and growth go up, but the interest rate remains the same.

The system can now be summarized by the following pair of reduced-form equations for the rates of optimal saving and endogenous growth:

$$
s = \frac{1 - \lambda + \left(\dfrac{\beta}{1-\beta}\right)\left(1 - \dfrac{\lambda\rho}{r}\right)}{1 - \lambda\left(1 - \dfrac{1}{\sigma}\right)},
\tag{20}
$$

$$
g = \frac{r\left[1 + (1-\lambda)\left(\dfrac{1-\beta}{\beta}\right)\right] - \lambda\rho}{1 - \lambda\left(1 - \dfrac{1}{\sigma}\right)}.
\tag{21}
$$

Equation (21) shows how the rate of growth is determined endogenously by tastes and technology in addition to the interest rate. An exogenous increase in the marginal product of capital (i.e., an increase in β) decreases the rate of growth and increases the saving rate, provided that $r > \lambda\rho$. Here, then, we have a case where saving and growth move in opposite directions. On the other hand, an increase in the interest rate increases both the saving rate and the rate of growth. Here we see again how saving, growth, and the rate of interest all move in the same direction for given technology (β) and tastes (σ and ρ). Changes in the taste parameters influence saving and growth without changing the interest rate. Once again, any conceivable pattern of interest rates and saving — and, now, growth — is possible, especially if two or more exogenous parameters change at the same time (see Table 3). But if r, s, and g move in opposite

Table 3. *The interest rate, saving, and endogenous growth: comparative statics*

	r	β	σ	ρ
s	+	+	+	−
g	+	−	+	−

directions, either tastes or technology must be changing in the background in this model.

A special case. Again, the case without assets in the utility function (i.e., with $\lambda = 1$) is of interest. In this case, as before, dynamic optimization yields the Ramsey rule and a corresponding saving function:

$$g = \sigma(r - \rho), \tag{22}$$

$$s = \left(\frac{\beta\sigma}{1-\beta}\right)\left(1 - \frac{\rho}{r}\right). \tag{23}$$

These equations are obtained by substituting $\lambda = 1$ into equations (20) and (21). Equation (23) implies that saving rises unambiguously in response to an increase in the rate of interest given the two basic taste parameters of the representative consumer, that is, the discount rate (ρ) and the intertemporal elasticity of substitution (σ), and also given productivity (β). Specifically, we now have

$$\frac{\partial s}{\partial r} = \frac{\beta\sigma\rho}{(1-\beta)r^2} > 0. \tag{24}$$

Therefore, the interest elasticity of the saving rate is

$$\varepsilon = \frac{\partial s}{\partial r}\frac{r}{s} = \frac{\rho}{r - \rho} \tag{25}$$

which is positive as long as $r > \rho$, that is, as long as the growth rate (g) and saving rate (s) are positive, compare equations (22) and (23). Notice also that there is no way for the saving rate to change by equation (23) without a change in either the taste parameters (ρ or σ) or in productivity (β) or in the interest rate triggered by a productivity shock on the supply side of the economy by equation (19). In other words, the saving rate reacts to external shocks or to changes in economic policy in this model only if the underlying parameters reflecting tastes and technology do so.

III. Discussion

The simultaneous endogeneity of saving and interest rates in the economic system makes it possible for them to move in the same direction or in opposite directions, over time and across countries, depending on the exogenous forces that affect both of them. In this light, it is not surprising that the structural links between saving and interest derived from the neoclassical theory of intertemporal choice have proven hard to establish in econometric research. (Similar difficulties are frequently encountered in other fields of economics: supply responses to price changes are notoriously hard to quantify with confidence, for example.) By computing the equilibrium values of the saving rate and the interest rate when the exogenous taste and technology parameters of the model are allowed to vary within a reasonable range, it is possible to demonstrate how saving and interest rates may seem to be *negatively* correlated in economic data (that is, in reduced form) despite a strongly *positive* structural link between the two by hypothesis.

What can monetary and fiscal authorities infer from this about the formulation of interest rate policies? In particular, does it make sense to maintain high real interest rates through monetary restraint, or to tax interest income lightly, in the hope of stimulating saving — and, perhaps, growth — if observed saving and interest rates are inversely related in practice?

The arguments presented in this paper suggest a twofold answer to these questions.

In the exogenous-growth version of the model presented here, the long-run relationship between saving and interest rates is influenced by three exogenous variables (cf. Figure 1): (i) growth, which is exogenous by assumption; (ii) the discount rate, which is essentially a psychological parameter; and (iii) the elasticity of intertemporal substitution, a quantity that can be influenced by institutional change. For example, a liberalization of borrowing constraints in the banking system (with a commensurate strengthening of bank supervision) would create conditions for increased flexibility in consumption and saving. Policies thus geared toward increased intertemporal substitution would increase saving and investment and lower interest rates at the same time. Moreover, if a distinction between gross and net interest and hence also between the return on saving and the cost of investment were introduced into the story, saving and investment could be stimulated by a favorable tax treatment, for instance. Also, a distinction between private and public saving would introduce a possible link between fiscal policy and total saving in the model.

However, even if the saving rate could be affected by fiscal policy and by institutional change, there is no way for high-interest policies through monetary restraint to promote saving in the long run in the exogenous–growth version of the model without further extension. Essentially, this is because real variables such as the real interest rate cannot be influenced in the long run by nominal variables such as money and credit in this version of the model. Put differently, the marginal product of capital is beyond the reach of the central bank in Solow's model of growth. In other words, the exogeneity of growth makes it impossible for the monetary authorities to influence saving and investment in the long run.

In the endogenous–growth version of the model, on the other hand, public policies to increase productivity and growth stimulate saving and increase interest rates at the same time (cf. Table 3). In this version, the marginal productivity of capital and the rate of growth of output and other real variables in the long run are modeled in a way that allows them to be influenced by a number of variables. These variables include employment, cf. equation (19); trade policy and research and development, cf. Grossman and Helpman (1991); fiscal policy, cf. Barro (1990) and Barro and Sala-i-Martin (1992); redistribution policies, cf. Persson and Tabellini (1991); and monetary policy, cf. Fischer (1991). The endogeneity of growth thus opens a new channel through which the government, including the monetary authorities, may be able to influence saving, investment, and interest rates, and, of course growth. Exogenous growth makes real interest rates immune to changes in monetary policy in the long run, whereas monetary policy can possibly be used to influence real interest rates, saving, investment, and endogenous growth permanently.

Even so, the contrast between the two versions of the growth model studied here, and between models of exogenous *versus* endogenous growth in general, should not be exaggerated. In practice, it may prove difficult to distinguish the properties of endogenous growth processes from the medium-term properties of neoclassical growth models where the rate of growth adjusts gradually along the transition path of the economy to a steady state.

References

Barro, R. J.: Government spending in a simple model of endogenous growth. *Journal of Political Economy 98* (5), S103–S125, Oct. 1990.

Barro, R. J.: World interest rates and investment. *Scandinavian Journal of Economics 94* (2), 323–34, 1992.

Barro, R. J. & Sala-i-Martin, X.: Public finance in models of economic growth. CEPR DP 630, Mar. 1992.

Baum, D. N.: Consumption, wealth, and the real rate of interest: A reexamination. *Journal of Macroeconomics 10* (1) 83–102, Winter 1988.

Blinder, A. S.: Distribution effects and the aggregate consumption function. *Journal of Political Economy 83* (3), 447–75, June 1975.

Blinder, A. S.: Temporary income taxes and consumer spending. *Journal of Political Economy 89* (1), 26–53, Feb. 1975.

Blinder, A. S. & Deaton, A.: The time series consumption function revisited. *Brookings Papers on Economic Activity 2*, 465–511, 1985.

Boskin, M. J.: Taxation, saving and the rate of interest. *Journal of Political Economy 86*, Part 2, S3–S227, Apr. 1978.

Campbell, J. Y. & Mankiw, N. G.: Consumption, income, and interest rates: Reinterpreting the time-series evidence. *NBER Macroeconomics Annual*, 185–216, 1989.

Campbell, J. Y. & Mankiw, N. G.: The response of consumption to income: A cross-country investigation. *European Economic Review 35* (4), 723–67, May 1991.

Carlino, G. A.: Interest rate effects and intertemporal consumption. *Journal of Monetary Economics 9* (2), 223–34, Mar. 1982.

Deaton, A.: *Understanding Consumption*. Oxford University Press, 1992.

Evans, O. J.: Tax policy, the interest elasticity of saving, and capital accumulation: Numerical analysis of theoretical models. *American Economic Review 73* (3), 398–410, June 1983.

Fischer, S.: Money and the production function. *Economic Inquiry 12* (4), 517–33, Dec. 1974.

Fischer, S.: Growth, macroeconomics, and development. *NBER Macroeconomics Manual*, 329–64, 1991.

Fisher, I.: *The Rate of Interest*. Macmillan, London, 1907.

Fisher, I.: *The Theory of Interest*. Macmillan, London, 1930.

Friend, I. & Hasbrouck, J.: Saving and after-tax rates of return. *Review of Economics and Statistics 65* (4), 537–43, Nov. 1983.

Fry, M. J.: Money and capital or financial deepening in economic development? *Journal of Money, Credit and Banking 10* (4), 464–75, Nov. 1978.

Giovannini, A.: The interest elasticity of saving in developing countries: The existing evidence. *World Development 11* (7), 601–7, July 1983.

Grossman, G. & Helpman, E.: *Innovation and Growth in the Global Economy*. MIT Press, Cambridge, MA: and London, 1991.

Gylfason, T.: Interest rates, inflation, and the aggregate consumption function. *Review of Economics and Statistics 63* (2), 233–45, May 1981.

Hall, R. E.: Stochastic implications of the life cycle–permanent income hypothesis: Theory and evidence. *Journal of Political Economy 86* (6), 971–87, Dec. 1978.

Hall, R. E.: Intertemporal substitution and consumption. *Journal of Political Economy 96* (2), 339–567, Apr. 1988.

Hansen, L. P. & Singleton, K. J.: Stochastic consumption, risk aversion, and the temporal behavior of asset prices. *Journal of Political Economy 91* (2), 249–66, Apr. 1983.

Heien, D. M.: Demographic effects and the multiperiod consumption function. *Journal of Political Economy 80* (1), 125–38, Jan./Feb. 1972.

Houthakker, H. S. & Taylor, L. D.: *Consumer Demand in the United States: Analyses and Projections*. 2nd ed., Harvard University Press, Cambridge, MA, 1970.

Howrey, E. P. & Hymans, S. H.: The measurement and determination of loanable-funds saving. *Brookings Papers on Economic Activity 3*, 655–85, 1978.

Juster, F. T. & Wachtel, P.: A note on inflation and the saving rate. *Brookings Papers on Economic Activity 3*, 765–78, 1972.

Kouri, P. J. K.: Profitability and growth. *Scandinavian Journal of Economics 84* (2), 317–39, 1982.

Mankiw, N. G.: The permanent income hypothesis and the real interest rate. *Economics Letters 7* (4), 307–11, 1981.

Mankiw, N. G.: Consumer durables and the real interest rate. *Review of Economics and Statistics 67* (3), 353–62, Aug. 1985.

Mankiw, N. G., Rotemberg, J. J. & Summers, L. H.: Intertemporal substitution in macroeconomics. *Quarterly Journal of Economics 99* (1), 225–51, Feb. 1985.

Montgomery, E.: Where did all the saving go? A look at the recent decline in the personal saving rate. *Economic Inquiry 24* (4), 681–97, Oct. 1986.

Persson, T. & Tabellini, G.: Is inequality harmful for growth? NBER WP 3599, 1991.

Phelps, E.: The golden rule of accumulation: A fable for growthmen. *American Economic Review 51* (4), 638–43, Sept. 1961.

Ramsey, F. P.: A mathematical theory of saving. *Economic Journal 38*, 543–59, Dec. 1928.

Rebelo, S.: Long-run policy analysis and long-run growth. *Journal of Political Economy 99* (3), 500–21, June 1991.

Romer, P. M.: Increasing returns and long-run growth. *Journal of Political Economy 94* (5), 1002–37, Oct. 1986.

Smith, Roger S.: Factors affecting saving, policy tools, and tax reform. *IMF Staff Papers 37* (1), 1–70, Mar. 1990.

Solow, R. M.: A contribution to the theory of economic growth. *Quarterly Journal of Economics 70* (1), 65–94, Feb. 1956.

Springer, W. L.: Did the 1968 surcharge really work? *American Economic Review 65* (4), 644–59, Sept. 1975.

Springer, W. L.: Consumer spending and the rate of inflation. *Review of Economics and Statistics 59* (4), 299–306, Aug. 1977.

Summers, L. H.: Capital taxation and accumulation in a life cycle growth model. *American Economic Review 71* (4), 533–44, Sept. 1981.

Taylor, L. D.: Saving out of different types of income. *Brookings Papers on Economic Activity 2*, 383–415, 1971.

Weber, W. E.: The effect of interest rates on aggregate consumption. *American Economic Review 60* (4), 591–600, Sept. 1970.

Weber, W. E.: Interest rates, inflation, and consumer expenditures. *American Economic Review 65* (5), 843–57, Dec. 1975.

Wright, C.: Some evidence on the interest elasticity of consumption. *American Economic Review 57* (4), 850–4, Sept. 1967.

Wright, C.: Saving and the rate of interest. In A. C. Harberger & M. J. Bailey (eds.), *The Taxation of Income from Capital*, Brookings Institution, Washington, DC, 1969.

Trade, Human Capital Accumulation and Growth in an Underdeveloped Economy

Tuomas Saarenheimo *

University of Helsinki, Finland

Abstract

This paper seeks to contribute to our understanding of the dynamic effects of trade, especially from a developing country's point of view. A model is constructed, in which a continuum of goods is produced using labor and human capital in different proportions. It is then examined how opening up trade changes the developing country's production structure towards labor intensive production and lowers the wage on human capital relative to the wage on labor. This, in turn, lowers the rate of human capital accumulation in the developing country. However, because of a favorable change in the terms of trade, the rate of growth may still rise as compared to the autarky level.

I. Introduction

For decades the policies of the IMF and the World Bank have rested on the assurance that free trade has beneficial effects on development. However, the empirical evidence supporting this assurance is mixed[1] and its theoretical underpinnings have been almost nonexistent. It was not until the recent emergence of endogenous growth theory that the theoretical literature on the relationship between trade and growth began to build up. This paper seeks to contribute to our understanding of the dynamic effects of trade, particularly from the point of view of a developing country. It examines how openness and the change in production structure induced by trade affect factor prices, and thereby the incentives to invest in educa-

---

* Detailed comments by an anonymous referee are gratefully acknowledged.

[1] For a recent and most thorough empirical study of the determinants of growth, see Levine and Renelt (1992). They did not find robust correlation between growth and any of several measures of trade. On the other hand, Helliwell (1992) reports that in Asia, open economies generally have significantly faster growth rates.

tion; conversely, it analyzes how human capital accumulation gradually changes the production structure. The theoretical framework is a multi-sector endogenous growth model, in which growth is driven by human capital accumulation.

Several recent papers conclude that trade does, indeed, increase growth; see, for example, Grossman and Helpman (1990a, 1990c and 1991, Ch. 7), Romer (1990) and Rivera-Batiz and Romer (1991). Almost without exception, the assumption underlying this result has been that the opening up of trade increases some kind of positive technological externality (or knowledge spillovers) between trading countries. In these models, free trade eliminates international differences in the level of technology and equalizes the long-run rates of growth regardless of the initial conditions.

An alternative line of research, which limits the extent of spillovers at the national level, produces more ambiguous results. With this kind of approach, the effect of trade on production structure becomes important. Grossman and Helpman (1990b, 1990c and 1991, Ch. 8) explored a multisector model in which knowledge spillovers were local. They found that the long-term pattern of trade is determined entirely by initial factor endowments. A country with a low initial endowment will never catch up with the more developed country. On the contrary, the more developed country will enjoy a higher rate of growth and the difference in endowments will grow over time. Other models that follow this approach include those of Buiter and Kletzer (1991), Feenstra (1990), Stokey (1991) and Young (1991).

The central role of assumptions about the extent of technology spillovers is somewhat disquieting. There are no universally applicable stylized facts concerning the diffusion of technology, and economic theory is certainly of very little help. In this paper, the spillovers are assumed to be purely national in scale. This assumption is based on the belief that, for an under-developed country, the importance of international knowledge spillovers is small.

To understand and justify this choice, it is necessary to clarify what is meant by international knowledge spillovers. These spillovers are usually associated with what might be called the social stock of technological knowledge, which consists of all technological information accessible at negligible cost. It includes the state of basic scientific knowledge and the quality of textbooks. It also includes that part of private, or commercial, technological knowledge which becomes public when new products are introduced. It seems likely that under even a moderate degree of integra-tion, the stock of available technological knowledge cannot vary to any large extent between countries. After all, everyone has access to the same textbooks, and if a firm cannot prevent a piece of technological information from becoming public domain domestically, there is little reason to believe that national borders are relevant obstacles either.

The social stock of technological knowledge is, however, only part of the story. There is a substantial difference between a piece of technological knowledge being available, and this technology being successfully applied in the particular environment of a developing country. This is where human capital, a knowledgeable and skilled workforce, is needed, i.e., to modify the technology suitable for local conditions, and to run and maintain it. Unlike the social stock of technological knowledge, the stock of human capital in a developing country is determined largely by local factors. It is hard to imagine what kind of international spillovers might be connected with this embodied type of knowledge. On the other hand, the transfer of human capital from developed countries to LDCs is difficult, first because of people's unwillingness to migrate, and second because the successful implementation of new technologies requires experience and knowledge of local circumstances; see Pack and Westphal (1986) for a profound discussion on this subject.

Thus, it is argued in this paper that the primary reason for the observed differences in labor productivity between countries is not so much the variation in the level of available technological knowledge, but the variation in the level of human capital embodied in individuals.[2] Particularly for undeveloped countries, the relevant bottleneck preventing the adoption of new technology is not the lack of technology *per se*, but the lack of human capital necessary to implement it in a productive fashion. This view is also supported by recent econometric studies stressing the importance of the local level of human capital on growth; see e.g. Barro (1991), Mankiw, Romer and Weil (1992) and Levine and Renelt (1992).

Using a model built on these considerations, it is found in this paper that free trade is likely to slow down human capital accumulation in a small, underdeveloped economy, leading the country to specialize in labor intensive production that requires little human capital input. Nevertheless, free trade may be optimal for the LDC, not only because of the static benefits from specialization, but also because the LDC can, in a way, free ride on the rising relative price of labor intensive goods, brought about by human capital accumulation in the more developed rest of the world.

It is illuminating to compare these findings to those obtained by the two previous studies that bear the closest resemblance to this paper: Grossman and Helpman (1990c) and Stokey (1991). In Grossman and Helpman (1990c), two countries produce a continuum of symmetric differentiated goods and a single homogeneous good. In addition, each country has a

---

[2] There are, of course, many other important determinants, such as political instability and the lack of economic infrastructure, which are not included in the model.

research sector that produces designs for new differentiated goods and keeps the economy growing. Under free trade, research will, in the long run, concentrate in the country that has an initial advantage in research. The conclusions obtained by Grossman and Helpman parallel the findings of this paper: although trade decreases the rate of technological progress in the less developed country, it does so, in many cases, without adverse welfare effects. However, while Grossman and Helpman conclude that, on the equilibrium path, growth is always slower in the less developed economy, the same is not necessarily true in this paper. Here it is quite possible that, over some periods of time, the underdeveloped country grows faster than the rest of the world.

Stokey (1991) uses a framework more similar to the one adopted here. In her model, a succession of finitely living generations allocate time between production and education. Education accumulates human capital and enables an individual to produce better quality goods. The efficiency of education for each generation depends on the level of human capital accumulated by the previous generation, thereby allowing for sustained growth. Stokey analyzes how opening up trade affects the dynamic behavior of a small open economy. Her model gives rise to a rather complicated dynamic behavior. For a low enough initial endowment of human capital in the small country, the model converges to steady state with zero rate of human capital accumulation in the small economy. In addition, the model may possess several other steady states. Stokey does not analyze welfare effects or effects on the rate of output growth. However, one feature of her model that tends to produce results different from those obtained in this paper is that low quality goods produced in the less developed country contain a subset of the "characteristics" of the high quality goods produced in the rest of the world. Since goods are valued according to the characteristics they possess, low quality goods are always cheaper than high quality goods. It is unlikely that this formulation allows for the terms of trade effects found in this paper.

The main difference in results between this paper and the two discussed above is the strong role of changing terms of trade. This effect may be strong enough that, despite a slowdown in education, the LDC may enjoy a faster rate of growth under free trade than under autarky, both in the short and in the long run. In an extreme case the citizens of the small under-developed country, allocating all their time to producing labor intensive goods, may enjoy a higher level of total income than the citizens of the developed rest of the world, who, although earning a higher wage per unit of time at work, spend a large fraction of their time educating themselves. While the previous papers conclude that despite a slowdown in growth, welfare effects for an underdeveloped economy may be positive, this model goes one step further by showing that it is possible that *both* welfare *and* the rate of growth increase.

The paper is organized as follows. The basic assumptions of the model are introduced in the next section. Section III examines the characteristics of a closed economy. The effects of international trade on growth are analyzed in Section IV, focusing on the case of a small open economy. Section V concludes.

II. The Model

The economy is modeled as consisting of L identical, infinitely living individuals. The individual indexed by i is assumed to have an inter-temporal utility function of the form

$$U_i(\tau) = \int_\tau^\infty e^{-\rho t} \log C_i(t)\, dt, \tag{1}$$

where $C_i(t)$ denotes the individual's consumption of the unique consumption good Y.[3] In what follows, the subscript i refers to an individual, while a variable with no subscript is an economy aggregate. There is no storage technology, so at each point in time

$$\int_0^L C_i(t)\, di = Y(t)$$

must apply. Besides the consumption good, there is a continuum of inter-mediate goods $M(j)$, where index j runs from zero to one. The intermediates are used to assemble the consumption good without other factor inputs. This is assumed to take Cobb–Douglas form which, with time indices suppressed, can be written as

$$\log Y = \int_0^1 \log M(j)\, dj. \tag{2}$$

Without loss of generality, index j in equation (2) is chosen so that the weight of intermediates stays constant over the whole range of j.

---

[3] Logarithmic utility is used because it produces a simple relation between the interest rate and the rate of output growth. Generalization to the constant elasticity case is straight-forward but does not add any insight.

The intermediates themselves are produced using two primary factors of production: raw labor L and human capital H. Again, this is done using Cobb–Douglas technology. Index j arranges the intermediates in increasing order of human capital intensity.[4] With the units chosen appropriately, the production function for intermediates can be written as:

$$M(j) = H(j)^{\beta(j)} L(j)^{1-\beta(j)}, \qquad 0 \le j, \beta(j) \le 1, \tag{3}$$

where $H(j)$ and $L(j)$ are the amounts of factors allocated to sector j and $\beta(j)$ is continuously differentiable and increasing. Since physical capital would not contribute to the analysis in any essential way, it is omitted from the production function.

Every individual is endowed with one unit of labor. The population, and thus the stock of raw labor, is constant at L. Human capital can be accumulated by schooling. An individual i can increase his stock of human capital h_i according to linear technology

$$\dot{h}_i = g(s_i)h \qquad g(0) = 0, \qquad g' > 0, \qquad g'' < 0, \tag{4}$$

where s_i is the individual's personal rate of investment in education, i.e., the fraction of time he allocates to education. Function g is assumed to be increasing and concave over the whole range $s_i \in [0, 1]$. $h \equiv H/L$ stands for the per capita stock of human capital in the economy. By incorporating the average stock of human capital as a determinant of human capital accumulation, equation (4) represents an attempt to capture the strong impact that family, friends, the neighborhood, the whole social environment all have on a person's attitude towards learning and his ability to absorb education.[5] ·

An atomistic individual is unable to affect h, so he correctly takes it as given when deciding his investment in education. The cost of acquiring education is the income foregone during it. If an individual allocates fraction s_i of his time to education, he spends fraction $1 - s_i$ at work, and receives a flow of income $(1 - s_i)(w_H h_i + w_L)$, where w_H and w_L denote the factor prices (in terms of the final output) of human capital and raw labor, respectively. Thus, the wage of an individual consists of a flat rate for physical labor input and an additional payment that depends on his human capital endowment.

The equality of supply and demand for the primary factors gives the two resource constraints in the economy:

---

[4] This multisector framework is similar to that in Dornbush, Fisher and Samuelson (1977, 1980).

[5] This fact is also emphasized by Lucas (1988): "Human capital accumulation is a *social* activity involving *groups* of people in a way that has no counterpart in the accumulation of physical capital".

$$(1-s)H \equiv \int_0^1 H(j)\, dj$$

$$(1-s)L \equiv \int_0^1 L(j)\, dj. \tag{5}$$

where s stands for the average rate of investment in education in the economy.

III. The Closed Economy

In the closed economy setting, the fact that there is a continuum of intermediates plays a negligible role — factor prices, and thus the behavior of the whole model, are fully determined by the average factor share of human capital over all intermediates, denoted by $\bar{\beta} \equiv \int_0^1 \beta(j)\, dj$. By utilizing cost minimization and perfect competition, (2), (3) and (5) can be combined to give the final output Y directly in terms of the stocks of primary factors of production H and L and the average rate of human capital investment s:

$$Y(H, L, s) = (1-s) H^{\bar{\beta}} L^{1-\bar{\beta}}, \tag{6}$$

or in per capita terms

$$y(h, s) = (1-s) h^{\bar{\beta}}. \tag{6'}$$

Differentiating (6) gives the factor prices (in terms of the final output) $w_H = \bar{\beta} h^{\bar{\beta}-1}$ and $w_L = (1-\bar{\beta}) h^{\bar{\beta}}$.

In what follows, the focus is on the balanced growth solution, characterized by the constant rate of investment s^c for all individuals (c for "competitive"), and the rate of human capital accumulation $g(s^c)$. The constant rate of accumulation combined with constant factor shares implies $\dot{w}_H / w_H = (\bar{\beta} - 1) g(s^c)$ and $\dot{w}_L / w_L = \bar{\beta} g(s^c)$. Since supply of human capital rises while the supply of raw labor stays constant, the price of the former falls and that of the latter rises. Moreover, aggregate output Y (as well as per capita output) grows at a rate $\dot{Y}/Y = \bar{\beta} g(s^c)$. Logarithmic utility implies that on the optimal consumption path, the growth rate of consumption is $\dot{C}/C = \dot{Y}/Y = \dot{R} - \rho$ where $\dot{R}$ is the instantaneous rate of interest.[6] On the balanced growth path, the interest rate is constant $\dot{R} \equiv r = \rho + \bar{\beta} g(s^c)$.

---

[6] This is obtained as the solution to maximizing (1) subject to the intertemporal resource constraint

$$\int_\tau^\infty e^{-R(t)} C_i(t)\, dt = \int_\tau^\infty e^{-R(t)} (Y(t)/L)\, dt.$$

Equality of supply and demand $C_i(t) L = Y(t)$ holds always if and only if $\dot{C}/C = \dot{Y}/Y = \dot{R} - \rho$.

Now consider the optimal investment program for an individual. The individual maximizes his discounted income

$$\max_{, s_i} \int_\tau^\infty e^{-r(t-\tau)}(1 - s_i(t))(w_H(t) h_i(t) + w_L(t))\, dt$$

s.t. $\dot{h}_i = g(s_i) h$

$$0 \le s_i \le 1 \tag{7}$$

$$r = \rho + \bar{\beta} g(s^c).$$

The solution to (7) is a mapping from the average rate of investment to the individual optimum. The equilibrium value s^c is the fixed point of this mapping. The maximization problem can be written as one of maximizing the current value Hamiltonian:

$$\max_{s_i} \mathcal{H} = \max_{s_i} [(1 - s_i)(w_H h_i + w_L) + \mu_i g(s_i) h], \tag{8}$$

where μ_i is the shadow price of human capital for the particular individual. The first-order conditions are

$$w_H h_i + w_L = \mu_i g'(s_i^c) h$$

$$\dot{\mu}_i = r\mu_i - (1 - s_i^c) w_H. \tag{9}$$

The first equation suggests that the cost of education — the foregone wage income — must be equal to the value of human capital multiplied by the amount of human capital produced by investing marginally more in education. Since the Hamiltonian is concave in h_i and s_i, the conditions in (9) are also sufficient for optimality.

Substituting the fixed-point conditions $h_i = h$, $s_i^c = s^c$ and $\mu_i = \mu$, and using the fact that $w_H h + w_L = w_H h + (1 - \bar{\beta}) h^{\bar{\beta}} = w_H h / \bar{\beta}$, simplifies the first equation of (9) to $\mu = w_H / (\bar{\beta} g'(s^c))$. Differentiating this and using $\dot{s} = 0$ produces

$$\frac{\dot{\mu}}{\mu} = (\bar{\beta} - 1) g(s^c). \tag{10}$$

The second line of (9) can be written

$$\frac{\dot{\mu}}{\mu} = r - (1 - s) \bar{\beta} g'(s^c). \tag{11}$$

Combining (10) and (11) and using $r = \rho + \bar{\beta} g(s^c)$ gives the final expression

$$\rho - (1 - s^c) \bar{\beta} g'(s^c) + g(s^c) = 0. \tag{12}$$

The expression in the l.h.s. of (12) is increasing in s^c, so if a solution exists, it is unique. Equation (12) has a solution in the feasible range $s^c \in [0, 1]$ if and only if the marginal productivity of investment at zero is high enough that $\rho - \bar{\beta} g'(0) \leq 0$ holds. Otherwise the optimal rate of investment is zero. The competitive solution can be written as

$$s^c = s^c(\bar{\beta}, \rho), \qquad s^c_{\bar{\beta}} > 0, \qquad s^c_{\rho} < 0. \qquad (13)$$

Thus, the competitive rate of investment s^c is an increasing function of $\bar{\beta}$, the share of human capital of output, and a decreasing function of time preference ρ.

Uncompensated positive externality leads almost certainly to an equilibrium which is not Pareto optimal. Thus, it is no surprise that here, too, a social planner could do strictly better than the competitive solution. The planner would choose the balanced growth path to maximize

$$\int_{\tau}^{\infty} e^{-\rho(t-\tau)} \log[(1-s)\bar{H}^{\beta}]\, dt$$

s.t. $\qquad \dot{h} = g(s)h \qquad (14)$

$\qquad 0 \leq s \leq 1,$

which has the solution s^o (for "optimum") given by

$$\rho - (1-s)\bar{\beta} g'(s^o) = 0. \qquad (15)$$

It is easy to check that s^o is higher than the competitive solution s^c given by (13). Since the difference is due to the failure of the market to reward investment in education according to its true social value, the obvious choice for policy intervention is to subsidize education. In the current setting, where all individuals are identical, there are many tax/subsidy schemes that attain the first best. For example, by levying a proportional income tax and subsidizing the time spent on education, a government can reach the optimal rate of investment without distorting the factor prices. A subsidy on human capital intensive goods would raise the rate of investment as well, but would lead to an inefficient static allocation of resources.

IV. Trade and Growth in the Small Open Economy

Suppose now that a small, previously closed economy, called the home country, starts trading in the world market, hereafter referred to as the foreign country. The focus is on competitive equilibrium. Optimal equilibrium differs only slightly from the competitive case, and is briefly analyzed later in the paper.

The small economy takes commodity prices as given. International borrowing and lending are allowed, so the interest rate is also exogenous for the home country. In every other respect, the small open economy is as described in Section II. The foreign country follows the closed economy balanced growth path. Preferences and technology are the same everywhere. Both raw labor and human capital are assumed to be immobile. Moreover, only the local average level of human capital matters for the efficiency of education.

The foreign country is allowed to subsidize education and finance the subsidy by a tax scheme that does not distort prices. It is assumed that the degree of subsidization is somewhere between zero and the optimum, so the balanced growth path of the foreign country can be characterized by the first-order condition

$$\rho - (1 - s^*)\bar{\beta}g'(s^*) + (1 - \theta^*)g(s^*) = 0, \qquad 0 \le \theta^* \le 1. \tag{16}$$

Here the foreign variables are indicated by a superscript asterisk. The parameter θ^* measures the degree of subsidization and $\bar{\beta}$ is defined as in the preceding section. $\theta^* = 0$ and $\theta^* = 1$ correspond to the competitive path in (12) and the optimal path in (15), respectively. Hence, the rate of human capital accumulation in the foreign country, $\bar{\beta}g(s^*)$, is between the closed economy competitive rate $\bar{\beta}g(s^c)$ and the closed economy optimal rate $\bar{\beta}g(s^o)$. The relative factor price in the foreign economy is

$$\frac{w^*_L}{w^*_H} = \frac{1 - \bar{\beta}}{\bar{\beta}} h^*, \tag{17}$$

where $h^* \equiv H^*/L^*$. The growth rates of the foreign variables are $\dot{h}^*/h^* = \dot{\omega}^*/\omega^* = g(s^*)$ and $\dot{Y}^*/Y^* = \bar{\beta}g(s^*)$. The interest rate is, according to (7), constant at $r^* = \bar{\beta}g(s^*) + \rho$. The world market price $p^*(j)$ of an intermediate j is obtained from the cost function corresponding to the production function $M(j) = H(j)^{\bar{\beta}}L(j)^{1-\bar{\beta}}$:

$$p^*(j) = \left(\frac{w^*_H}{\beta(j)}\right)^{\beta(j)} \left(\frac{w^*_L}{1 - \beta(j)}\right)^{1-\beta(j)}. \tag{18}$$

The world market price p^*_Y of the final good can be similarly solved from (2):

$$p^*_Y = \exp\left(\int_0^1 \log p(j)\, dj\right). \tag{19}$$

In the home country, maximization of profits by individual firms will allocate resources in a way that maximizes the real GNP. Since GNP is linear in intermediates, this allocation is generally not unique. We can simplify the exposition by restricting attention to choosing a single input to export. Then the static resource allocation problem can be written as

$$\max_{j} \; p^*(j) \cdot h^{\beta(j)},$$

where h is the per capita human capital in the home country and $p^*(j)$ is given by (18). Routine calculations show that if an interior solution exists, it is unique and given by $\hat{j}$, which satisfies

$$\beta(\hat{j}) = \frac{w^*_H h}{w^*_L + w^*_H h}. \tag{20}$$

Denoting the relative stock of human capital in the home country by $x \equiv h/h^*$, and using (17), the optimal $\hat{\beta} = \beta(\hat{j})$ can be written as a function of x:

$$\beta = \frac{\bar{\beta} x}{(1 - \bar{\beta}) + \bar{\beta} x}. \tag{20'}$$

As long as the solution is an interior one and equation (20) holds, factor prices are equalized between countries. If, on the other hand, the stock of human capital in the home country is very small relative to the stock of human capital in the foreign country, and $\beta(0) > 0$, an interior solution may not exist. In this case, the factor prices in the home country will diverge from their world market value, adjusting to preserve the equality

$$\frac{w_L}{w_H} = \frac{1 - \beta(0)}{\beta(0)} h.$$

and to satisfy the budget constraint $p^*(0) h^{\beta(0)} = w_L + w_H h$.

It is assumed for the moment that $\beta(0) = 0$ and $\beta(1) = 1$, i.e., there are some goods that can be produced using one factor only. In this case (18') always holds and the factor prices are the same in both countries. Output (and income) per capita in the home country, measured in terms of the final good, can be written as

$$
\begin{aligned}
y &= (1 - s) \frac{p(\hat{j})}{p^*_Y} h^{\beta} \\
&= (1 - s) \frac{w^*_L + w^*_H h}{p^*_Y}.
\end{aligned}
\tag{21}
$$

The term $p(\hat{j})/p^*_Y$ can be interpreted as the terms of trade of the home country. The static gains of trade can be calculated by subtracting the per capita production in the closed economy, given in $(6')$, from (21). It can be checked that, for a given h, output under free trade is greater than the autarky output everywhere except at the point $h = h^*$, where the free trade income and the autarky income coincide.

The intertemporal maximization problem for an individual in the home country is

$$\max_{s_i} \int_{\tau}^{\infty} e^{-r^*(t-\tau)}(1 - s_i)(w_H^* h_i + w_L^*)\, dt$$

$$\text{s.t.} \qquad \dot{h}_i = g(s_i)\, h,$$

(22)

along with the nonnegativity condition $s \geq 0$. This problem is solved in the Appendix. The solution is a system of two nonlinear differential equations in variables s and x. Proposition 1 characterizes the solution to this control problem.

Proposition 1. *Let* $\beta(0) = 0$ *and* $\beta(1) = 1$ *and let the relative per capita stock* x *initially be smaller (greater) than a threshold value* x_e. *Then (i) the initial value of* s *is smaller (greater) than* s^*, *and (ii) both* x *and* s *will decline (increase) monotonically over time.*

Proof: See Appendix.

Proposition 1 states that, if at the moment when trading starts, the stock of human capital in the home country is smaller than a threshold value (given in the Appendix), then the home country will invest less in education than the foreign country, and the rate of investment declines over time. Consequently, the stock of human capital grows slower than in the rest of the world, i.e., x falls over time. This, in turn, changes the production structure, determined by $(20')$, towards more and more labor intensive production. If $g'(0)$ is finite, the country will reach a zero rate of investment in finite time. Otherwise, s approaches zero asymptotically.

Figure 1 illustrates the dynamics of the model in (x, s) space. The locus BB' is the equilibrium path. After opening up trade, a country with initial relative stock of human capital x' initially invests at rate s'. Over time, the equilibrium moves along the locus BB' to the left and down. Figure 1 is drawn under the assumption that $g'(0)$ is finite. If $g'(0)$ is infinite, the locus BB' is strictly increasing for all values of x.

In the case $\beta(0) > 0$ and $\beta(1) < 1$, two additional threshold values of x are needed. Let $\underline{x}$ and $\bar{x}$ denote the points where $\beta = \beta(0)$ and $\beta = \beta(1)$, respectively, where β is given by $(20')$. Thus, $\underline{x}$ is the value of x at which the small country exports good 0, and $\bar{x}$ the value at which it exports good

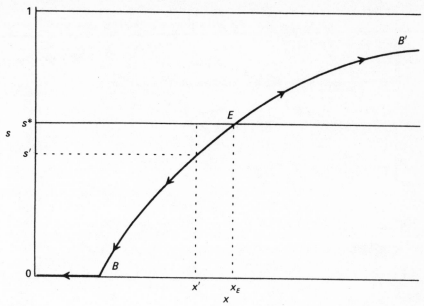

Fig. 1.

1. When x is between $\underline{x}$ and $\bar{x}$, factor pirces are equalized. On the other hand, for values of x smaller than $\underline{x}$, the price of labor is lower and the price of human capital exceeds the corresponding world market values. The equilibrium dynamics of this case are given in Proposition 2.

Proposition 2. *Let the initial value of x be smaller (greater) than a threshold value x_E. Then (i) the initial value of s is smaller (greater) than s^*, and (ii) x and s decline (increase) monotonally until $x = \underline{x}$ ($x = \bar{x}$), after which s stays constant and x approaches zero (infinity).*

Proof: The proof is very similar to the proof of Proposition 1 and is omitted.[7]

The dynamics of this case are illustrated in Figure 2. The only difference to the former case is that when x hits the value $\bar{x}$ and the home country specializes to good $\beta(0)$, the rate of investment ceases to fall. The intuition behind this result is loosely the following. Incentive to invest in education is positively related to the future price of human capital. As long

---

[7] The proof is available from the author on request.

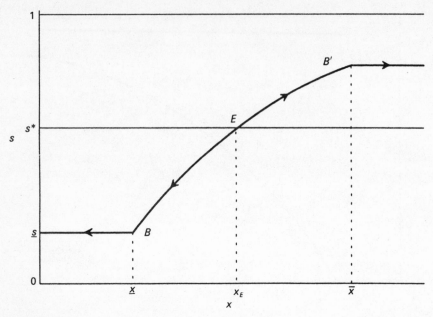

Fig. 2.

as $x > \underline{x}$, the price of human capital, given in the world market, keeps falling (relative to the price of the final good) at a rate determined by the rate of human capital accumulation in the foreign country. Once x falls below $\underline{x}$, the price of human capital in the home country diverges from the price in the foreign country. More precisely, it will decline more slowly at home than abroad, and may even start to rise again. The anticipation of this change in the trend offsets the slow improvement in the efficiency of education, and stabilizes the rate of investment at level $\underline{s}$.

Once the dynamics of the stock of human capital are known, the next aspects to consider are the behavior of GNP and the welfare effects of trade. In the following, it is assumed that the home country is less developed relative to the rest of the world, so that it will follow the path characterized by a decreasing investment rate and slow growth in human capital. While the results on the dynamics in the previous propositions are qualitatively robust to changes in functional specification, most of the welfare analysis relies on the assumed functional forms. Asymptotic behavior will also depend on whether $\beta(0)$ is zero or strictly positive, so these cases will be dealt with separately.

Assume first that $\beta(0) = 0$ so that the factor prices are always equalized. The logarithmic differential of the output equation (21) gives the growth rate of the real GNP:

$$\frac{\dot{y}}{y} = \frac{\dot{p}^*(j)}{p^*(j)} - \frac{\dot{p}^*_Y}{p^*_Y} - \frac{\dot{s}}{1-s} + \beta \frac{\dot{h}}{h}. \tag{23}$$

The first term on the r.h.s. of (23) is the change in the export price. The second term gives the change in the price of the final good, i.e., import price. Together these two represent the change in real GNP resulting from the change in the terms of trade. The third term demonstrates the effect of the change on allocation of resources between education and production. The fourth term gives the part of the growth due to human capital accumulation. Notice that since $\beta = \beta(\hat{j})$ has already been chosen to maximize output, it follows from the envelope theorem that the change in $\hat{j}$ can be ignored here. Normalizing p^*_Y to unity, equation (23) can be written as

$$\frac{\dot{y}}{y} = (\bar{\beta} - \beta)g(s^*) - \frac{\dot{s}}{1-s} + \beta g(s). \tag{24}$$

Since $\bar{\beta} > \beta$, the first term is positive, indicating that the terms of trade of the home country improve over time. The reason for this improvement is that when human capital grows more abundant in the rest of the world, the relative price of labor intensive intermediates rises. The second term is also positive; the shift of resources from education to production increases output. The adverse effects of this shift show up in the third term. Since free trade lowers both the rate human capital accumulation and the human capital intensity of production, the rate of productivity growth due to human capital accumulation, $\beta g(s)$, is clearly smaller than it would be under autarky.

It is not generally clear whether the output growth in (24) is above or below the autarky rate. In the long run, however, as β and s approach zero, the rate of growth in the home country approaches the foreign rate of growth $\bar{\beta}g(s^*)$, which is greater or equal to the competitive autarky rate, depending on the rate of subsidization in the foreign country. In the limit, all income in the home country will be payments for raw labor, and the growth in the value of output is due solely to improving terms of trade. This improvement in terms of trade allows for a curious possibility: when x goes to zero, the income in the home country relative to the rest of the world approaches $(1 - \bar{\beta})/(1 - s^*)$. If education is sufficiently subsidized in the foreign country, it is possible, in principle, that $s^* > \bar{\beta}$, in which case the income (at the limit) would be higher in the undeveloped home country than in the more advanced foreign country.[8] The logic behind this is that,

---

[8] In practice, this is not likely to happen. Mankiw, Romer and Weil (1992) conjecture that 50 to 70 per cent of total labor income represents return to human capital, so $\bar{\beta}$ should be between 0.5 and 0.7. It is highly unlikely that the share of resources devoted to education comes close to that.

by subsidizing education, the foreign country not only increases its future output, but also keeps the price of human capital intensive intermediates falling relative to the price of labor intensive intermediates. The home country enjoys improving terms of trade without needing to withdraw resources from production. Thus, even when there is no direct international externality in human capital accumulation, there is an indirect positive externality which works through changes in relative prices and lets the home country benefit from the investment in human capital abroad.

The welfare effects of a shift in the trade regime from autarky to free trade are also ambiguous. The static effects are clearly beneficial, and the long-run rate of growth is greater or equal to the autarky rate. Between the short and the long run, there may be a period with a slower rate of growth than under autarky, and the path of income in the long run may be above or below the path of income under autarky. It is possible, however, to cite some special cases in which the effects of opening up trade is less ambiguous.

Proposition 3. *Let $\beta(0) = 0$, and let the initial stock of human capital in the home country, relative to that of the foreign country, be $x_0 < x_E$. Then the output in the home country will be (i) higher at every point in time under free trade than under autarky if $x_0 < (1 - \tilde{\beta})^{1/\tilde{\beta}}$ and (ii) higher in the long run if $x_0 < [(1 - \tilde{\beta})/(1 - s_c)]^{1/\tilde{\beta}}$.*

Proof: See Appendix

In case (i) the output of the home country will always be above the autarky level, so trade will unambiguously improve welfare. Hence, a sufficiently poor country always benefits from trade. The weaker condition in case (ii) guarantees that, after a finite time, the output of the country will exceed and stay above the autarky level.

Proposition 3 is sensitive to the assumption that $\beta(0) = 0$, i.e., there is always room for the home country to move towards more labor intensive production.[9] Now consider the case where $\beta(0) > 0$. Again, x will approach zero, but this time the long-run investment rate $\underline{s}$ may be non-zero. As long as $x > \underline{x}$, the rate of output growth is as given in equations (23) and (24). However, when $x < \underline{x}$, factor prices are no longer equalized, and instead of

---

[9] This assumption is not necessarily unreasonable. After all, there are many tasks that can be performed without a day of education.

(24), the rate of output growth is constant at

$$\frac{\dot{y}}{y} = (\bar{\beta} - \beta(0))g(s^*) + \beta(0)g(\underline{s})$$

$$< \bar{\beta}g(s^*).$$

(24')

If the foreign country does not subsidize education, $\bar{\beta}g(s^*)$ equals the home country's autarky rate of growth, and the long-run effect of trade on growth is clearly negative. However, if the foreign country subsidizes education sufficiently and $\beta(0)$ is small, then the improvement in the terms of trade may, once again, more than outweigh the decline in the rate of human capital accumulation, resulting in a rate of long-run growth that exceeds the autarky rate.

Without further assumptions about the shape of function $g(s)$, it is impossible to give complete conditions under which opening up trade improves welfare. It would not be difficult to show that, as in the case $\beta(0) = 0$, for a sufficiently poor country, the static gains from trade always more than outweigh any dramatic losses, so opening up improves welfare. As is often the case with welfare analysis, this result hinges on the specific functional forms, so it will not be elaborated further here.

The qualitative properties of the equilibrium remain the same when a social planner chooses the rate of investment in the home country. The only difference is that the threshold value x_E, above which the economy settles on a path with high rate of human capital accumulation, is smaller than in the competitive case. When the level of development in the home country is close to that of the rest of the world, the initial level of subsidy may determine whether the country settles on a path with low investment in human capital and labor intensive production or on a path with high investment and human capital intensive production. For an LDC, the long run rate of growth under trade in the optimal case is unambiguously (weakly) smaller than the optimal rate of growth under autarky. If $\beta(0) = 0$, these two coincide; otherwise, the inequality is strict. The welfare implications in the optimal growth case are simple: opening up will unambigously increase welfare. This is obvious since the social optimizer could have chosen the autarky rate of investment s^* under free trade as well. Then the home country would have enjoyed static gains from trade while maintaining the autarky rate of human capital growth.

To summarize the results, when a developing country moves from autarky to free trade, something like the following should be observed. Initially, the "static" gains from trade take place, and the flow of resources from the home market sector to the export sector keeps output growing rapidly. Once these traditional gains from specialization are fully exploited, there are still three sources of growth. The first is the growth of human capital which slows down gradually. The second is the shift of resources from education to production. The last, and according to the model, eventually the most important, is the change in the prices of the intermediates. If education is subsidized more in the rest of the world than it was in the developing country under autarky, this effect alone may well keep the long-run rate of growth in the developing country above its autarky rate of growth.

V. Conclusions

It is concluded in several recent papers that positive international spillovers under free trade increase growth in the trading countries. Other studies which limit the scope of externalities at the national level, suggest that the effects of free trade may be asymmetric, and that well developed countries are more likely to benefit from trade than their underdeveloped partners. This paper uses the latter approach to construct a model that, even in the absence of international spillovers, allows for the possibility of free trade to boost growth in an underdeveloped economy.

As in several other models following this approach, trade has adverse effects on the production structure in the LDC. In the particular setting of this paper, trade changes the production structure toward low-tech goods and lowers the factor price of human capital. This, in turn, lowers the rate of investment in education which, over time, shows up in a decreasing level of human capital relative to the rest of the world and a further specialization in labor intensive goods.

Despite these structural effects, trade always improves welfare if education is subsidized sufficiently to correct the inefficiencies in education technology. Even if education is not subsidized in the LDC, effects on welfare, as well as on output growth, may still be positive. Static benefits may outweigh any potential dynamic losses, and if human capital accumulation in the rest of the world is fast enough, the continuing improvement in the terms of trade may result in an increased rate of GNP growth in the LDC.

Even in a case where trade decreases welfare, barriers to trade would, of course, be an inappropriate remedy. The potential source of problems for the LDC is not free trade itself, but the spillovers involved in education technology. Under free trade, this inefficiency may simply do more damage than under autarky. This interpretation, and thus the analysis in this paper, supports the trade-oriented policies of the IMF and the World Bank. At the same time, it stresses the importance of a proper structural policy, which, in this paper, means subsidizing education. From a broader point of view, structural policy may involve subsidizing various forms of production or investment, to the extent that these activities improve the country's ability to adapt new technologies.

Appendix

Solution to problem (22)

Writing the Hamiltonian, solving for the first-order conditions, and substituting the fixed point conditions $s_i = s$ and $h_i = h$ gives

$$w_{II}^* = \beta \mu g'(s)$$

$$\frac{\dot{\mu}}{\mu} = r - (1-s)\beta g'(s). \tag{A1}$$

Differentiating the first equation of (A1) gives

$$\frac{\dot{\mu}}{\mu} = \frac{\dot{w}_{II}^*}{w_{II}^*} - \frac{\dot{\beta}}{\beta} - \frac{g''(s)\dot{s}}{g'(s)}. \tag{A2}$$

Suppose first that $\beta(0) = 0$. Then, by differentiating (20) it can be seen that $\dot{\beta}/\beta = (g(s) - g(s^*))(1 - \beta)$. It is also known that $\dot{w}_H^*/w_H^* = (\bar{\beta} - 1)g(s^*)$. Substituting these in (A2), subtracting (A2) from the second line of (A1), and rearranging gives the dynamics for s, $0 < s < 1$:

$$\dot{s} = -\frac{g'(s)}{g''(s)} [\rho - (1-s)\beta g'(s) + (1-\beta)g(s) + \beta g(s^*)]. \tag{A3}$$

Differentiating the definition of x gives,

$$\dot{x} = [g(s) - g(s^*)]x. \tag{A4}$$

Equations (A3) and (A4) define a system of nonlinear differential equations characterizing the behavior of the model. The locus $\dot{s} = 0$ is upward sloping over the range of x where $s > 0$, and horizontal at $s = 0$ for low values of x. Above this locus $\dot{s} > 0$ and below it $\dot{s} < 0$. The locus $\dot{x} = 0$ is horizontal at $s = s^*$. Above this locus $\dot{x} > 0$ and below it $\dot{x} < 0$. The two loci intersect at the point $E = (x_F, s_F)$ where $s_E = s^*$, and x_E can be solved from the first-order conditions to be

$$x_E = \frac{(1 - \bar{\beta})\bar{\beta} + \theta^*(1 - \bar{\beta})G}{(1 - \bar{\beta})\bar{\beta} - \theta^* \bar{\beta} G}$$

where

$$G = \frac{g(s^*)}{(1 - s^*)g'(s^*)}.$$

If $\theta^* = 0$, then the point of intersection is $(1, s^*)$. If $\theta^* > 0$, then $x_E > 1$ at the intersection points. The Jacobian of the differential system reveals that the intersection is an unstable node.

If $\beta(0) > 0$, the dynamics are otherwise as in (A3) and (A4), but when x falls below $\underline{x}$, the relative factor prices diverge between the countries and the small country specializes in the good indexed by 0. Equation (23) is then replaced by

$$\dot{s} = -\frac{g'(s)}{g''(s)}[\rho - (1-s)\beta(0)g'(s) + g(s^*)], \qquad \text{for } s > 0. \tag{A3'}$$

The part of the locus $\dot{s} = 0$ given by (A3') is horizontal in (x, s) space. Similarly, for values of x higher than $\bar{x}$,

$$\dot{s} = -\frac{g'(s)}{g''(s)}[\rho - (1-s)\beta(1)g'(s) + g(s^*)]. \tag{A3''}$$

Thus the locus $\dot{s} = 0$ jumps discontinuously at the threshold values $\underline{x}$ and $\bar{x}$.

Proof of Proposition 1

For the maximumization problem defined in equation (22), the conditions of Theorem 15 in Seierstad and Sydsæter (1987) hold. Thus, the existence of an admissible path implies the existence of an optimal path. Since the existence of an admissible path was shown above, the existence of an optimal path is established. In order to prove that this path is monotonic, it only needs to be shown that no nonmonotonic trajectory can be optimal.

Define a function $z: x \to s$ as follows: z maps each x to the value of s for which the implicit function

$$\rho - (1-s)g'(s)\hat{\beta}(x) + g(s^*) = 0 \tag{A5}$$

holds. It can be readily checked that $z(x)$ is single valued, monotonically increasing, passes through the node E and lies below $\dot{s} = 0$ locus for values of $x < x_E$, and above it for $x > x_E$. Implicit differentiation of (A5) gives

$$\frac{dz(x)}{dx} = -\frac{g'(s)}{g''(s) - (1-s)g'(s)} \cdot \frac{\bar{\beta}}{1 - \bar{\beta} + \bar{\beta}x}. \tag{A6}$$

Let $\tilde{x}$ be an arbitrary value of x and define $\tilde{s} \equiv z(\tilde{x})$. Using equations (A3) and (A4), the slope of the trajectory passing through the point $(\tilde{x}, \tilde{s})$ can be solved to be

$$\left.\frac{\dot{s}}{\dot{x}}\right|_{(\tilde{x}, \tilde{s})} = -\frac{g'(\tilde{s})}{g''(\tilde{s})} \cdot \frac{\bar{\beta}}{1 - \bar{\beta} + \bar{\beta}\tilde{x}}$$

$$> \left.\frac{dz(x)}{dx}\right|_{x = \tilde{x}}. \tag{A7}$$

Thus, at any point on the curve $s = z(x)$, the trajectory passing through it is steeper than the curve itself. Similarly, since the curve $\dot{s} = 0$ slopes upwards, and every trajectory intersecting it is horizontal at the intersection point, then at that point, the curve is steeper than the trajectory. Therefore, starting from any point above both the $\dot{s} = 0$ locus and the $s = z(x)$ curve, s will increase (weakly) monotonically over time. Likewise, starting from a point below the $\dot{s} = 0$ locus and the $s = z(x)$ curve, s will decrease over time.

Finally, it will be shown that any point in the (x, s) plane which is not either the equilibrium point E or strictly between the loci $\dot{s} = 0$ and $s = z(x)$ implies a contradiction in the sense that the shadow price of human capital implied by the future paths of variables does not coincide with the shadow price implied by the first-order conditions.

For this purpose, μ, the private value of an additional unit of human capital at time τ, is written as the discounted value of factor payments on it:

$$\mu(\tau) = \int_{\tau}^{\infty} e^{-r^*(t-\tau)} (1 - s(t)) w_H(t) \, dt.$$

Assume first that initially (at time τ), $s(\tau) \geq z(x(\tau))$ and $\dot{s}(\tau) \geq 0$. In other words, the economy is at a point $(x(\tau), s(\tau))$ which lies above both the loci $\dot{s} = 0$ and $s = z(x)$. Using $r^* = \rho + \bar{\beta} g(s^*)$ and $\dot{w}_H / w_H = (\bar{\beta} - 1) g(s^*)$,

$$\mu(\tau) = \int_{\tau}^{\infty} e^{-(\rho + g(s^*))(t-\tau)} (1 - s(t)) w_H(\tau) \, dt$$

$$\leq \int_{\tau}^{\infty} e^{-(\rho + g(s^*))(t-\tau)} (1 - s(\tau)) w_H(\tau) \, dt \tag{A8}$$

$$= \frac{(1 - s(\tau)) w_H(\tau)}{\rho + g(s^*)}.$$

Substituting the necessary condition $\mu \bar{\beta} g'(s) = w_H$ produces

$$(1 - s(\tau)) \bar{\beta} g'(s(\tau)) > \rho + g(s^*). \tag{A9}$$

By using the definition of the function $z(x)$ it can be shown that (A9) holds only if $s(\tau) < z(x(\tau))$, which contradicts the initial assumption. Thus, no point for which $s \geq z(x)$ and $\dot{s} \geq 0$ apply simultaneously, can be on the optimal path. Similarly, it can be shown that $s < z(x)$ and $\dot{s} < 0$ holding simultaneously imply a contradiction. Therefore, every point of the optimal trajectory must lie between the loci $\dot{s} = 0$ and $s = z(x)$. This implies that on the optimal trajectory, $\dot{s} < 0$ and $\dot{x} < 0$ if $x < x_E$, whereas $\dot{s} > 0$ and $\dot{x} > 0$ if $x > x_E$, and the proof is complete. $\square$

Proof of Proposition 3

Since education is not subsidized in the home country, the rate of human capital investment in the foreign country is equal (if $\theta^* = 0$) or greater (if $\theta^* > 0$) than in the home country under autarky, i.e., $s_c \leq s^*$. Thus, without trade, the ratio of GNP per capita in the home country relative to the foreign country is intially $((1 - s_c)/(1 - s^*))x_0^{\bar\beta}$, and decreases over time. Under free trade, the ratio of outputs can be shown to be

$$\frac{1-s}{1-s^*}[(1-\bar\beta)+\bar\beta x] \geq \frac{1-s}{1-s^*}(1-\bar\beta).$$

Thus, the ratio of GNP in the small open economy relative to that under autarky is greater or equal to

$$\frac{1-s}{1-s_c}\frac{1-\bar\beta}{x_0^{\beta}}.\tag{A10}$$

If $x_0 < (1-\bar\beta)^{1/\beta}$, the second fraction of (A10) is greater than one. But the first fraction is also greater than one, since if $s > s_c$, then substituting $\beta < \bar\beta$ (follows from $x_0 < 1$) and the closed economy first-order condition (12) into (A2) would give $\dot s > 0$, which was shown in Proposition 1 not to be optimal for $x_0 < 1$. Thus, (A10) is greater than one and result (i) is established.

In the long run s goes to zero and (A10) approaches $(1 - \bar\beta)/((1 - s_c)x_0^{\beta})$. Result ($ii$) follows. □

References

Barro, R. J.: Economic growth in a cross section of countries. *quarterly Journal of Economics 106*, 407–44, 1991.

Buiter, W. H. & Kletzer, K. M.: Persistent differences in national productivity growth rates with common technology and free capital mobility. NBER WP 3637, 1991.

Dornbush, R., Fisher, S. & Samuelson, P. A.: Comparative advantage, trade and payments in a Richardian model with a continuum of goods. *American Economic Review 67*, 823–39, 1977.

Dornbush, R., Fisher, S. & Samuelson, P. A.: Heckscher–Ohlin trade thoery with a continuum of goods. *Quarterly Journal of Economics 45*, 203–24, 1980.

Feenstra, R.: Trade and uneven growth, NBER WP 3276, March, 1990.

Grossman, G. M. & Helpman, E.: Comparative advantage and long run growth. *American Economic Review 80*, 796–815, 1990a.

Grossman, G. M. & Helpman, E.: Trade, knowledge spillovers, and growth. NBER WP 3485, 1990b.

Grossman, G. M. & Helpman, E.: Hysteresis in the trade pattern. NBER WP 3526, 1990c.

Grossman, G. M. & Helpman, E.: *Innovation and growth in the global economy.* MIT Press, Cambridge, MA, 1991.

Helliwell, J. F.: International growth linkages: Evidence from Asia and the OECD. NBER WP 4245, 1992.

Levine, R. & Renelt, D.: A sensitivity analysis of cross-country growth regressions. *American Economic Review 82*, 942–63, 1992.

Lucas, R. E.: On the mechanics of economic development. *Journal of Monetary Economics 22*, 3–42, 1988.

Mankiw, N. G., Romer, D. & Weil, D. N.: A contribution to the empirics of economic growth. *Quarterly Journal of Economics 107*, 1992.

Pack, H. & Westphal, L. P.: Industrial strategy and technological change. *Journal of Development Economics 22*, 87–128, 1986.

Rivera-Batiz, L. M. & Romer, P. M.: Economic integration and endogenous growth. *Quarterly Journal of Economics 106*, 531–56, 1991.

Romer, P. M.: Endogenous technological change. *Journal of Political Economy 98*, 71–103, 1990.

Seierstad, A. & Sydsæter, K.: *Optimal control theory with economic applications.* North-Holland, Amsterdam, 1987.

Stokey, N. L.: Human capital, product quality and growth. *Quarterly Journal of Economics 106*, 587–616, 1991.

Young, A.: Learning by doing and the dynamic effects of international trade. *Quarterly Journal of Economics 106*, 369–407, 1991.

Egalitarianism and Growth[*]

Jonas Agell

Uppsala University, Sweden

Kjell Erik Lommerud

University of Bergen, Norway

Abstract

Are competitive wage premia an obstacle to growth? The answer of the architects of the Scandinavian "model" in the 1950s and 1960s was in the affirmative. By punishing expansive and growth enhancing sectors of the economy, competitive wage premia imposed an unwarranted drag on the rate of structural change. We formalize this intuition using a two sector endogenous growth model, considering both open and closed economy cases. We also show that egalitarian pay compression, combined with active labor market policies, works in the same way as an industrial policy of subsidizing sunrise industries.

I. Introduction

Scandinavia in the decades following World War II is regarded by many as a success story. Growth was rapid and unemployment remained spectacularly low. At the same time powerful and centralized labor unions pursued strongly egalitarian wage policies, and apparently succeeded in establishing a more even distribution of wages and income than in most other countries. This is in stark contrast to standard economics, which suggests

---

[*] We appreciate skillful research assistance from Kerstin Johansson. Without implicating them, we would like to thank Per-Anders Edin, Nils Gottfries, Assar Lindbeck, Torsten Persson, Lars E. O. Svensson and two anonymous referees for helpful comments on an earlier version of the paper. We have also benefited from presenting the paper at the Institute for International Economic Studies, University of Stockholm; Center for Research in Economics and Business Administration, Bergen; the labor market seminar at the Swedish Institute for Social Research (SOFI), University of Stockholm; University of Bergen; Uppsala University; Trade Union Institute for Economic Research (FIEF); the 1992 EEA congress in Dublin; and University of Munich. The paper was written when Jonas Agell was at the Institute for International Economic Studies.

that compression of wages relative to productivities should lead to more or less severe efficiency losses. Today there are many signs of economic distress in both Norway and Sweden. As faith in the Scandinavian "model" falters, it seems warranted to look back on its heyday. How was it possible to combine egalitarianism with growth and strong economic performance?

Our focus is on how egalitarian wage policies, like those pursued in Norway and Sweden, can have a beneficial effect on structural change and growth. This said, it should be stressed that we do not believe that labor market institutions constitute the only explanation for the comparative economic success of these countries until recently. Nor do we believe that labor market institutions are solely to blame for the present productivity slowdown and rising unemployment. We have no quibbles with the argument that a generous welfare state and a rapid expansion of public sector employment might require tax levels that are detrimental to growth; see e.g. Lindbeck (1990).

The 1980s have witnessed a revival of interest in trade union theory. Much of this literature is best viewed as portraying bargaining between a firm–specific union and the employer side, but there has also been some focus on large, centralized unions and their interaction with the government. For example, Olson (1982) and Calmfors and Driffill (1988) claim that with highly centralized unions, efficiency is less likely to be harmed than with intermediate centralism. The argument is that a large encompassing union is more likely to internalize some of the negative macroeconomic externalities present in wage setting. There is probably some truth in this, but the story still seems rather incomplete as a description of union centralism in, for instance, Norway and Sweden. *Ceteris paribus*, if wage moderation is the key characteristic of centralized unions, we should expect countries with highly centralized unions to be low-wage economies. This does not seem to fit the facts; cf. Landesmann and Vartiainen (1990).

In contrast, the intellectual architects of the Scandinavian model were much more preoccupied with the dynamic effects of centralized trade unionism. The crux of the matter was a deeply held suspicion of the role of competitive wage premia in the growth process. In the words of Rehn (1988, p. 325), labor is not "... like mercury, requiring only small level differences between two areas in order to float quickly, and in large quantities, from one of them to the other" (our translation). As a consequence firms in expanding sectors of the economy have to pay more or less substantial competitive wage premia to attract workers from firms in old and stagnating sectors. However, by increasing the wage bill of expansive firms, these wage premia impose an unwarranted drag on the rate of structural change.[1]

---

[1] The idea that intersectoral wage gaps create efficiency losses is also standard in the development literature; see e.g. Williamson (1988).

The suggested remedy was "solidary" wage policies.[2] By compressing wage differentials between low-productivity and high-productivity sectors, a central union can help to speed up growth and structural change. And as high-productivity sectors expand and low-productivity sectors are driven out of existence, redundant workers can find a better paid job in the expanding sectors of the economy. There is also a close link between solidary wage policies and the traditionally strong emphasis on active labor market policies, especially in Sweden. To speed up the reallocation of redundant workers, the government should pay outright mobility grants and subsidize retraining directed at work in the expanding sector.

For decades, however, most academic economists have had trouble with this dynamic approach to union centralism. The belief has been that a system of competitive markets would provide us with the right speed of structural change, and — as a corollary — that pay compression could only create inefficiencies. In the absence of market imperfections, competitive wage differentials simply reflect the true opportunity cost of intersectoral labor mobility.[3] Thus, while solidary wage policies remained an important (many would say the most important) ingredient of the Scandinavian model for several decades, it seems safe to conclude that most economists consider their theoretical underpinnings as at best shaky.[4]

The purpose of this paper is to show that these shaky views about growth and the role of competitive wage premia and union wage policy can be tied together using the tools of endogenous growth theory. Following the pioneering work of Romer (1986) and Lucas (1988), a key focus in much of this literature is that there can be socially increasing returns and positive externalities from producing in certain sectors rather than in others. This provides a rationale as to why structural change might be suboptimal in a laissez-faire economy. One policy implication might be that the government should subsidize employment in the externality-

---

[2] The intellectual origins for the notion of solidary wage policies can be traced to the writings of the Swedish trade union economists Gösta Rehn and Rudolf Meidner in the late 1940s and early 1950s. For an English translation of some of the key essays, see Turvey (1952). Hibbs and Locking (1991) summarize some of the main institutional developments, and provide a very thorough empirical examination of the impact of solidarity bargaining on the Swedish wage structure.

[3] For forceful presentations of this view, see Flam (1987), Kierzkowski (1982, 1984) and Knies and Herberg (1988).

[4] While observations of pay compression within union sectors are plentiful, and not confined to the Nordic countries, see e.g. Freeman and Medoff (1984), there is scant theoretical work on the subject. For recent attempts, see e.g. Agell and Lommerud (1992), analyzing pay compression as an insurance device, and Moene and Wallerstein (1992), analyzing the interaction of bargaining institutions, pay compression and structural change.

generating sector, or education that is geared towards the needs of this sector. This could easily lead to larger income differentials — for the sake of faster growth. However, a radically different policy might also work. By compressing wage differentials between e.g. a high-tech, externality-generating modern sector and a low-tech traditional sector, people will be forced out of the traditional sector into the modern one.

A first interesting analysis along these lines is provided by Chadha (1991). Chadha's focus is on Singapore, but Singapore's policy of promoting growth through certain "wage correction" policies closely parallels ideas prevailing in Norway and Sweden in the 1950s. Our analysis shares the spirit of Chadha's model, but differs in important respects. First, whereas Chadha envisages workers to be perfectly mobile across sectors, we introduce mobility costs that give rise to a well defined competitive wage differential. This allows us to explore the effects of competitive wage premia on growth in some detail, and to formalize the notion of wage premia as a tax hindering structural change.

Second, sluggish labor adjustments affect the allocation of labor *and* capital, and hence the functional distribution of income. In order to explore the distributional dynamics during a process of structural change, we incorporate capital in our model. This links our analysis to the old-age debate on whether or not economic development requires increased inequality as a prerequisite. Perhaps the most famous concept in this context is Kuznets' "U-hypothesis": when the development process gets started, inequality increases — only when economic development is well under way will society start to become more egalitarian again. On the face of it, the view of wage compression as a dynamic force in the growth process may seem to be in complete contradiction of the Kuznets hypothesis. However, the degree of equality does not only depend on the degree of wage dispersion among workers; the functional distribution of income also matters.

Invoking sector-specific externalities to explore the effects of such a multifaceted phenomenon as solidary pay compression is, of course, a procedure open to some criticism. First, one would be hard-pressed to argue that the Scandinavian proponents of pay compression actually had externalities in mind when they made their case in the late 1940s. Our topic, however, is not doctrinal criticism, but rather the potential effects of union egalitarianism put into practice. Second, our argument that external economies of scale are more important in a "modern" manufacturing sector (engineering, electronics, etc.) than in a "traditional" sector (agriculture, textiles, etc.) is not airtight. Clearly, there is a marked disparity between the burgeoning theoretical literature on endogenous growth, often based on assumptions about externalities, and the relatively scant empirical investigation into the importance of externalities in the real world.

However, we do believe that the available evidence is sufficiently rich to prevent our conjecture from being dismissed offhand. Caballero and Lyons (1989, 1990) report comprehensive evidence on significant externalities in U.S. and European manufacturing. In a follow-up, Bartelsman, Caballero and Lyons (1991) try to disentangle different sources of externalities. Overall, their results provide evidence that both fluctuations-oriented and growth-oriented external economies are important in U.S. manufacturing. Their findings also support the idea that external economies vary considerably across sectors. This idea also seems to be in line with common beliefs. Given the freedom of choice, why does almost everyone prefer electronics to textiles, and engineering to agriculture? To us, it is quite natural to think of electronics and engineering as activities more likely to generate positive knowledge spillovers. The importance of knowledge externalities is studied in the literature on R&D spillovers; for some recent empirical evidence, cf. Griliches and Lichtenberg (1984), Bresnahan (1986) and Jaffe (1986).

The remainder of the paper is organized as follows. Section II outlines the main elements of our endogenous growth model. In Section III we study the properties of equilibrium growth in a laissez-faire economy, and go on to analyze the effects of competitive wage premia. Section IV analyzes the consequences of solidary wage compression within this framework. Section V turns to the limitations of our analysis, and examines the extent to which our results survive when we relax certain key assumptions. A final section provides some concluding remarks.

II. The Basic Model

Production and Learning

Our basic setup builds on Lucas (1988). The main difference is that we incorporate physical capital into the model, and assume that labor mobility across sectors is less than perfect. There are two competitive production sectors, a modern one denoted by subscript m, and a traditional one denoted by subscript t. Both sectors use labor and capital, in fixed total supplies, to produce consumption goods c_m and c_t. To this standard Heckscher–Ohlin setup we add dynamic learning effects in the modern sector. As these learning effects cumulate over time, so will the economy's aggregate production possibilities.

The two consumption goods are produced according to the Cobb–Douglas production functions

$$c_m = h l_m^\beta k_m^{1-\beta} \tag{1}$$

$$c_t = l_t^\beta k_t^{1-\beta}, \tag{2}$$

where l_i and k_i denote the labor and capital employed in sector i, and h is the human capital used in modern sector production. Of course, it would not be difficult to allow the share parameter β to differ between sectors. However, for our purposes it is convenient to suppress all kinds of inter-sectoral production heterogeneity related to factors other than dynamic learning effects.

As Krugman (1987) and Lucas (1988), we assume that learning effects in the modern sector represent an industry phenomenon, entirely external to individual firms. Following Lucas, the rate of learning-by-doing (i.e., the rate of human capital accumulation) is specified as an increasing function of the size of the modern sector work force:

$$\dot{h}/h = \delta l_m, \tag{3}$$

where a dot over a variable defines a time derivative, and δ measures the intensity of our linear learning technology. The simple form of the learning equation is not crucial for our analysis. What we do need for our results to go through is a positive link between the resource base of the modern sector and its rate of external knowledge formation. Such a link occurs in a variety of endogenous growth models.

Factor Markets and Labor Mobility

Students of structural change and growth processes often seem to focus on the role of sluggish *capital* reallocations across sectors. The concept of solidary wage policy builds on the polar view that insufficient *labor* mobility constitutes a major obstacle to growth.[5] However, sluggish labor force adjustment is regarded as having unwarranted side effects on the intersectoral allocation of capital. As old and stagnating sectors of the economy can pay lower than average wages, they can also afford to pay the going rental rate of capital. As a consequence, capital gets stuck in the wrong industries.

While intersectoral mobility costs may come in a variety of forms, ranging from necessary re-education to meet job requirements in the modern sector to outright travel expenses, in the following we focus on locational preferences as a source of imperfect labor mobility. Apart from

---

[5] For an interesting recent paper discussing sectoral adjustment in the presence of restricted labor mobility, see Matsuyama (1992). Matsuyama focuses on irreversible educational decisions as a mobility obstacle. As there are no externalities in his model, the rate of structural change is always efficient.

lending itself to a simple analytical treatment, locational preferences also seem to come close to the kind of mobility obstacles emphasized by critics of the solidary wage policies pursued in Norway and Sweden. By speeding up the deindustrialization of large, and often distant, areas of the country, solidary wage policies unduly forced, it was argued, a sizable portion of the population to abandon their preferred ways of living.

To pinpoint these arguments, we assume that workers always prefer to work (and consume) in the traditional sector.[6] A convenient way of formalizing this is to assume a utility function of the form

$$U_t = \gamma U(c_m, c_t), \qquad \gamma \gtrless 1 \tag{4}$$

$$U_m = U(c_m, c_t), \tag{5}$$

where U_m is utility from living in the modern sector and U_t utility from living in the traditional sector. $U(\cdot)$ is homogeneous of degree one in the consumption of modern and traditional sector output. The parameter γ is a multiplicative shift factor, representing the location-dependence of utility. In short, any given consumption bundle gives higher utility if consumed in the traditional sector. For any given choice of geographical location, workers maximize utility by allocating their wage income across the two consumption goods. Assuming that each worker supplies one labor unit regardless of his sectoral affiliation, the resulting conditional indirect utility functions become $V_m = Rw_m$ and $V_t = \gamma Rw_t$, where V_i is the indirect utility of living (and consuming) in sector i, w_i is the corresponding wage and R is some function of output prices.

Consider the mobility decision of a traditional sector worker. To accept a job in the modern sector it must be the case that $V_m \geq V_t$, implying that the required wage premium must satisfy $w_m \geq \gamma w_t$. With competitive labor markets we then obtain the marginal mobility condition

$$w_m = \gamma w_t, \tag{6}$$

which must be satisfied at every point in time during a process of structural change, where resources gradually move from the traditional to the modern sector.[7] Capital, on the other hand, is perfectly flexible across sectors:

$$r_m = r_t \equiv r. \tag{7}$$

---

[6] More realistically, locational preferences would depend on the whole history of where one has lived, so that a newcomer to the modern sector gradually adjusts her preferences. But as we focus on an ongoing migration process from the traditional to the modern sector, we find this simplification acceptable.
[7] See Katz and Stark (1989) for an example from the migration literature where receiving sector wages are discounted when compared with source sector wages.

To simplify algebra without loss of generality, we set total supplies of labor and capital equal to unity.[8] The full employment conditions for factor markets then become

$$l_m + l_t = 1 \tag{8}$$

$$k_m + k_t = 1. \tag{9}$$

The Demand Side

To close the model we assume a utility function of the constant elasticity form:

$$U(c_m, c_t) = [c_m^{-\rho} + c_t^{-\rho}]^{-1/\rho}, \tag{10}$$

where $\rho > -1$ and $\sigma = 1/(1+\rho)$ is the elasticity of substitution between c_m and c_t.[9] Denoting the relative price of traditional sector output in terms of modern sector output by q, the optimal consumption bundle must satisfy

$$c_t/c_m = q^{-\sigma}. \tag{11}$$

In our capital and labor economy, as in the pure labor model of Lucas (1988), the value of σ turns out to be crucial for the rate (and even direction) of structural change. Holding the factor allocation constant across sectors, the learning equation (3) implies that unit costs in the modern sector decrease over time. If σ is small ($\sigma < 1$), this bonus will be used to allow increased consumption of both goods, meaning that resources will move from the modern to the traditional sector. If σ is large ($\sigma > 1$), resource transfers will go in the other direction, and the absolute size of the traditional sector will decrease over time. As this situation seems to come closest to mind when considering structural change in the real world, we henceforth follow Lucas in assuming that $\sigma > 1$.

III. Competitive Wage Premia, Growth and Distribution

The equilibrium dynamics of our model are simple. As our representative agents face no intertemporal tradeoffs, there is no role for forward-looking

---

[8] While common in Heckscher–Ohlin type models, the assumption of a fixed amount of capital which can move without friction across sectors is, of course, rather questionable. We do not suggest that intertemporal savings decisions and capital formation are unimportant factors for understanding growth and structural change in the real world. We do, however, believe in Ockham's razor — our formulation permits a clean-cut analysis of growth and competitive wage differentials.

[9] With purely external human capital formation and no physical capital accumulation, all relevant aspects concerning consumer preferences are captured by the single period utility function depicted in (10).

expectations in deciding equilibrium growth patterns. In the terminology of Krugman (1991) "history" is all that matters. Given the initial conditions, the entire future growth path is uniquely determined.

It is useful to start out by characterizing equilibrium factor allocations. It takes just a few lines of algebra to show that perfect competition in factor markets must imply that[10]

$$\frac{k_m/l_m}{k_t/l_t} = \gamma,$$ (12)

at each instant τ. Due to the proportional (and constant) wage premium γ, capital intensity in the modern sector always exceeds capital intensity in the traditional sector. Equation (12) is suggestive of the view of wage premia as a potential obstacle to growth. As the rate of external learning formation is directly tied to the size of the modern sector work force, the wage premium γ slows growth by promoting capital intensive production in the modern sector.[11]

To derive expressions for factor uses in absolute terms, we have to invoke the demand side. Substituting (1) and (2) into (11), and using (12), we obtain

$$q = [h^{-1} \gamma^\beta (k_t/k_m)]^{-1/\sigma}.$$ (13)

Perfect competition in output markets implies that q must equal relative unit costs. With our Cobb–Douglas production functions, this means that

$$q = h\gamma^{-\beta}.$$ (14)

Combining (13) and (14) we have that

$$\frac{k_m}{1 - k_m} = h^{\sigma - 1} \gamma^{\beta(1 - \sigma)}$$ (15)

$$\frac{l_m}{1 - l_m} = h^{\sigma - 1} \gamma^{\beta(1 - \sigma) - 1},$$ (16)

---

[10] We use the fact that perfect competition in factor markets implies $w_m = mpl_m$, $w_t = q \cdot mpl_t$, $r_m = mpk_m$ and $r_t = q \cdot mpk_t$, where mpl_i and mpk_i are the marginal products of labor and capital in sector i. Manipulating (1), (2), (6) and (7), we then obtain (12).

[11] In general, the competitive wage premium also creates a scale effect, as it decreases the overall size of the modern sector. This scale effect explains why the simple form of the learning equation (3) is less crucial. Had we rather chosen to specify knowledge formation as a function of modern sector output, or of some weighted average of factor inputs, we would thus still obtain a negative link between competitive wage differentials and external learning.

where we have used (8) and (9), and where the last expression follows from combining (12) and (15). Equations (15) and (16) underline the key role of human capital as a vehicle of structural change. At each date, the inter-sectoral allocation of production factors is directly linked to the stock of external human capital in the modern sector. To obtain the evolution of human capital, we substitute (16) in (3):

$$\frac{\dot{h}}{h} = \delta \frac{A}{1+A},\tag{17}$$

where

$$A = h^{\sigma-1}\gamma^{\beta(1-\sigma)-1}.\tag{18}$$

Given an initial endowment $h(0)$, the nonlinear differential equation (17) implicitly defines the stock of human capital at each instant, and hence from (15) and (16) the time paths for the allocation of labor and capital. In the following we assume that $h(0) > 0$. Our model then implies a process of ongoing structural change (if $h(0) = 0$, the economy gets stuck in an equilibrium where all production takes place in the traditional sector). As external human capital steadily accumulates in the modern sector, labor and capital gradually shift towards this sector. To further characterize the solution of (17), we note that A is, given our assumption on σ, a monotonically increasing function of h. The growth rate of human capital, $\dot{h}/h$, therefore increases over time, and reaches an upper bound δ when time approaches infinity.

As in other models with external learning effects, the competitive equilibrium path is not efficient. The higher growth potential in the modern sector is not accounted for by private agents. As a consequence, the rate of transformation from traditional to modern sector production is too slow. From (17) and (18) we also note that the growth rate of human capital is a decreasing function of the wage premium γ. If γ is sufficiently large, the growth process comes to a standstill.

Figure 1 illustrates the point. It shows the time path for the stock of human capital for different values of γ. In all cases we assume $\sigma = 2$, $\beta = 0.75$, and $h(0) = 1$. We set $\delta = 0.02$, which reflects an annual steady-state growth rate of two per cent. As time goes by, competitive wage premia impose a cumulative drag on human capital formation. In effect, they operate as a tax on learning formation in the modern sector. Interpreting τ as calendar time and using the growth path for an economy without wage differentials (i.e., when $\gamma = 1$) as the benchmark case, we note that the

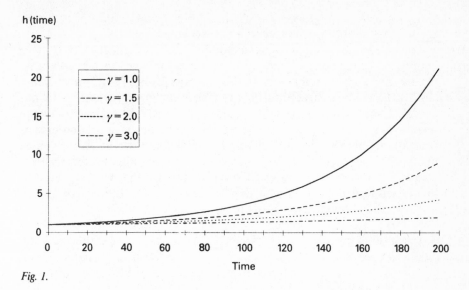

h (time)

Fig. 1.

human capital stock at year 200 is about 80 per cent smaller for an economy with $\gamma = 2$.

Are economies with smaller wage premia better off than those with larger ones? Clearly, at any given instant an economy is better off in a state with a large, rather than a small, stock of human capital; *ceteris paribus*, a larger human capital stock simply implies a more generous aggregate resource constraint. In this particular sense smaller wage premia are better than larger ones. While tempting, it is still inappropriate, however, to identify the growth paths of Figure 1 with different levels of economic well-being. Economies with larger wage differentials have a preference for less rapid growth, and undertake smaller sacrifices in terms of current reallocations in order to reap future gains. Although the external nature of human capital formation means that the competitive growth path for any particular economy (characterized by a certain value for γ) falls short of its optimal one, there is no meaningful way of ranking growth paths across different economies.

Which growth rate would be chosen by a benevolent planner? As the planner internalizes the externality in modern sector production, the optimal rate of structural change will always be larger than that provided in the competitive equilibrium. However, it will not be infinitely large either. Along the optimal growth path the planner must set the shadow value of transferring workers to the externality generating sector against current marginal costs in the form of a less desirable mix of consumption goods and a less desirable locational pattern of workers.[12]

The idea that sluggish intersectoral factor adjustments may have important consequences for the distribution of income is well known from the literature on international trade; see e.g. Mussa (1982) and Neary (1978). How does structural change affect income distribution in our model? Labor incomes in the two sectors are locked to each other by the relationship $w_m = \gamma w_t$. As the economy grows, the wage differential is constant in percentage, but increasing in absolute terms. However, in utility terms workers are always equally well-off in either sector: the very concept of a competitive wage differential implies that workers become indifferent to their sectoral affiliation. Clearly, this result does not fit very well with the U-hypothesis of Kuznets.

Matters become more interesting when we turn to the functional distribution of income. With perfectly mobile labor ($\gamma = 1$), it follows from (15) and (16) that the capital–labor ratio is unity at each date in both production sectors. With capital intensities thus given, both wage rates and the rental rate must increase in tandem with the stock of external learning capital; i.e., $\dot{w}/w = \dot{r}/r = \dot{h}/h$. With imperfect labor mobility ($\gamma > 1$) factor intensities change over time. From (12) capital intensity in the modern sector always exceeds capital intensity in the traditional sector by the multiplicative factor γ. During the growth process, when resources gradually get released from the traditional sector, capital intensity must therefore decrease in both sectors; this can be shown by repeated use of (15) and (16). As the changes in factor intensities are favorable to capital owners, it follows that $\dot{w}/w < \dot{h}/h < \dot{r}/r$.

During the modernization phase, competitive wage differentials affect the dynamics of functional factor shares. An increasing share of the fruits of structural change will accrue to capital owners. Over time, however, rates of factor price increase converge. As time approaches infinity, both capital returns and wages converge to the common growth rate $\dot{h}/h$. The implied pattern of factor returns is roughly consistent with a modified version of Kuznets' U-relation between development and inequality.

---

[12] Consider a benevolent planner maximizing workers' utility (including capital owners in the welfare function would not alter the intuition). At any instant τ the return function is $R = l_m U_m + (1 - l_m) U_t$, where $U_m = U(c_m^m, c_t^m)$, $U_t = \gamma U(c_m^t, c_t^t)$, and c_j^i denotes the amount of sector i production allocated to workers in sector j. Given some social discount factor, the planner maximizes the integral of $R(\tau)$ from time zero to infinity, subject to (3) and the resource constraints $h l_m^\beta k_m^{1-\beta} = l_m c_m^m + (1 - l_m) c_m^t$ and $(1 - l_m)^\beta (1 - k_m)^{1-\beta} = l_m c_t^m + (1 - l_m) c_t^t$. Setting up the corresponding Hamiltonian and deriving the relevant first-order conditions (treating l_m, k_m and the c_j^is as controls, and $h(\tau)$ as a state variable), it is straightforward to derive the intuition of the text.

However, while Kuznets focused on the uneven development of wages in different sectors, the modified U-result that comes out of our analysis pertains to the uneven development of functional factor shares. It should also be noted that our modified U-result pertains to growth rates of inequality, and not to absolute levels. Thus, even though the growth rate of wages eventually catches up with that of capital, the inequality gap created during the transition phase will not be closed.

IV. Solidary Wage Policies

While pay compression is a prerequisite for the Scandinavian approach to industrial restructuring, it has to be complemented by two other measures to be effective. First, wages must be set at such a level that firms at the low end of the productivity distribution are under constant pressure to restructure and reallocate. Second, union wage policy must be accompanied by active labor market policies, designed to speed up restructuring and mitigate the individual consequences of structural change. Do these policies make economic sense?

Consider the laissez-faire equilibrium of the preceding section. To highlight the mechanics of solidary wage policies, we now introduce its component parts in sequential order. First, think of a central union as fixing the wage differential at unity (implying a uniform wage rate w across sectors), but letting the wage level be determined in the market. While this removes the differential wage tax on skill formation in the modern sector, it also affects the mobility decision of workers. Allowing for remigration to the traditional sector, our economy will collapse to a one-good equilibrium. Labor will rush back to the traditional sector, and capital must follow suit. The economy gets locked into a low-productivity equilibrium, which is sustained forever.

The dual role of wage premia, stimulating intersectoral labor mobility but taxing modern sector firms, underscores that a policy of pay compression may, on its own, create more problems than it solves. To be successful, labor somehow has to be induced to return to the modern sector, despite the lack of migration incentives. Solidary wage policy solves the problem in a harsh way: if the carrot does not work, why not use the stick instead? Full employment wages in the one-good equilibrium are too low, as they do not reflect labor's alternative use in the modern externality–generating sector. By raising the overall wage level, a central union forces traditional sector firms to economize on labor. The net outcome is traditional sector unemployment — the stick.

Now, traditional sector unemployment does not translate directly into a willing line of modern sector job seekers. Depending on the distribution of reservation wages, some workers may prefer to stay on in the traditional sector despite unemployment; other workers may, using an out-of-the-model argument, need some retraining to satisfy modern sector job requirements, etc. This is where active and mobility–oriented labor market policies enter. By introducing extensive retraining programs and providing mobility grants, the government would promote rapid and efficient reallocation of unemployed workers in the traditional sector.

Assume that the active labor market policies operate as intended, meaning that every unemployed worker in the traditional sector is willing to apply for a modern sector job.[13] Within the context of our model, a central union then has some latitude in determining the growth rate. By accepting the full employment wage rate in the specialized equilibrium (i.e., when all production takes place in the traditional sector), the union opts for zero growth. However, at real wages higher than the full employment wage in the traditional sector the union is, at any given instant, confronted with a menu of growth–wage combinations; by increasing the wage level the union speeds up the rate of reallocation of workers to the modern sector. Obviously, there is an upper limit to such growth oriented wage policies. If real wages are too high, only some fraction of unemployed workers in the traditional sector can find new jobs in the modern sector — the net outcome is aggregate unemployment.

It is easy to characterize the maximum growth path compatible with solidary wage policies. Denote the implied wage rate by w^*. At this wage, labor demand of modern sector firms is just sufficient to absorb the unemployment in the traditional sector. Formally, we then have that

$$l_m(w^*) = u, \tag{19}$$

$$l_t(w^*) = 1 - u, \tag{20}$$

where u is the fraction of workers expelled from the traditional sector, and $l_i(w^*)$ denotes the labor demand of sector i in a general equilibrium conditioned on the wage rate w^*. Consolidating (19) and (20) we obtain

$$l_m(w^*) + l_t(w^*) = 1. \tag{8'}$$

Equation (8′) is formally equivalent to the full employment condition (8) in the laissez-faire economy, the only difference being that involuntary mobility at a uniform wage w^* replaces voluntary mobility at a given wage differential γ. This immediately suggests a simple rule for determining w^*.

---

[13] In the following, we assume that the reservation wage of unemployed workers in the traditional sector is always lower than the modern sector wage plus mobility grants. The implied rapid reallocation of unemployed traditional sector workers is not all that unrealistic. In the 1950s and 1960s (decades of rapid structural change), the average Swedish unemployment rate was about 1.5 per cent; see e.g. Lindbeck (1975).

Let w_c denote the equilibrium wage in a laissez-faire economy *without* wage differentials (i.e., when $\gamma = 1$). From the preceding section we know that equations (15)–(18) then summarize the competitive dynamics, holding γ at unity. Clearly, as long as $w^* = w_c$ at each instant τ, the economy with solidary wage policies will replicate the competitive outcome. As time goes by, the union must then increase w^* at the same rate as the stock of external learning capital in the modern sector.[14]

The bottom line is the following. Starting in a competitive equilibrium with imperfect labor mobility, a central union may short-cut the potentially adverse effects of competitive wage premia on growth. By mimicking the Walrasian outcome in a world with perfectly mobile labor, properly devised pay compression may promote growth. Returning to the figure, we may now think of the different growth paths as referring to one particular economy, operating under alternative wage setting regimes. Depending on the value of γ, the difference between any of the broken curves and the solid curve represents the maximum additional growth potential provided by solidary wage policies.[15]

Solidary wage policies were designed to combine growth and income equality. Our analysis suggests that this dual purpose strategy may make economic sense. In the laissez-faire economy with imperfect labor mobility the modified U-result holds, implying that returns to capital owners increase at a faster rate than wages throughout the growth process. Along the maximal growth path (where $w^* = w_c$) wages are equalized across sectors, and the overall wage level grows in tandem with capital returns. However, income equality is not the same as equality of welfare. While pay compression may, relative to laissez-faire, lead to a more even development of functional factor shares, it may also create new inequalities among different groups of workers. This possibility, so often stressed in the policy debate in Norway and Sweden, is also clear from our analysis. Equalization of intersectoral wages means that workers always prefer a rationed job in the traditional sector to a job in the modern sector. In this sense, the gainers from pay compression belong to the (ever decreasing) number of workers that manage to keep a job in the traditional sector.

---

[14] This follows directly from the dynamics of factor returns in the laissez-faire equilibrium with perfect labor mobility. As discussed in the previous section, the w_c equilibrium is characterized by constant factor intensities over time, and hence a uniform development of factor returns.

[15] For reasons discussed in the preceding section, growth does not necessarily coincide with welfare. While laissez-faire growth is surely too slow, the solid curve in the figure may well be associated with too rapid growth. A benevolent union may then adopt a less growth-oriented wage policy, and set the uniform wage rate somewhere below w^*, but above the full employment wage rate in the specialized no-growth equilibrium.

Solidary pay compression is not the only feasible growth promotion strategy in our model. In fact, the growth path associated with the w^*-policy can also be obtained through a policy of payroll subsidies to firms in the modern sector. (Consider the effects of giving firms in the modern sector a subsidy directly proportional to the competitive wage differential.) We denote this latter strategy "industrial policy". When the two policies are measured out to give the same rate of structural change, and when pay compression is combined with full compensation to movers, they are in fact formally identical. The only cosmetic difference is that under solidary wage policy, movers get compensation when leaving the traditional sector, while industrial policy involves paying out the compensation upon arrival in the modern sector in the form of a (subsidized) wage premium.

All this is quite intuitive. Full compensation transforms solidary pay compression into a "pull" policy for labor mobility. Moving is then voluntary, just as when modern sector employment is subsidized. With less than full compensation, however, important differences occur. While industrial policy and pay compression still deliver the same growth rate, they have different implications for equity and government revenue raising. As pay compression with incomplete compensation means that involuntary movers have to pay part of their mobility costs themselves, it is less costly for the government than industrial policy. From an equity point of view, however, industrial policy has the obvious advantage of never interfering with the mobility condition (6), meaning that utility is always the same for all workers. Before condemning pay compression without compensation as unsolidary, we must recognize that a complete welfare analysis should also take into account the effects of distortionary taxes, made necessary by full compensation.[16]

V. Omissions and Extensions

Are our results robust? Let us briefly discuss some of the key simplifying assumptions:

Open economy considerations. What are the effects of introducing international trade into our model? Consider the case of a small open economy facing internationally given output prices.[17] At any given instant τ, world prices are $(1, q)$. Perfect competition then implies the zero-profit

---

[16] In discussing the relative merits of pay compression and industrial policy, we may also note that international agreements to an increasing extent seem to block a country from subsidizing its "modern" sectors. Though conceptually similar, solidary wage policy does not seem to meet any international retaliation.

[17] The following argument owes much to Lucas (1988).

conditions

$$1 \leq Bh^{-1} w_m^\beta r^{1-\beta} \tag{21}$$

$$q \leq Bw_t^\beta r^{1-\beta}, \tag{22}$$

where the right-hand terms give the unit cost functions corresponding to (1) and (2), B is some function of β, and $w_m = \gamma w_t$. Unit costs in the traditional sector, relative to unit costs in the modern sector, are then $h\gamma^{-\beta}$. Everything else equal, competitive wage premia decrease relative unit costs, while human capital formation works in the other direction. At any instant, there are three possible competitive equilibria. Consider first the case where $q > h\gamma^{-\beta}$, implying that the price of traditional sector output in terms of modern sector output is higher than the corresponding relative unit cost. Our small open economy will then specialize in the production of traditional sector output (meaning that (22) reduces to an equality, and (21) to a strict inequality). In the converse case, where $q < h\gamma^{-\beta}$, our economy will specialize in modern sector production. Finally, in the knife-edge case where $q = h\gamma^{-\beta}$, we obtain a — at least momentarily — diversified equilibrium, with production taking place in both sectors.

The effects of competitive wage premia on growth appear even more dramatic in the open economy. Consider two small trading countries, having the same initial human capital stock $h(0)$, but differing in terms of γ. Clearly, the country with the higher value of γ is the one most likely to specialize in the production of traditional sector goods. Thus, initial comparative advantages depend crucially on γ. High-γ countries have a comparative advantage in traditional sector production, while low-γ countries have a comparative advantage in modern sector production. As countries specialize accordingly, low-γ countries will accumulate external learning capital and settle on a path of sustained growth, while high-γ countries get locked into a stationary equilibrium.

If output trade underscores the case for pay compression, international factor mobility is an altogether different story. It is probably no coincidence that the concept of solidary wage policies was developed at a time when the Nordic countries adopted far-reaching capital controls, and when international labor mobility was severely restricted. With internationally mobile factors, any policy aiming at affecting domestic factor prices will, of course, be hard to implement.[18]

Equal pay for unequal work. In our model workers can be thought of as a pool of homogeneous carpenters (or university professors), requiring a

---

[18] As part of its wage correction policy, Singapore also adopted measures to limit the inflow of low-skilled foreign workers; see Chadha (1991).

wage premium to incur the cost of moving to the modern sector. In this one-job economy, pay compression simply means that carpenters are paid the same regardless of their sectoral affiliation, which speeds up industrial restructuring. This form of *intra*-job wage equalization captures well the solidary wage policies actually pursued in Sweden up to the mid-1960s; see Hibbs and Locking (1991). Under the catchy slogan "equal pay for equal work", the Swedish confederation of blue-collar workers squeezed wage differentials within occupations, but not across occupations.

The original idea of intra-job wage leveling was transformed in a radically egalitarian direction in .the late 1960s. For ideological and political reasons, solidary wage policy then became an instrument for a drastic compression of wages *across* occupations and skill groups, thus transforming the notion of equal pay for equal work into something more like "equal pay for unequal work". As such it may have been overly successful. Available empirical studies indicate that the return to education in Sweden may have fallen by about 50 per cent from the late 1960s to the mid-1980s; see Björklund (1986) and Edin and Holmlund (1993). While this decline may have come about for a number of reasons, it is still suggestive of potentially large educational disincentive effects. To shed further light on this latter, and more aggressively egalitarian, type of pay compression we would need a richer model, that formalizes the role of educational decisions in the growth process.[19]

VI. The Demise of the Scandinavian Model?

We have formalized some unorthodox but influential Scandinavian notions of competitive wage premia as a potential hindrance to growth. We have also argued that solidary wage policies (the suggested policy response) may make more economic sense than is commonly believed. Indeed, properly devised pay compression may produce growth *and* a more even development of factor returns. We also demonstrated the close conceptual similarity between pay compression and a general industrial policy of "picking the winners". However, solidary wage policies are not a universal formula that a country — whether Scandinavian, European or Asian — can apply to promote economic development and equality at all times. As the

---

[19] In analyzing the effects of "equal pay for unequal work", it is far from obvious that educational disincentive effects will be crucial. Smaller wage premia to education will also change relative labor demands, as firms substitute educated workers for relatively expensive uneducated workers. The resulting slack in the market for uneducated workers may then induce people to acquire education, in spite of a less favorable monetary return. This, of course, is nothing but a variation of our basic push argument for pay compression.

nature of external constraints and knowledge formation change over time, so will the appropriate policies to foster growth and structural change.

We have emphasized that wage compression is favorable for growth only when combined with overall real wage moderation. Such wage moderation is perhaps easier to achieve in already fast-growing societies, like Scandinavia in the years after World War II or Southeast Asia of today. In countries where the overall wage level is too high — perhaps the current situation in many Eastern European countries — things are quite different. Wage compression then only drives people out of the stagnant sectors and into unemployment, to the benefit of no one.

In Sweden, the highly centralized wage bargaining system dissolved in 1983. As industry and local level bargaining replaced bargaining at the national level, the main union confederation lost its instrument to enforce egalitarian wage agreements. In Norway, the dominant trade union confederation was challenged in the 1980s, and two competing confederations grew rapidly in membership. The lesson to be learned seems to lie as much on the political as on the economic side. A high unionization rate is a necessary but not a sufficient condition for solidary wage policy. The internal cohesion and organizational strength of the union movement must also be high, and the links between unions and government must be close, with the latter providing the right kind of labor market policies. Although these conditions prevailed in Norway and Sweden in the 1950s and 1960s, and may also prevail today in *dirigiste* market economies like Singapore and Taiwan, they are clearly more of an exception than a rule. *Why* these prerequisites come forth in some countries, in some time periods, is a crucial question, well beyond this paper.[20]

References

Agell, J. & Lommerud, K. E.: Union egalitarianism as income insurance. *Economica 59*, 295–310, 1992.

Bartelsman, E. J., Caballero, R. J. & Lyons, R. K.: Short and long run externalities. NBER WP 3810, Cambridge, MA, 1990.

Björklund, A.: Assessing the decline of wage dispersion in Sweden. In IUI Yearbook 1986–87, *The Economics of Institutions and Markets*. IUI, Stockholm, 1986.

---

[20] In fact, this issue is central in the political science literature on whether "social democratic corporatism" (which some argue is the essence of the Scandinavian model) is growth stimulating; see e.g. Lange and Garrett (1985), Jackman (1986) and Hicks (1988). From the viewpoint of economics, Persson and Tabellini (1991, 1992) and Saint-Paul and Verdier (1991) provide very interesting perspectives on the interaction of politics and growth. Their emphasis, very different from ours, is on how the degree of equality influences political decision processes, which in turn might have important consequences for growth.

Bresnahan, T.: Measuring spillovers from technical advance: Mainframe computers in financial services. *American Economic Review 76*, 741–55, 1986.

Caballero, R. J. & Lyons, R. K.: The role of external economies in U.S. manufacturing. Mimeo, Columbia University, 1989.

Caballero, R. J. & Lyons, R. K.: Internal versus external economies in European industry. *European Economic Review 34*, 805–26, 1990.

Calmfors, L. & Driffill, J.: Bargaining structure, corporatism and macroeconomic performance. *Economic Policy 6*, 14–61, 1988.

Chadha, B.: Wages, profitability, and growth in a small open economy. *IMF Staff Papers 38*, 59–82, 1991.

Edin, P.-A. & Holmlund, B.: The Swedish wage structure: The rise and fall of solidaristic wage policy. NBER WP 4257, Cambridge, MA, 1993.

Flam, H.: Equal pay for unequal work. *Scandinavian Journal of Economics 89*, 435–50, 1987.

Freeman, R. B. & Medoff, J. L.: *What Do Unions Do?* Basic Books, New York, 1984.

Griliches, Z. & Lichtenberg, F.: Interindustry technology flows and productivity growth: A reexamination. *Review of Economics and Statistics 66*, 324–9, 1984.

Hibbs, D. & Locking, H.: Wage compression, wage drift, and wage inflation in Sweden. FIEF WP 87, Stockholm, 1991.

Hicks, A.: Social democratic corporatism and economic growth. *Journal of Politics 50*, 677–704, 1988.

Jackman, R.: The politics of economic growth in industrial democracies. *Journal of Politics 48*, 242–56, 1986.

Jaffe, A. B.: Technological opportunity and spillovers of R&D: Evidence from firms' patents, profits, and market value. *American Economic Review 76*, 984–1001, 1986.

Katz, E. & Stark, O.: International labour migration under alternative informational regimes: A diagrammatic approach. *European Economic Review 33*, 127–42, 1989.

Kierzkowski, H.: Wage relativities in an open economy. *Weltwirtschaftliches Archiv 118*, 690–705, 1982.

Kierzkowski, H.: Trade unions, wage relativities and employment. *Australian Economic Papers 23*, 91–104, 1984.

Knies, D. & Herberg, H.: The employment effects of a rigid wage ratio in small open economies with sector-specific capital. *Journal of Institutional and Theoretical Economics 144*, 671–83, 1988.

Krugman, P.: The narrow mowing band, the Dutch disease, and the competitive consequences of Mrs Thatcher. *Journal of Development Economics 27*, 41–55, 1987.

Krugman, P.: History versus expectations. *Quarterly Journal of Economics 106*, 651–67, 1991.

Landesmann, M. & Vartiainen, J.: Social corporatism and long-term economic performance. DAE WP 9020, University of Cambridge, 1990.

Lange, P. & Garrett, G.: The politics of growth. *Journal of Politics 47*, 792–827, 1985.

Lindbeck, A.: *Swedish Economic Policy.* Macmillan, London, 1975.

Lindbeck, A.: The Swedish experience. IIES Seminar Paper 482, University of Stockholm, 1990.

Lucas, R. J.: On the mechanics of economic development. *Journal of Monetary Economics 22*, 3–42, 1988.

Matsuyama, K.: A simple model of sectoral adjustment. *Review of Economic Studies 59*, 375–88, 1992.

Moene, K. O. & Wallerstein, M.: The process of creative destruction of the scope of collective bargaining. Memorandum 29/92, Department of Economics, University of Oslo, 1992.

Mussa, M.: Imperfect factor mobility and the distribution of income. *Journal of International Economics 12*, 125–41, 1982.

Neary, J. P.: Short-run capital specificity and the pure theory of international trade. *Economic Journal 88*, 488–510, 1978.

Olson, M.: *The Rise and Decline of Nations.* Yale University Press, New Haven, 1982.

Persson, T. & Tabellini, G.: Is inequality harmful for growth? Theory and evidence. Mimeo, University of Stockholm, 1991.

Persson, T. & Tabellini, G.: Growth, distribution and politics. *European Economic Review 36* (Papers and Proceedings), 593–602, 1992.

Rehn, G.: *Full sysselsättning utan inflation. Skrifter i urval.* (Full Employment without Inflation. Selected Writings.) Tidens Förlag, Stockholm, 1988.

Romer, P. M.: Increasing returns and long-run growth. *Journal of Political Economy 94*, 1002–37, 1986.

Saint-Paul, G. & Verdier, T.: Education, growth and democracy. Mimeo, DELTA, Paris, 1991.

Turvey, R., (ed.): *Wages Policy under Full Employment.* William Hodge and Company, London, 1952.

Williamson, J. G.: Migration and urbanization. In H. Chenery & T. N. Srinivasan (eds.), *Handbook of Development Economies*, vol. 1, North Holland, Amsterdam, 1988.

Talent, Growth and Income Distribution

Ragnar Torvik *

University of Oslo, Norway

Abstract

A model with heterogeneous individuals and bequests between generations is constructed to analyze income distribution and educational choice. The introduction of an imperfection in the credit market is shown to influence the allocation of talent. Both ability and bequest are of relevance in deciding whether or not to invest in education. With learning by doing between generations, the allocation of talent affects not only the level of production, but also the growth rate.

I. Introduction

Bequests and earning capacity of individuals are both important determinants of income distribution. As regards bequests, income distribution in each generation depends on the income distribution in the parents' generation. Atkinson and Stiglitz (1980, Ch. 3 and 9) provide an overview of models where earning capacity is generated randomly. Loury (1981) develops the theory further, adding the training offspring receive from their parents to explain earning capacity. Since investments in offspring are dependent on parents' income, a link is established between income distribution over generations.

A study by Galor and Zeira (1988), and new growth theory in general, have contributed to renewed interest in income distribution over generations and growth. Recent papers include Aghion and Bolton (1991), Banerjee and Newman (1991), Perotti (1990) and Saint-Paul and Verdier (1991). Galor and Zeira (1988) develop an overlapping generations model where parents give bequests to their children. Each of the identical individuals decides whether or not to invest in education. Investing in education is associated with a cost in the first period of life. Two sources

---

*I am grateful for stimulating discussions with seminar participants at the Department of Economics, University of Oslo.

are available for raising the educational expenditure, inheritance from parents and borrowing in the market. However, there is a capital market imperfection. An individual can only borrow at an interest rate which is higher than the lending rate. As a result, educational choice becomes dependent on the amount an individual inherits from his parents. Individuals with inheritance higher than a critical level invest in education, individuals with inheritance below this level do not. The wage an individual receives is dependent on his education. Consequently, as the bequest from individuals with education is higher, their children are more likely to invest in education, and so on. The dynamic equilibrium is characterized by zero growth. Each individual belongs to one of two groups, high income or low income. The income distribution from the parent generation to the child generation reproduces itself exactly. Aghion and Bolton (1991) and Banerjee and Newman (1991) go one step further by analyzing reasons for capital market imperfections. According to Aghion and Bolton (1991), unobservable effort gives rise to moral hazard problems. The result is that the interest rate is increasing in the amount an individual borrows, and therefore decreasing in the bequest from parents. With a more specific treatment of the credit market, many of the qualitative results from Galor and Zeira (1988) are reproduced.

Models with voting and heterogeneous agents are analyzed by Perotti (1990) and Saint-Paul and Verdier (1991). The median voter decides how much should be redistributed through the tax system or how much public education should be provided. Since the transfer or the amount of public education is the same for everyone, agents with the highest ability also have the highest earning capacity. These voting models preclude a situation where individuals with low ability invest in education, while individuals with high ability do not. In this sense, talent is allocated in an optimal way.

The model developed in this paper is close in spirit to that of Galor and Zeira (1988). A credit market imperfection is introduced in its simplest form, by a difference between the lending and borrowing rates of interest. The most important dissimilarity between our static model and the model of Galor and Zeira is that agents differ not only in the amounts they inherit from their parents, but also in their heterogeneity with respect to ability. In contrast to the papers discussed above, this allows us to consider the allocation of talent. Do the agents who will increase their productivity the most by investing in education in fact choose education? In this model, we will see that, in general, the answer is no. Educational choice is determined by a combination of bequests and ability. Equal ability does not produce equal educational opportunities.

In the dynamic specification, I incorporate an endogenous growth model in its simplest form with "Learning By Doing" (LBD) between generations. It is realistic to assume that the greater the number of people who invest in eduation in one generation, the stronger the LBD to the next generation. Education represents an increase in the human capital endowments in society that benefits not only the present generation, but also future generations. For example, an engineer working today will learn about production processes and perhaps make new inventions that can be used in the future. We should expect such learning effects to be strongest from someone with education — and stronger, the higher the ability of an educated individual. With this in mind, I study how the growth rate is affected by the allocation of talent.[1]

Furthermore, will the economy converge to a situation where only ability matters for educational choice? As will be shown, this is not necessarily the case. I also discuss the question of the optimal number of people who invest in education. In the presence of LBD, there is an externality between generations that has to be taken into account.

The model is presented in Section II, and then used to study income distribution and the allocation of talent in Section III. Section IV is devoted to the dynamics of income distribution and educational choice. The steady state of the model is shown to be dependent on initial conditions. The steady-state growth rate is derived in Section V; some of its properties are discussed there and in Section VI, which concludes.

II. The Model

The economy under consideration is small and open, with all prices except wages given on the world market. The total output in the economy at time t, Y_t, is given by the aggregate production function $Y_t = F(h_t L_t, K_t)$, where h_t is overall labor productivity or human capital, L_t a labor aggregate, and K_t capital at time t. The production function is assumed to be homogeneous of degree one in $h_t L_t$ and K_t. Capital is fully mobile and the interest rate r is given exogenously and constant on the world market. The amount of effective labor $h_t L_t$ is always known one period in advance, and consequently the capital stock adjusts to achieve

$$F_{K_t}\left(\frac{h_t L_t}{K_t}, 1\right) = r . \tag{1}$$

The effective labor-capital ratio is constant over time. This determines the time invariant price of effective labor, w. The price of one unit of the labor aggregate is then $h_t w$.

---

[1] Although in a different context, allocation of talent and growth is also analyzed by Baumol (1990) and Murphy et al. (1991). These papers study the case where agents choose either productive or unproductive (rent-seeking) work from the point of view of the society.

There is a continuum of agents of given total mass in the economy. Each agent lives for one period and leaves one child with the same ability for the next period. The physical population is therefore constant over time. The ability of an agent i denoted $a(i)$, and the child of agent i is denoted i, and so on. The agents are distributed according to ability with some density function $f(a)$, continuous and positive on the interval $<1, a']$. The total physical population is then given by the integral of $f(a)$ over this interval.

Workers are either unskilled or skilled. At each period in time there are both unskilled and skilled workers. The density functions are given by $f_{ut}(a)$ and $f_{st}(a)$, respectively, and must satisfy $f_{ut}(a) + f_{st}(a) = f(a)$ for all a. Since agents can enter and leave the group with education over generations, the density functions are in general time dependent, even if the density function for the population as a whole is not. The labor aggregate L_t is given by

$$L_t = \int_1^{a'} f_{ut}(q)\,dq + \int_1^{a'} a(q) f_{st}(q)\,dq. \tag{2}$$

A skilled worker has a higher productivity than an unskilled worker, $(a(i)>1)$. The higher the ability, the larger the difference in productivity between being unskilled and skilled.

When a car is produced, production results in more than just a car; it also leads to new insight and increased knowledge, thereby benefiting later production. This important aspect of production is represented in the model by the LBD mechanism

$$\frac{h_t - h_{t-1}}{h_{t-1}} = \delta L_{t-1} \Rightarrow h_t = h_{t-1} \delta L_{t-1} + h_{t-1} = z_{t-1}\, \delta \geq 0. \tag{3}$$

Equations (2) and (3) clarify the two effects of education in the model. The static effect is to increase the relative productivity of the workers who invest in education. There is also a dynamic effect of education, i.e. it raises the productivity of the whole workforce. Since $a(i)>1$, the strongest LBD is from a worker with education, the higher the ability, and the stronger the LBD. This captures central aspects of education. It not only raises the productivity of those who choose it, but also lays a foundation for increased knowledge and productivity in the future.[2]

---

[2] The formulation of LBD is similar to Lucas (1988) and Young (1991), except that the model presented here has heterogeneous agents and education. As pointed out by Arrow (1962), it is most realistic to assume that the learning in a good is bounded. Young (1991) shows how bounded learning in each good can lead to unbounded learning at the aggregate level. The reason is that new goods are set into production over time. An alternative way of modelling LBD here would be to assume that there is LBD only from people with education.

In the beginning of each period, an agent decides whether to invest in education or not. Without education he works as an unskilled worker, earning a wage equal to his marginal productivity

$$w_{ut} = h_t w. \tag{4}$$

If he decides to invest in education, he has to pay a cost e_t in the beginning of the period.

$$e_t = \beta h_t w \qquad \beta > 0. \tag{5}$$

The cost of education is related to the wage level in the period.[3] Since w is the wage per efficiency unit, a skilled worker yields the wage

$$w(i)_{st} = a(i) h_t w. \tag{6}$$

At the end of the period, all individuals decide how much to consume and how much to leave as a bequest to the child. The individuals have the same homothetic utility function $U = U(c, b)$ in consumption c and bequest to the child b. The share of consumption and bequest out of income is then a function of the relative price only. Since the "price" of bequests and consumption is the same, an individual will leave a constant fraction of his total income x as a bequest to the child

$$b = (1 - a)x \qquad 0 < a < 1. \tag{7}$$

An individual can lend at the world market interest rate r in the beginning of each period. We assume an imperfect capital market in the sense that if an agent wants to borrow in the beginning of the period, he has to repay the amount at a higher interest rate than r at the end of the period.[4]

This does not alter the results of the model. The key element is that the learning effects are increasing in the amount of people investing in education, and that the learning effects from a worker are stronger, the higher his ability is. However, as in other endogenous growth models, the results are not robust against changing the assumption of unbounded learning at the aggregate level. If aggregate learning is bounded, learning is not strong enough to produce continuous growth.

[3] Then, the relative importance of the cost will be the same over time. The assumption of a cost of education related to the wage level can be justified by the fact that production of education calls for labor resources, or that education requires time and that the cost of time is related to the wage level.

[4] Galor and Zeira (1988) show one possible way this can result from costs of keeping track of borrowers so that they do not default. Perhaps the easiest way to model such an imperfection is to assume tracking costs proportional to the amount an agent borrows. The costs of keeping track of a borrower can then be written ρd, where d is the amount borrowed. The interest rate r^* paid by a borrower must be such that the net return from lending to him equals the return on the world market, i.e., $rd = r^* d - \rho d$. We then get $r^* = r + \rho$.

III. Income Distribution and the Allocation of Talent

Consider an agent i in period t. If he decides to work as an unskilled worker, his income equals the wage he receives plus the amount he inherited with interest:

$$x(i)_{ut} = h_t w + (1 + r) b(i)_{t-1}. \tag{8}$$

If the agent decides to invest in education, he is a net borrower if the bequest he got is lower than the cost of education. He then has to borrow at the interest rate $r^* > r$. If the bequest is higher than the cost of education, he is a net lender:

$$x(i)_{st} = a(i) h_t w - (1 + r(i))(e_t - b(i)_{t-1}),$$
$$r(i) = r^* \text{ if } b(i)_{t-1} < e_t \wedge r(i) = r \quad \text{if } b(i)_{t-1} > e_t. \tag{9}$$

An individual chooses education if the income from doing so is higher as compared to not choosing education. If the bequest is higher than the cost of education, an individual invests in education if the r.h.s. of (9) with $r(i) = r$ is larger than the r.h.s. of (8). This is equivalent to

$$a(i) > (1 + r)\beta + 1. \tag{10}$$

Next we consider the case where the bequest is not high enough to cover the cost of education. For an individual to invest in education, the r.h.s. of (9) with $r(i) = r^*$ must be larger than the r.h.s. of (8), equivalent to

$$b(i)_{t-1} > \frac{z_{t-1} w[(1 + r^*)\beta - (a(i) - 1)]}{r^* - r}. \tag{11}$$

Expressions (10) and (11) determine those of the individuals who will choose education. From (10) we see that if the bequest is larger than the cost of education, then ability — and ability alone — determines the education choice. If ability is higher than a critical level, $a_s = (1 + r)\beta + 1$, an individual will invest in education. From (11) it is clear that ability need not be the only aspect of relevance if the inheritance is less than the cost of education. Consider first the case where ability is higher than $a_H = (1 + r^*)\beta + 1$. Then, the r.h.s. of (11) is negative. Therefore, an agent with ability above a_H will invest in education even if he does not receive a bequest. For sufficiently high ability, the imperfection in the credit market is not strong enough to prevent an agent from choosing education. Consider next the case where the ability level is above a_s, but below a_H. For a given ability level in this interval, the bequest from the parent determines whether an agent decides to invest in education or not. The higher the bequest from the parent, the less an individual has to borrow, and the higher the net return on education.

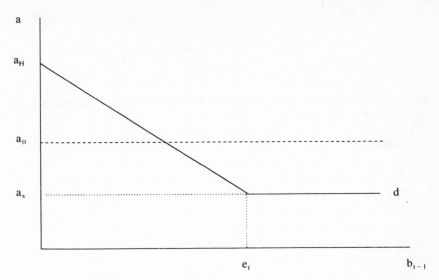

Fig. 1.

By equality in (10) and (11), we get the combination of ability and bequest where agents are indifferent between investing in education or not, depicted as the curve d in Figure 1. The curve intersects the vertical axis at a_H. Agents having higher ability than a_H will choose education regardless of the bequest they receive. The curve is downward sloping in the interval from a_H to a_s. For an agent to be indifferent between investing in education or not, lower ability has to be compensated by a higher bequest. At a_s the curve is horizontal. When the inheritance is larger than the cost of education, the education choice is independent of bequest from the parent. Agents above the curve will invest in education, those below will not.

It is obvious that talent is not allocated in an optimal way.[5] Optimal allocation of talent requires the educational choice to be independent of bequest from the parent. The only relevant attribute is an agent's ability. For the same number of individuals investing in education, production would be higher if all the agents with ability above, say, a_0 were educated, and the agents below a_0 were not. a_0 is determined so that the number of

---

[5] In this context, "optimal allocation of talent" implies the following. If a given number of people invest in education, are agents with and without education distributed so that production is maximized? In other words, allocation of talent is not the same as optimizing the number of people investing in education. The latter is denoted here by "optimal number of people investing in education", where it is implicitly assumed that talent is allocated in an optimal way.

individuals choosing education is the same as in the actual economy, depicted as the dotted curve in Figure 1.

As regards the distribution of bequests and the allocation of talent, it should be noted that an egalitarian distribution will in general give an optimal allocation of talent. If everyone receives the same bequest, the agents' ability determines whether or not they invest in education. All agents above a critical ability level will choose education, all agents below will not. We may also find some properties of the distribution that maximize the number of individuals choosing education for a given amount of total bequests. This is the same as a distribution that lifts as many of the individuals as possible above the curve d in Figure 1. For agents above a_s, this distribution is characterized by lower bequests, the higher the ability. If the total level of bequests is low (a "poor" economy), the distribution is also characterized by zero bequest to agents below a_s and above a_H. Therefore, in poor economies, there may be a serious tradeoff between education and income distribution. The distribution which favors education implies that little of the total bequest is left to the people with the lowest ability and income.

IV. The Dynamics of Income Distribution and Educational Choice

It is most convenient to solve the model with respect to bequest divided by overall labor productivity. Define this as $b_t/h_t = b_t/z_{t-1} = \zeta_t$. Inserting from (8) into (7) and taking (3) into account, the bequest for agents without education is

$$\zeta_t = (1-\alpha)\left[w + (1+r)\frac{z_{t-2}}{z_{t-1}}\, \zeta_{t-1}\right]. \tag{12}$$

Inserting from (9) into (7), and then using (3) and (5), bequests for agents with education are

$$\zeta_t = (1-\alpha)\left[a(i)w - (1+r(i))\left(\beta w - \frac{z_{t-2}}{z_{t-1}}\,\zeta_{t-1}\right)\right], \tag{13}$$

$$r(i) = r^* \text{ if } \frac{z_{t-2}}{z_{t-1}}\,\zeta_{t-1} < \beta w \wedge r(i) = r \text{ if } \frac{z_{t-2}}{z_{t-1}}\,\zeta_{t-1} > \beta w.$$

Using (3) the term z_{t-2}/z_{t-1} can be written

$$\frac{z_{t-2}}{z_{t-1}} = \frac{1}{\delta L_{t-1}+1} = \gamma_{t-1} < 1. \tag{14}$$

For simplicity, I assume in the following that this term is time independent and equal to γ, meaning that adjusted for differences in ability, the flow in and out of the group with education is equal. This will be the case in the steady state, but nothing guarantees that this will be fulfilled in the movement towards the steady state. The general case with a time dependent γ is analyzed in the Appendix.

Equations (12) and (13) are the first-order differential equations determining the dynamics of the bequests and educational choice in the economy. Since the bequests are a constant share of income, the dynamics of income measured in labor productivity units can be found by dividing by $(1 - \alpha)$. Furthermore, the development of income measured in income units is obtained by multiplying both sides of the equations by labor productivity.

In the following, equations (15) and (16) are assumed to be satisfied. The first inequality in (15) is the stability condition for (12) and (13) with $r(i) = r$. If this is not fulfilled, the differential system would explode. The second inequality in (15) below is assumed to hold for the model to be of any interest in studying the allocation of talent. If this inequality is not satisfied, only ability would matter for the educational choice in the steady state.[6] Expression (16) implies that the cost of education is higher than the steady state bequest for agents without education. This assumption is also made to enhance the interest of the analysis. If this were not the case, all agents with $a > a_s$ would choose education in the steady state.[7]

$$(1 - \alpha)(1 + r)\gamma < 1 < (1 - \alpha)(1 + r^*)\gamma \tag{15}$$

$$\frac{\beta}{\gamma} > \frac{1 - \alpha}{1 - (1 - \alpha)(1 + r)\gamma}. \tag{16}$$

Consider two groups of agents with different ability, $a(l)$ and $a(u)$ such that

$$a_s < \frac{\beta}{(1 - \alpha)\gamma} < a(l) < a(u) < (1 + r^*)\beta + \frac{1 - (1 + r^*)(1 - \alpha)\gamma}{1 - (1 + r)(1 - \alpha)\gamma} < a_H. \tag{17}$$

---

[6] This, of course, is an interesting result in itself. If the capital market imperfection is weak in the sense that there is a small difference between r and r^*, the ability effect will dominate over the bequest effect in the long run. For a given number of people investing in education, talent will be allocated in the optimal way. In the remainder of the paper, I focus on the situation where the capital market imperfection is in fact so strong that the second inequality in (15) holds.

[7] Again, if the assumption does not hold, this is an interesting result in itself. If the cost of education is sufficiently low, all agents with $a > a_s$ would invest in education in the steady state. In the rest of the analysis, I assume that the cost of education is high enough to preclude this.

It can be verified that the rest of the inequalities in (17) follow from (15) and (16). I begin with this case because it shows, in a clear-cut way, an interesting result of the model: also in the steady state, the allocation of talent will not be optimal. (The general case with agents of all ability levels is studied below). Figure 2 shows the phase diagram for the two groups. From (11) we see that when the bequest in period $t-1$ is at a low level, the agents in both groups will choose not to invest in education. When agents do not choose education, (12) is the relevant equation, with the slope of the curve given by $(1-\alpha)(1+r)\gamma$. The agents in the group with ability $a(u)$ invest in education if $\zeta_{t-1} > D$. The agents in this group are net borrowers in the interval from D to H. Here (13) with $r(i) = r^*$ is the relevant equation, with the slope of the curve given by $(1-\alpha)(1+r^*)\gamma$. Above H they are net lenders. (13) gives the slope of the curve as $(1-\alpha)(1+r)\gamma$.

The curve in Figure 2 is similar for the agents in the group with ability $a(l)$. However, the important difference here is that these agents will not choose education if $\zeta_{t-1} < F$, where $F > D$. Because of the lower ability of the agents in this group, the level of bequest from the parent necessary to invest in education is higher than for the agents with $a(u)$.

For each group in Figure 2, there are two stable dynamic equilibria: A and C for agents with $a(u)$, and A and B for agents with $a(l)$. Individuals in

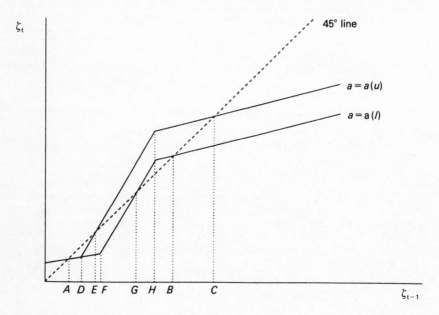

Fig. 2.

A will not choose education, while individuals in B and C will. Individuals without education will all have the same income level and leave the same bequest to their child. For agents with education, income and bequests will be higher, the higher the ability. For given ability, the income group to which each individual belongs is fully determined by the initial conditions. For the group with ability $a(u)$, the individuals initially in the interval up to E will be without education. For the group with ability $a(l)$, individuals initially in the interval up to G will be without education.[8]

For the same reason as in the static equilibrium, it is easy to see that talent is not allocated in an optimal way. Switching one individual with education and ability $a(l)$ for one individual without education and ability $a(u)$ would increase production.

The general case with individuals of all ability levels and initial levels of bequest is illustrated in Figure 3. There is a continuum of curves in the phase diagram. I limit the discussion to the five different principal cases in the model. Case 1 is the situation where ability is below a_s. Individuals in this group will not invest in education under any circumstances, and in the long-run equilibrium all individuals in the group will be in A. In case 2, ability is somewhat higher, but below $\beta/(1-a)\gamma$. For a sufficiently high inheritance, the individuals in this group will choose education. However, in the long-run equilibrium all agents in this group will also be in A. Their ability is not high enough to maintain bequests at a level sufficient for them to invest in education over time. In order for individuals in a group to choose education in the long-run equilibrium, ability has to be at least $\beta/(1-a)\gamma$, as in case 3. Here the agents with inheritance sufficient to cover the cost of education in the first period will also choose education in steady state. Case 4 is the situation where ability is sufficiently high for all the agents to invest in education in the long-run equilibrium, even if some of the agents do not choose education initially. Here ability is at least as high as the l.h.s. of the last inequality in (17). Finally, some of the agents have a high enough ability to invest in education regardless of the bequest from their parent. This is illustrated in case 5 in Figure 3. For individuals to be in this group, ability must be at least a_H.

In the steady state we will have a group of individuals without education in A, where

$$A = \frac{(1-a)w}{1-(1-a)(1+r)\gamma}. \tag{18}$$

---

[8] Note that if β is falling over time (e.g. due to technical progress in education), the point H would move to the left in the figure over time. Then, at some point in time, all agents would choose education.

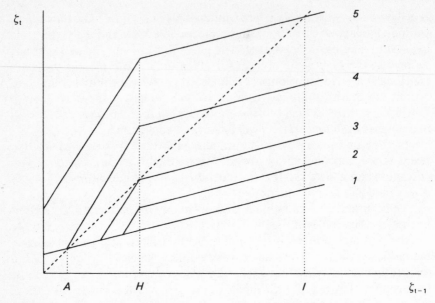

Fig. 3.

There will be a continuum of individuals with education on the interval from H up to the point I determined by the group of individuals with the highest ability, a^I. For individuals with education, the bequest (and income) in labor efficiency units is higher, the higher the ability. The bequest in labor productivity units for an agent i with education will converge to

$$\frac{(1-\alpha)w(a(i)-(1+r)\beta)}{1-(1-\alpha)(1+r)\gamma}.$$

Hence, also in steady state, the allocation of talent is in general not optimal. Production would be higher if the individuals who invest in education were those with the highest ability.

V. The Allocation of Talent and Growth

The growth rate of labor in efficiency units, g_t, is determined by

$$g_t = \frac{h_t L_t - h_{t-1} L_{t-1}}{h_{t-1} L_{t-1}}. \tag{19}$$

In steady state the labor aggregate L is constant. From (3) we then get the steady-state growth rate of labor in efficiency units as $g = \delta L$. From (1) the growth rate for capital is the same. Then, the steady-state growth rate of production is also $g = \delta L$.

We see from (4) and (6), respectively, that this is also the growth rate in wages for unskilled and skilled workers. From (5) the cost of education grows by the same rate, and from (12) and (13) we note that g is also the steady-state growth rate of bequests. Then, it follows from (7) that the total income for each agent grows by the same rate g.

Note that the steady-state growth rate is dependent on the allocation of talent. For a given number of individuals investing in education, the better the allocation of talent, the higher the degree of LBD, and the higher the growth rate. For the same reason, the growth rate is higher, the greater the number of people choosing education.[9] For given total bequests in the economy, the income distribution that maximizes the number people investing in education also maximizes growth.

We may also ask what would be the optimal number of people who invest in education. Consider first the case where $\delta = 0$, so that there is no LBD. If the education cost reflects the social cost, all agents with $a > a_s$ should choose education. Consider next the case where $\delta > 0$. Education then represents a dynamic externality. The more people who invest in education in one period, the stronger the LBD to the next period. If an individual with $a < a_s$ chooses education, there would be a static loss because the increase in labor productivity does not compensate for the cost of investing in education. On the other hand, there would be a dynamic gain due to higher LBD. For instance, if we introduce a social planner with preferences in income over generations, we would in general have the result that the lower the discount rate, the lower the optimal a.

VI. Concluding Remarks

When the agents in an economy cannot borrow and lend at the same interest rate, the allocation of talent will in general not be optimal. People

---

[9] It is also clear that as the model is formulated, the size of the economy measured in terms of the number of people will have a positive impact on the growth rate. This is a common feature of many endogenous growth models, but here it should be regarded as a result of convenient modelling instead of economic realism. Restating equation (3) as

$$\frac{h_t - h_{t-1}}{h_{t-1}} = \frac{\delta L_{t-1}}{\displaystyle\int_1^{a'} f(q)\, dq}$$

would give all the same results in the model, except that the growth rate would be independent of the number of people in the economy.

with high inheritance from their parent may choose education even if their ability is lower than that of other individuals who do not choose education. The capital market imperfection prevents the education choice from being dependent on ability only, which it otherwise would be in an optimal situation. Bequests between generations tend to preserve the income distribution over time. Even in the steady state, individuals with higher ability than others may have less income because they are locked out of education.

With LDB between generations, the allocation of talent influences not only the level of production, but also the growth rate. The better the allocation of talent, the greater the extent of learning, and the higher the growth rate. In addition, the number of people choosing education has a positive impact on the growth rate.

Consider two countries that differ only in the initial conditions for total bequests (wealth) in the economy. The poorer country has a low level of bequests and the richer country a high level. Then, more people will invest in education in the rich country, making the growth rate higher than in the poor country. The result is diverging rather than converging growth paths. For the same reason, shocks to the economy may have permanent effects in the model. A shock that erodes the level of bequests can have a permanently negative impact on the growth rate.

The model may also be able to clarify other aspects regarding differences between rich and poor countries. If poor countries face stronger market imperfections in credit markets, the difference in the rate of interest between borrowing and lending may be higher. Fewer people invest in education. This is also the case if the cost of education is relatively higher compared to the wage in poor countries (higher β).

If total bequests are at a low level, there may be a more pressing tradeoff between income distribution and growth than if initial wealth is at a high level. The income distribution that favors education implies that little of the bequest is left to agents with low income and ability. Breaking the link between bequests and educational choice could reduce this tradeoff. Public education may provide part of the solution.

Appendix

This appendix focuses on the case where the term γ in general is time dependent. From (2) and (14) it follows that γ is bounded above and below at γ_H and γ_s, respectively, where

$$\gamma_H = \frac{1}{1 + \delta \int_1^{a^i} f(q)\, dq}, \tag{A1}$$

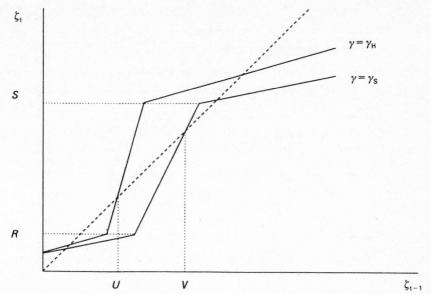

Fig. A1.

$$\gamma_s = \frac{1}{1 + \delta \int_1^{a'} a(q) f(q) \, dq}. \tag{A2}$$

The discussion is limited to a group of agents with given ability. The same argument could easily be applied to agents at all levels of ability, but would not provide any new intuition as compared to the case presented here. The phase diagram for a group with some given ability is depicted in Figure A1. This group of agents is represented by two curves in the figure. The upper curve refers to the case $\gamma = \gamma_H$, and the lower curve to the case $\gamma = \gamma_s$. For each period in time, the actual curve has to lie somewhere between the two curves.

The upper and lower curves start out at the same point $w(1-\alpha)$. The curve where $\gamma = \gamma_H$ has a steeper slope than the curve where $\gamma = \gamma_s$. It can be verified that the switching points at the ζ_t axis from the curve given by (12) to the curve given by (13) with $r(i) = r^*$, and from the curve given by $r(i) = r^*$ to the curve given by $r(i) = r$ in (13) are independent of γ. In the figure, these switching points are denoted R and S, respectively.[10]

---

[10] Figure A1 may give the impression that agents in a slow growing economy are more likely to invest in education than agents in a fast growing economy, since the lower the growth rate, the higher the curve in the diagram. This is not what the figure shows, however. The curve in a slow growing economy is higher precisely because fewer people invest in education. The figure in fact shows that in a slow growing economy, the bequest measured in labor productivity necessary to invest in education is lower than in a fast growing economy. The reason for this is the higher increase in the cost of education from one period to the next in a fast growing economy.

Since the curve in each period of time has to be between the two curves in Figure A1, it is clear that the agents initially in the interval up to U in the figure will be without education in the steady state, regardless of how the actual curve shifts from one period to the next in the phase diagram. Furthermore, it is clear that the agents initially above the point V will choose education in the steady state under any circumstances. As regards the agents initially in the interval from U to V, without further information we cannot in general say how large the fractions with and without education will be in the steady state. Among the agents in this interval, those who end up in the groups with and without education will be dependent on how the actual curve in the phase diagram shifts over time. This is again dependent on the initial simultaneous distribution of ability and bequests for all the agents in the economy. When we reach the steady state, γ is constant over time and we are back in the case analyzed earlier.

Allowing γ to be time dependent does not alter the basic conclusions in the paper. The only difference is that we have a group of agents where determination of who ends up in which group will be dependent on the initial simultaneous distribution of bequests and ability for all the agents. All the qualitative results in the model will still be valid. The movement towards the steady state may be somewhat different, but when the economy reaches the steady state, γ will in fact be independent of time.

References

Aghion, P. & Bolton, P.: A trickle-down theory of growth and development with debt-overhang. Mimeo, DELTA, Paris, 1991.

Arrow, K. J.: The economic implications of learning by doing. *Review of Economic Studies* 29, 155–73, 1962.

Atkinson, A. B. & Stiglitz, J. E.: *Lectures on Public Economics.* McGraw-Hill, London, 1980.

Banerjee, A. V. & Newman, A. F.: Risk-bearing and the theory of income distribution. *Review of Economic Studies* 58, 211–35, 1991.

Baumol, W. J.: Entrepreneurship: Productive, unproductive and destructive. *Journal of Political Economy* 98, 893–921, 1990.

Galor, O. & Zeira, J.: Income distribution and macroeconomics. Brown University WP 89–25, 1988.

Loury, G. C.: Intergenerational transfers and the distribution of earnings. *Econometrica 49*, 843–67, 1981.

Lucas, R. E. Jr.: On the mechanics of economic development. *Journal of Monetary Economics 22*, 3–42, 1988.

Murphy, K. M., Shleifer, A. & Vishny, R. W.: The allocation of talent: Implications for growth. *Quarterly Journal of Economics 106*, 503–30, 1991.

Perotti, R.: Political equilibrium, income distribution and growth. Mimeo, MIT, 1990.

Saint-Paul, G. & Verdier, T.: Education, democracy, and growth. Mimeo, DELTA, Paris, 1991.

Young, A.: Learning by doing and the dynamic effects of international trade. *Quarterly Journal of Economics 106*, 368–405, 1991.

Living with Lobbying: A Growth Policy Co-opted by Lobbyists Can Be Better than No Growth Policy at All

*Knut Anton Mork**

Norwegian School of Management, Sandvika, Norway

Abstract

The social effects of lobbying are studied in a model where growth can be improved by policy, but only at the cost of lobbying. Three results are derived: (i) the growth rate in an equilibrium with lobbying is higher than if lobbying and policy are both banned; (ii) if the subjective discount rate is low enough, welfare is improved; and (iii) the equilibrium approaches the first-best solution if the response function for lobbying is initially very steep, but flattens out very quickly.

I. Introduction

A common theme in much of the theory of endogenous growth is that markets are less than fully efficient, so that policy can improve welfare. Furthermore, in a growth context, the gains from the right policy tend to be much larger than what economists are used to because growth rates and not just income levels are affected. When policy matters this much, lobbying can become very persuasive and thus potentially lucrative. However, lobbying itself is nothing but rent seeking, and time spent on lobbying represents a pure waste of society's resources. Grossman (1990, p. 119) considers this problem serious enough to remark, "The success of an industrial policy program hinges as much on the protection that it builds into the process to prevent it from being co-opted by interested

*The research underlying this paper was started while I was at the Centre for Research in Economics and Business Administration in Oslo. Financial support from the Centre is gratefully acknowledged. Kjetil Bjorvatn provided valuable research assistance. Seminar participants at the University of Oslo and the Norwegian School of Management, two anonymous referees and the editors of the Journal provided useful comments and suggestions.

parties as it does on the ability of economists and policy makers to identify market failures and to propose appropriate remedies under idealised analytical conditions. The potential societal gains from an activist policy can easily be sacrificed if opportunities for wasteful rent seeking are created ...".

It is suggested here, however, that this view may be unduly pessimistic. I analyze a case where firms lobby for subsidies to the extent that they find profitable, and where policy makers set policies only in response to lobbying, without regard for the public good. In this equilibrium, the growth rate is unambiguously higher than if lobbying and growth policy were both banned. If the subjective discount rate is low enough, social welfare is higher as well.

These results depend crucially on the endogeneity of the growth rate and thus do not carry over to the case of a static externality. They should not be interpreted as a general defence for rent seeking. Moreover, if the model had been extended to allow an industry to lobby for a subsidy under the *pretence* of a growth externality, the result most likely would be reversed. To consider such possibilities, the model would need to be expanded to include asymmetric information. Such an extension could be quite interesting, but lies beyond the scope of this paper.

Rent seeking and growth have been analyzed in a different context by Murphy, Schleifer and Vishny (1991). If their model were extended such that the output of the rent-seeking sector was a policy to improve the allocation of talent in the rest of the economy, we would expect it to be desirable that the technology in the rent-seeking sector be productive enough to attract some talent, but concave enough to keep the sector from attracting too much and too good talent.

A similar feature is found here. Because lobbying leads to desirable policies, it is in the public's interest for politicians to be responsive to lobbying. However, to minimize waste, this responsiveness should flatten out quickly as the lobbying effort increases.

II. A Growth Model with Lobbying

Like Romer (1986), I model growth as the result of knowledge accumulation and assume that knowledge is imperfectly appropriable so that an externality exists. The model can also be interpreted as a reduced form of the model of growth from increasing returns due to specialization in Romer (1987). That model has no true externality but behaves as if it did because competition is imperfect. In either model, first-best efficiency can be achieved by a subsidy that equals the (apparent) externality. One of the attractive features of the second model is that it implies constant returns to capital in the aggregate in a reduced-form sense. I use this assumption for analytical convenience. For additional simplicity, I assume that employment is exogenous. By further normalizing it to unity, I effectively ignore it.

All firms in the model are identical and have the Cobb–Douglas production function

$$y = \gamma k^a K^{1-a}, \qquad 0 < a < 1, \tag{1}$$

where k denotes the internal and K the external stock of knowledge capital, which, for brevity, is henceforth referred to simply as capital (in Romer's 1987 model, this interpretation is literal). The external capital is measured in units per firm, so that $K = k$ in equilibrium. For each firm, production is subject to decreasing returns to the privately controlled capital; however, in the aggregate, there are constant returns, implying endogenous growth at a constant rate.

Firms rent capital in competitive markets at a rate that, in the absence of taxes and subsidies, equals the market interest rate r. The rental rate takes this simple form because capital and consumer goods are perfect substitutes (with a relative price of unity) and the depreciation rate is assumed to be zero. A constant depreciation rate could be included, but would not add any insight.

However, firms are allowed to lobby for a subsidy on the use of capital. To keep matters simple, I assume that each firm lobbies for its own subsidy and pays the full cost of that lobbying. Thus, firms do not collude — for example, in industry associations — to take advantage of economies of scale in lobbying. This assumption tends to exaggerate the cost of lobbying. It also simplifies by eliminating the possibility of free riding.

I assume that the cost of lobbying is a percentage x of the firms' output for a given level of lobbying effort, so that x can be used as an indicator of this effort. This cost represents pure waste and may be thought of as the output lost by reallocating talented people from production to lobbying. In the real world, lobbying may involve additional private costs in the form of pure transfers to rent-seeking politicians. By modelling private lobbying costs as pure waste, I bias my results further in the direction of emphasizing the social cost of lobbying.

With the cost of lobbying specified as a percentage of output, an equilibrium with a constant lobbying effort over time is consistent with a constant rate of economic growth. This specification implies yet another exaggeration of the costs of lobbying because it implicitly assumes that the same percentage of GDP must be wasted on lobbying each year if a certain subsidy is to be implemented *and* maintained. There is thus no presumption to the effect that the lobbying effort may be reduced when the policy has been approved and implemented. Furthermore, because the cost of lobbying is defined as a percentage of GDP, it grows over time as GDP grows.

On the other hand, lobbying is favoured somewhat in the model by the fact that the use of capital is the only activity that can be subsidized. Thus, there is no issue of subsidizing activities that do not generate positive growth externalities. While this feature limits the analysis, it also highlights the unique characteristics of growth externalities because the results of this paper are closely tied to the endogeneity of the growth rate and do not carry over to the static case.

The subsidy is assumed to be financed by a lump-sum tax. This assumption simplifies the analysis and allows us, for example, to ignore the labour market. However, the cost x also may be interpreted as including the losses caused by a distorting tax.

The "technology" for the "production" of subsidies is modelled in the form of a response function relating the relative subsidy s to the effort indicator x. I assume this function to be increasing and differentiable, so that $s'(x) > 0$. I also assume that policy makers are unwilling or unable to devise and implement a growth policy on their own without lobbying (or without encouraging lobbying), so that $s(0) = 0$. As usual, the function s must be concave for an equilibrium to exist. In this case, it turns out that we must also require the elasticity of $(1 - s)$ with respect to $(1 - x)$,

$$e(x) = \frac{1-x}{1-s(x)} s'(x), \tag{2}$$

to be a declining function of x.

The firm's optimization problem amounts to choosing the level of capital use k and the lobbying effort that maximizes the profit function

$$\pi(k, x) = (1 - x)\gamma k^a K^{1-a} - [1 - s(x)] rk \tag{3}$$

for a given level of external capital K. Setting the partial derivative with respect to k equal to zero and using the condition that external and internal capital be equal in equilibrium makes the real interest rate equal to

$$r = \frac{1-x}{1-s(x)} \alpha\gamma, \tag{4}$$

which is constant over time provided x is.

The corresponding condition for lobbying is obtained similarly. After substitution from (4) and (2), it can be written as:

$$\frac{\partial \pi}{\partial x} = \gamma k \left\{ \alpha \left[\frac{1-x}{1-s(x)} \right] s'(x) - 1 \right\} = \gamma k [\alpha e(x) - 1] = 0. \tag{5}$$

This condition indicates that the elasticity e must be a decreasing function of x for this stationary point to represent a maximum rather than a minimum.

For the problem to be interesting, the equilibrium level of x must be positive. This is the case when $s(0) > 1/\alpha$, which I assume in the following. For lobbying costs to absorb less than 100 per cent of GDP, we furthermore must have $e(1) < 1/\alpha$.

For the internal equilibrium, (5) implies

$$e(x) = 1/\alpha > 1. \tag{6}$$

From this condition, we note that the equilibrium level of lobbying is constant over time. Equation (4) then implies that the interest rate is constant as well.

Consumers maximize a time separable logarithmic utility function:

$$U = \rho^2 \int_0^\infty e^{-\rho t} \ln c(t) \, dt, \qquad \rho > 0, \tag{7}$$

where the factor ρ^2 is included to ensure the finiteness of the welfare criterion for values of ρ close to 0 (it may be thought of as a way of incorporating an overtaking criterion for $\rho = 0$). This function is maximized subject to the usual budget constraint. Since labour is ignored, consumers' income is the sum of the rents they receive from leasing capital to firms and the dividend they receive from firms' profits. Consumers treat both sources as exogenous because the stock of capital is predetermined. The first-order condition for maximization implies that the growth rate for consumption is $g = r - \rho$, which is constant over time. After substitution from (4), it can be written as:

$$g = \frac{1-x}{1-s(x)} \alpha\gamma - \rho. \tag{8}$$

As is well known, the initial consumption level in this type of model is determined by the saddle-point property of the consumption–capital dynamics. In fact, the economy jumps immediately to the saddle-point path so that the growth rates of capital and consumption are equal from the beginning. The growth rate of capital is derived from the GDP identity and the constant-returns production function (1) as:

$$\frac{\dot{k}}{k} = (1-x)\frac{y}{k} - \frac{c}{k} = (1-x)\gamma - \frac{c}{k}.$$

When this growth rate is set equal to that of consumption we obtain, after substitution from (8), the following condition for the initial consumption level:

$$c_0 = [(1-x)\gamma - g]k_0 = \left\{ \left[1 - x - \frac{1-x}{1-s(x)}\, \alpha \right] \gamma + \rho \right\} k_0. \qquad (9)$$

In (8) as well as (9) the value of x is understood to be the equilibrium level implied by (6).

III. Growth Rate and Welfare

The equilibrium solution with lobbying-based growth policy may be compared to the equilibrium that would have been obtained if both lobbying and growth policy had somehow been banned, so that x and s were both constrained to be zero. We then obtain the following result: *The equilibrium growth rate with lobbying-based growth policy is higher than the growth rate when lobbying and growth policy are both banned.*

From (8), we see that this result follows immediately if we can prove that $s(x) > x$ in equilibrium. Suppose there exists an $x_0 > 0$ for which $s(x_0) = x_0$. From the concavity of s and the condition that $s'(0) > 1/\alpha > 1$, it follows that the graph of s intersects the 45°-line from above at x_0, so that $e(x_0) = s'(x_0) < 1$. However, (6) then implies that x_0 cannot be an equilibrium. Because e decreases in x, the equilibrium must lie to the left of x_0. But this means that $s(x) > x$ in equilibrium. Although it may be possible for lobbying to be carried out to a point where it decreases the growth rate, firms would not be interested in paying the costs of going that far. Considering the many assumptions in this paper that bias the analysis against finding benefits of lobbying, this result seems likely to be fairly robust.

However, a higher growth rate does not automatically imply higher social welfare. Integration of (7), making use of the fact that the growth rate is constant over time, shows that the realized value of the utility function is

$$U^* = \rho \ln c_0 + g, \qquad (10)$$

where c_0 and g are the equilibrium values in (9) and (8), respectively. Furthermore, considering the result that $s(x) > x > 0$ in equilibrium, we can tell from (9) that lobbying unambiguously *reduces* the initial consumption level. As time passes, the consumption level with lobbying will eventually overtake the level without lobbying, but it starts out lower. The reduction in the initial consumption level comes partly from increased saving, as it would in the first-best case, but the real cost of lobbying adds an additional element.

Thus, unlike the first-best case, the relative magnitude of the dynamic costs and benefits is ambiguous *a priori*. Because the consumption levels unambiguously become higher far enough into the future, the tradeoff becomes a question of discounting. If the future is discounted heavily enough, lobbying entails a net cost. However, if the discount rate is low enough, we expect the future gains to dominate and lobbying to produce a net gain to society.

This result can be seen immediately from (10), according to which the value of the social welfare function approaches the growth rate for $\rho \to 0$, provided the growth rate is defined for $\rho \to 0$ and the logarithm of the initial consumption level does not go to zero faster than ρ.

From (8) we easily see that the growth rate is defined for $\rho \to 0$. From (9) we note that, given $x < 1$ in equilibrium, the initial consumption level is at least equal to ρk_0 as long as the subsidy at most equals its first-level $1 - \alpha$. Given this condition, $\rho \ln c_0 \geq \rho \ln k_0 + \rho \ln \rho$, so that $\rho \ln c_0 \to 0$ for $\rho \to 0$. Then, *lobbying unambiguously improves social welfare for* $\rho \to 0$.

IV. The Form of the Response Function for Lobbying

The magnitude of any such improvement clearly must depend on the form of the function s, which indicates the policy makers' response to lobbying efforts. In order to explore this form, I specify a functional form for this function and analyze how the equilibrium solution depends on its parameters.

The requirement that the elasticity e be decreasing in x restricts this choice considerably. A suitable form is the quadratic translog:

$$s(x) = 1 - (1-x)^{\beta + (1/2\sigma)\ln(1-x)}, \qquad \beta > 1, \qquad \sigma > 0, \tag{11}$$

for which

$$e(x) = \beta + \frac{1}{\sigma}\ln(1-x), \tag{12}$$

which decreases in x. It is easy to see that (11) satisfies $s(0) = 0$ and that the constraints on β and σ ensure convexity. s is increasing for $x < 1 - e^{-\beta/\sigma}$, which is sufficient for an internal equilibrium, provided that also $s'(0) = \beta > 1/\alpha$.

With this functional form the equilibrium level of lobbying is

$$x = 1 - e^{-\sigma(\beta - 1/\alpha)}, \tag{13}$$

the equilibrium subsidy is

$$s(x) = 1 - e^{-(\sigma/2)(\beta^2 - 1/\alpha^2)}, \tag{14}$$

and the implied realized value of the utility function becomes

$$U^* = \rho \ln\{[e^{-\sigma(\beta - 1/\alpha)} - \alpha e^{(\sigma/2)(\beta - 1/\alpha)(\beta + 1/\alpha - 2)}]\gamma + \rho\} + \rho \ln k_0$$
$$+ \alpha\gamma e^{(\sigma/2)(\beta - 1/\alpha)(\beta + 1/\alpha - 2)} - \rho. \tag{15}$$

Intuition suggests that welfare should be improved if the s-function is very steep for small values of x but then flattens out quickly, in other words if the function is both steep and concave. Then, low levels of activity should result in a substantial subsidy at the same time as the flattening out would contain the amount of lobbying. Lobbying would be limited, but effective.

A steep, but highly concave function s involves a combination of a large β and a low σ. Because these parameters appear multiplicatively in (13)–(15), we need to make some kind of choice as to which parameter goes faster to infinity and zero, respectively. Since two out of the three formulae contain the product of σ and the *square* of β, it seems natural to explore the case where this product remains finite as σ approaches zero.

Specifically, I specify $\beta = \sqrt{\mu/\sigma}$. Then, as $\sigma \to 0$, we obtain

$$x \to 0, \tag{13'}$$

$$s(x) \to 1 - e^{-\mu/2}, \text{ and} \tag{14'}$$

$$U^* \to \rho\{\ln[(1 - \alpha e^{\mu/2})\gamma + \rho] + \ln k_0\} + \alpha e^{\mu/2} - \rho. \tag{15'}$$

Viewing now social welfare as a function of μ, we see that this function is maximized for $\mu = -2 \ln \alpha$. Then, as a limiting solution, $x \to 0$ and $s \to 1 - \alpha$. But this is nothing other than the first-best solution! In other words, the system where growth policy is created by equilibrium lobbying can approach the first-best policy solution if the response function is such that it is extremely steep for values of x close to zero, but then flattens out very quickly. Thus, the point is not to have a system where policy makers are unaffected by lobbying. Rather, the public interest is best served by policy makers who respond strongly to moderate lobbying efforts, but whose marginal interest cools off quickly if the effort is raised significantly.

V. Concluding Comments

It is true that lobbying contains an element of rent seeking, which represents a waste of society's resources. However, lobbying also may lead policy makers to take advantage of welfare-improving opportunities that might otherwise have been ignored. Thus, although costly, lobbying for growth policies can be expected to raise the growth rate and quite possibly the level of social welfare as well.

There are two important reasons for this result. First, the policies promoted by lobbyists in this paper improve welfare. Welfare would have been improved even more if the same policy had been implemented without lobbying; however, given the workings of modern democracies, it is hardly realistic to expect policy makers to act simply as benevolent planners. Thus, the waste caused by lobbying may be an unavoidable price that society has to pay for desirable policies. Second, the prospects for welfare improvements are particularly promising in the case of growth policies. When growth rates are increased, the improvements in income levels over time can be considerable; and unless the discount rate is too high, the discounted benefits can easily exceed the initial costs.

However, the analysis of Section IV emphasizes that the response function s does not represent a true technological constraint, but the workings of the political system. Thus, even if we accept the (admittedly extreme) assumption that day-to-day policy making is determined by lobbying alone, it seems important to discuss practical ways to modify policy makers' response to lobbying in such a way as to serve the public interest better. Such a modification should seek to make the policy makers more responsive to lobbying at moderate levels, but at the same time less responsive on the margin to more intense lobbying. A discussion of these aspects, however, is beyond the scope of this paper.

References

Grossman, G. M.: Promoting new industrial activities: A survey of recent arguments and evidence. *OECD Economic Studies*, 87–125, 1990.

Murphy, K. M., Schleifer, A. & Vishny, R.: The allocation of talent: Implications for growth. *Quarterly Journal of Economics CVI* (2), 503–30, 1991.

Romer, P. M.: Increasing returns and long-run growth. *Journal of Political Economy 94* (5), 1002–37, 1986.

Romer, P. M.: Growth based on increasing .returns due to specialization. *American Economic Review, Papers and Proceedings 77* (2), 56–62, 1987.

Dynamic Analysis of an Endogenous Growth Model with Public Capital*

Koichi Futagami

Ritsumeikan University, Kyoto, Japan

Yuichi Morita

Osaka University, Toyonaka, Japan

Akihisa Shibata

Osaka City University, Osaka, Japan

Abstract

This paper develops an endogenous growth model with productive public capital along with private capital in a spirit similar to that of Barro (1990). Since our model includes two stock variables, it has transitional dynamics, unlike most of the previous studies on endogenous growth including Barro's, where concerns are restricted to the steady state analysis. First, we show that the transitional path is unique and stable. Second, the character of the transitional path is explored. Third, we show that the optimal tax rate is smaller than the rate which maximizes the national growth rate with a log-linear utility function.

I. Introduction

As has been stated by Atkinson and Stiglitz (1980), we should consider how taxation may discourage — or encourage — the long-term *rate of growth* of the economy. In the usual neoclassical growth models, the long-term rate of growth is determined by the exogenous growth rates of labor supply and of technical progress. Hence, these models cannot explain the

---

*Our special thanks go to two anonymous referees for their valuable comments and suggestions. We are also indebted to Takashi Fukushima, Hiroaki Hayakawa, Masaaki Homma, Toshihiro Ihori, Colin McKenzie, Kazuo Mino, Jim Raymo, Yoshihiko Seoka and seminar participants at Osaka, Osaka City and Hiroshima Universities for their helpful suggestions. Of course, any remaining errors are ours.

effect of taxation on the rate of growth. Fiscal policy can affect only the per-capita *levels* of capital and income in the long run.

New attempts to explain the long-term rate of growth endogenously were initiated by Romer (1986) and Lucas (1988). Since then, many researchers have examined the effects of fiscal policy using endogenous growth models along the lines suggested by Atkinson and Stiglitz.[1] Their models commonly assume that tax revenue is redistributed to households. However, it is unclear why the government conducts such distortionary policies as capital income taxation in some of these models. Barro (1990), on the other hand, develops a simple and elegant model of endogenous growth in which the government uses tax revenue to finance government expenditure and this expenditure enters into the production function as a productive input.[2] Furthermore, Barro proves that in his model, maximizing the national growth rate is equivalent to maximizing social welfare.

Along the same lines as Barro, this paper develops an endogenous growth model which incorporates public capital along with private capital and focuses on the following three issues. First, we prove the existence and uniqueness of the steady-growth equilibrium under certain conditions. Second, we characterize the steady-growth equilibrium and the stability of the transitional dynamics. Third, we investigate the dynamic effects of a change in the income tax on the transitional path of the economy and on lifetime welfare.

The model developed in this paper departs from the Barro model in one important respect. Barro regards public services which are flow variables as a productive input in private production and, as a result, his model essentially reduces to a version of the "AK" model in which there are no transitional dynamics. In contrast with his model, our model includes two state variables: private and public capital stocks; hence it has transitional dynamics. Therefore it is of interest to reexamine, for example, Barro's result on the optimal policy as well as the character of the transitional dynamics.[3] Indeed, some of Barro's results do not hold in our model.

---

[1] See, for example, Jones and Manuelli (1990), King and Rebelo (1990), Mino (1990a) and Rebelo (1991).

[2] The economic implications of public inputs are examined in a number of studies. In a static small open country model, Abe (1991) investigates the effect of tariff reform in a public goods economy. Constructing an endogenous growth model with threshold externalities, Futagami and Mino (1992) examine the relation between infrastructure accumulation and long run growth, and show the possibility of multiple equilibria.

[3] There are surprisingly few studies which examine the transitional dynamics of endogenous growth models analytically without relying on numerical simulations. Exceptions are Mino (1990a) and Mulligan and Sala-i-Martin (1992) who examine the dynamics of two-sector endogenous growth models.

Furthermore, we are able to rationalize our modeling strategy of incorporating public capital into the model instead of public services for the following reasons. First, many public infrastructures such as highways, airports, and electrical and gas facilities are stock variables in nature. Indeed, in the theoretical literature on public investment, it is commonly assumed that the stock of public capital, instead of the flow of public services, is a productive input to private production;[4] see e.g. Arrow and Kurz (1970) and Uzawa (1974). Second, and more importantly, there are several empirical studies supporting the importance of public capital in private production. For example, Aschauer (1988) finds empirically that public capital raises the marginal productivity of private capital. Estimating a version of the Cobb–Douglas production function with public capital for the Japanese economy, Iwamoto (1990) also finds a significant effect of public capital.

The paper is organized as follows. Section II sets up the model which incorporates public capital. Section III characterizes the steady-growth equilibrium and proves the uniqueness of the transitional path. Section IV examines the effects of income taxation on the long-term rate of growth, the steady-growth equilibrium and the transitional dynamics. We also present a general result of comparative dynamics on the transitional path. Using the comparative dynamics result obtained in Section IV, Section V examines the welfare effect of income taxation under a specific form of consumer utility function. Section VI contains some concluding remarks and prospects for the direction of future research.

II. The Model

The representative infinitely lived household maximizes the discounted sum of utility, as given by:

$$\int_0^\infty u(c)e^{-\rho t}\, dt, \tag{1}$$

where c and ρ are consumption per person and the subjective discount rate, respectively. Assume that population, which corresponds to the number of workers and consumers, is normalized to one and that the

---

[4] Indeed, Barro recognizes this point but argues that the difference between public capital and the flow of public services is not substantive. However, as we show below, the difference causes some significant modifications of Barro's results.

instantaneous utility function takes the form of:

$$u(c) = \frac{c^{1-\sigma} - 1}{1 - \sigma}, \text{ for } \sigma > 0, \qquad \sigma \neq 1,$$

$$= \ln c, \qquad \text{for } \sigma = 1,$$

where σ is the inverse of the elasticity of intertemporal substitution.

Following Barro (1990), we formulate the production function as follows. The production function exhibits constant returns to scale with diminishing returns with respect to each factor:

$$q = f(k, g) = k\phi(g/k), \qquad \phi' > 0, \qquad \phi'' < 0, \tag{2}$$

where q, k and g denote, respectively, output, private capital and public capital provided to the household–producer without user charges. Moreover, ϕ is assumed to satisfy the Inada conditions;

$$\lim_{x \to 0} \phi'(x) = \infty \quad \text{and} \quad \lim_{x \to \infty} \phi'(x) = 0, \quad \text{where} \quad x \equiv g/k.$$

Assume that the public expenditure consists only of public investment and is financed by a flat-rate income tax:

$$\dot{g} = T = \tau q = \tau k \phi(x), \tag{3}$$

where T is the government revenue and τ is the tax rate.[5] This is the only expression differs from Barro's model. However, this difference creates the need to examine certain problems.[6] In order to maintain tractability, we follow Barro in making the assumption that τ is time invariant.[7]

The representative household maximizes (1) subject to:

$$\dot{k} = (1 - \tau) f(k, g) - c. \tag{4}$$

---

[5] If we allow geometric depreciation, none of the main results obtained below would be modified except for the case of complete instantaneous depreciation, which is analyzed by Barro.

[6] Mino (1990b) and Lee (1992) investigate models similar to the one in this paper. However, the concern of their paper is the character of the steady-growth path. See also Barro and Sala-i-Martin (1992).

[7] This assumption may not be irrelevant. The optimal tax schedule may be time variant in the same way as proved by Chamley (1986) in an exogenous growth model. However, this issue is beyond the scope of this paper. Instead, we analyze the welfare effect of a marginal change in this time invariant tax rate in Section V.

As is well known, this maximization problem gives the following condition:

$$\frac{\dot{c}}{c} = \frac{1}{\sigma}[(1-\tau)f_k - \rho] = \frac{1}{\sigma}[(1-\tau)\phi(g/k)(1-\eta) - \rho], \tag{5}$$

where η is the elasticity of q with respect to g (for a given value of k), that is, $\eta \equiv x\phi'/\phi$ $(0 < \eta < 1)$.[8]

Summarizing the equations (3), (4) and (5), we get the following dynamic equations:

$$\frac{\dot{x}}{x} \equiv \frac{\dot{g}}{g} - \frac{\dot{k}}{k} = \tau\frac{\phi}{x} - (1-\tau)\phi + y \tag{6}$$

$$\frac{\dot{y}}{y} \equiv \frac{\dot{c}}{c} - \frac{\dot{k}}{k} = \frac{1}{\sigma}[(1-\tau)(1-\eta)\phi - \rho] - (1-\tau)\phi + y, \tag{7}$$

where $x \equiv g/k$ and $y \equiv c/k$. These equations describe the dynamics of the economy.

III. The Steady-Growth Equilibrium

In characterizing the steady state of the model, we begin by showing that there exists a unique stationary state which satisfies $\dot{x} = \dot{y} = 0$. The stationary state is defined by the following equations:

$$y^* = \left[(1-\tau) - \frac{\tau}{x^*}\right]\phi(x^*) \tag{8}$$

$$y^* = \frac{1}{\sigma}[(1-\tau)(\sigma + \eta^* - 1)]\phi(x^*) + \frac{\rho}{\sigma}, \tag{9}$$

where variables with asterisks represent the steady-state values of the variables.

This stationary state is called *steady-growth equilibrium*, because consumption per capita, private capital per capita, public capital per capita, and national product per capita grow at the same rate γ, that is, $\gamma = \dot{c}/c = \dot{k}/k = \dot{g}/g = \dot{q}/q$.

---

[8] Note that equations (4) and (5) can be derived from private optimization in perfectly competitive markets.

Subtracting (8) from (9), we obtain:

$$\Gamma(x^*) \equiv [\tau/x^* - (1 - \tau)(1 - \eta^*)/\sigma]\phi^* + \rho/\sigma,$$

where $\phi^* \equiv \phi(x^*)$. At the steady-growth equilibrium, $\Gamma = 0$; hence we first examine whether there is a value of x^* which satisfies $\Gamma = 0$. Differentiating Γ with respect to x^*, we obtain:

$$\tau(\phi^{*\prime}x^* - \phi^*)/x^{*2} + (1 - \tau)\phi^{*\prime\prime}x^*/\sigma < 0.$$

Moreover, it is easy to see that $\Gamma > 0$ when x^* is sufficiently small and $\Gamma < 0$ when x^* is sufficiently large since $(1 - \eta^*)$ can vary only within the range $(0, 1)$, while τ/x^* can vary within the range $(0, \infty)$. Therefore, there is a unique positive value of x^* which satisfies $\Gamma = 0$. The next problem to be considered is whether y^* is positive. From (8) x^* must be greater than $\tau/1 - \tau$ for y^* to be positive. Since $\Gamma(x^*)$ is a monotonically decreasing function of x^*, if

$$\Gamma((\tau/1 - \tau)) = [(1 - \tau)(\sigma + \bar{\eta} - 1)]\bar{\phi}/\sigma + \frac{\rho}{\sigma} > 0,$$

where $\bar{\eta} \equiv \eta((\tau/1 - \tau))$ and $\bar{\phi} \equiv \phi((\tau/1 - \tau))$, then there exists a unique steady growth equilibrium in which $y^* > 0$.

Summarizing the preceding argument, we can state:

Proposition 1. *When*

$$[(1 - \tau)(\sigma + \bar{\eta} - 1)]\bar{\phi}/\sigma + \frac{\rho}{\sigma}$$

is positive, there exists a unique steady-growth equilibrium.

Roughly speaking, the condition in proposition 1 requires the growth rate of consumption to be relatively small. In order to see this, by rewriting (9) we have $y^* = (1 - \tau)\phi^* - (1/\sigma)[(1 - \tau)(1 - \eta^*)\phi^* - \rho] = (1 - \tau)\phi^* - (\dot{c}/c)^*$. Thus $(\dot{c}/c)^*$ must be relatively small in order for y^* to be positive.

Second, we investigate the transitional dynamics. In order to examine the local stability of the transitional path, let us rewrite (6) and (7) as follows:

$$\dot{x} = \left[\tau\frac{\phi}{x} - (1 - \tau)\phi + y \right] x \tag{10}$$

$$\dot{y} = \left(\frac{1}{\sigma}[(1 - \tau)(1 - \eta)\phi - \rho] - (1 - \tau)\phi + y \right) y. \tag{11}$$

Linearizing (10) and (11) around the steady-growth equilibrium, we obtain:

$$\begin{bmatrix} \dot{x} \\ \dot{y} \end{bmatrix} = \begin{bmatrix} [-(1-\tau)\phi^{*'} + \tau(\phi^{*'}x^* - \phi^*)/x^{*2}]x^* & x^* \\ [-(1-\tau)(\phi^{*'} + \phi^{*''}x^*/\sigma)]y^* & y^* \end{bmatrix} \begin{bmatrix} x - x^* \\ y - y^* \end{bmatrix}.$$

Calculating the determinant of this coefficient matrix J, we get:

$$\det J = x^* y^* [\tau(\phi^{*'}x^* - \phi^*)/x^{*2} + (1-\tau)\phi^{*''}x^*/\sigma] < 0.$$

Therefore, one of the eigenvalues of the coefficient matrix is positive and the other is negative, that is, the steady-growth equilibrium is a saddle point. This means that there is a one-dimensional stable manifold. Since the initial value of $y = c/k$ is not predetermined, we can choose a unique initial value of y on this stable manifold for a given initial value of $x = g/k$. Thus we can state:

Proposition 2. *When there is a unique steady-growth equilibrium, there exists a unique stable path converging to the steady-growth equilibrium.*

Next, we depict the phase diagram of the dynamic system. As shown below, the dynamic property of the equilibrium path depends on whether the sum of σ and η^* is greater than one. Thus, we separately analyze the two cases: case (i) $\sigma + \eta^* > 1$ and case (ii) $\sigma + \eta^* < 1$.[9] The equilibrium stable manifold is depicted by the curve with multiple arrowheads in Figure 1a for case (i) and Figure 1b for case (ii).[10]

Note that the results obtained in this section do not depend on the specific form of the production function.

IV. Effects of Income Taxation

We now consider the effects of a change in the income tax rate on the long-run rate of growth.

Setting $\dot{x} = \dot{y} = 0$ in (6) and (7) and totally differentiating them, we get the following:

$$\frac{dx^*}{d\tau} = -\frac{x^* y^*}{\det J} \left[\frac{\phi^*}{x^*} + \frac{(\phi^* - \phi^{*'} x^*)}{\sigma} \right] > 0. \tag{12}$$

---

[9] Analysis of the case $\sigma + \eta = 1$ is trivial, hence we omit this case. For example, in Section IV, where η is assumed to be constant, the equilibrium value of y remains constant over time.

[10] The paths which do not converge to the stationary state are not optimal because they violate the transversality condition.

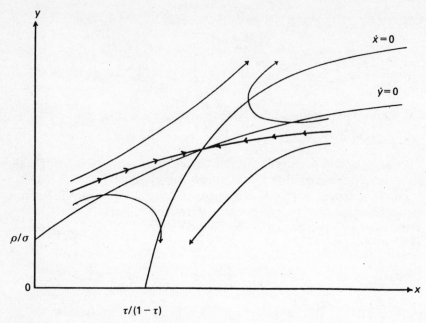

Fig. 1a. Case (i) $\sigma + \eta > 1$.

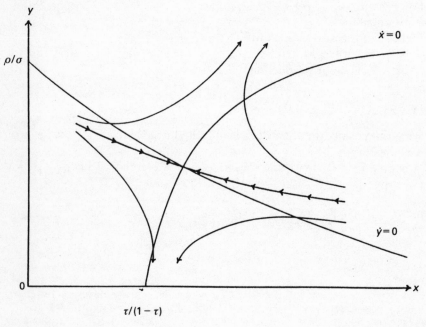

Fig. 1b. Case (ii) $\sigma + \eta < 1$.

When η is constant, that is, $\phi(x) = x^\eta$, we can calculate $dy^*/d\tau$ as follows;[11]

$$\frac{dy^*}{d\tau} = -\frac{x^* y^*}{\det J \cdot \sigma}(\sigma + \eta - 1)(\eta - \tau)x^{*2\eta-2}. \tag{13}$$

In case (i), that is, if $\sigma + \eta > 1$, the following holds:

$$\frac{dy^*}{d\tau} \gtreqless 0 \quad \text{when} \quad \eta \gtreqless \tau.$$

In case (ii), that is, if $\sigma + \eta < 1$, the following holds:

$$\frac{dy^*}{d\tau} \gtreqless 0 \quad \text{when} \quad \eta \lesseqgtr \tau.$$

Next we consider the effect of income taxation on the long-run rate of growth. An increase in τ has the following two opposite effects on the growth rate. The negative effect comes from the fact that an increase in τ reduces the level of private disposable income and thereby the level of private investment, as can be seen from (4). The positive effect is due to the fact that an increase in τ raises the ratio of public capital to private capital and thus the marginal productivity of private capital, f_k, at the steady-growth equilibrium; see equation (5). Although these two effects act on the national growth rate in opposite directions, when the elasticity of output with respect to government expenditure η is constant, we can derive a clear result. The growth rate in the steady-growth equilibrium γ^* is calculated by depicting (3) as

$$\gamma^* = \tau \frac{\phi^*}{x^*}.$$

Differentiating this formula with respect to τ, we get:

$$\frac{d\gamma^*}{d\tau} = \left[1 - \frac{(1 - \eta)\tau}{x^*} \cdot \frac{dx^*}{d\tau} \right] \frac{\phi^*}{x^*}.$$

By using (12), we can calculate the elasticity of x^* with respect to τ as follows:

$$\frac{\tau}{x^*} \cdot \frac{dx^*}{d\tau} = \frac{1}{(1 - \eta)} \left[1 + \frac{(1 - \eta)x^*}{\sigma} \right] \cdot \left[1 + \frac{(1 - \tau)\eta x^*}{\sigma \tau} \right]^{-1}.$$

---

[11] In the subsequent analysis we maintain the assumption that η is constant.

Here, let us compare the coefficient of x^*/σ in the numerator with the one in the denominator. Subtracting the latter value from the former value we get $(1 - \eta) - (1 - \tau)\eta/\tau = (\tau - \eta)/\tau$. Therefore, the following relation holds:

$$\frac{d\gamma^*}{d\tau} \gtreqless 0 \leftrightarrow \frac{(1 - \eta)\tau}{x^*} \cdot \frac{dx^*}{d\tau} \gtreqless 1 \leftrightarrow \tau \gtreqless \eta . \tag{14}$$

As a result of the preceding argument, we have proved the following proposition:

Proposition 3. *If η is constant, the growth rate of steady-growth equilibrium attains its maximum when $\tau = \eta$.*

Since η represents the ratio of public capital to national product and τ equals the ratio of public investment to national product, this proposition implies that in order to maximize the national growth rate, the government should set these two ratios at the same rate. This result is essentially the same as Barro's. Even in the model where public capital is taken into account, Barro's result on the maximum growth rate holds.

Second, we investigate the character of the transitional path after a change in the rate of income tax, τ. We assume that the economy is initially in the steady-growth equilibrium, and that an unanticipated increase in the rate of income tax occurs at time 0. In order to make the dependence of c, g, k, x and y on τ as well as time explicit, hereafter we denote them by $c(t, \tau)$, $g(t, \tau)$, $k(t, \tau)$, $x(t, \tau)$ and $y(t, \tau)$, respectively. Applying Judd's (1982, 1985) method of comparative dynamics, we can obtain the following proposition on the effect of the change in τ:

Proposition 4. *Suppose that η is constant. Then, if $\eta \leq \tau$, we get the following comparative dynamics result:*

$$\frac{\partial y(0, \tau)}{\partial \tau} \gtreqless 0 \quad \text{when} \quad \sigma + \eta \gtreqless 1.$$

Proof: See Appendix. It should be noted that even if τ is smaller than η, the results of proposition 4 holds when the value of τ is close to that of η. In the following, for simplicity, we assume that τ is larger than or close to η.

We can now explore the character of the transitional path. In case (i), $\sigma + \eta > 1$, when τ rises, the graph of (8) shifts downward and that of (9) also shifts downward. Figure 2a depicts these shifts. From proposition 4, y initially jumps downward and then increases, and x gradually increases. Therefore, $\dot{x}/x = \dot{g}/g - \dot{k}/k > 0$ and $\dot{y}/y = \dot{c}/c - \dot{k}/k > 0$ on the transitional path, and the initial level of consumption decreases. The initial impact of a

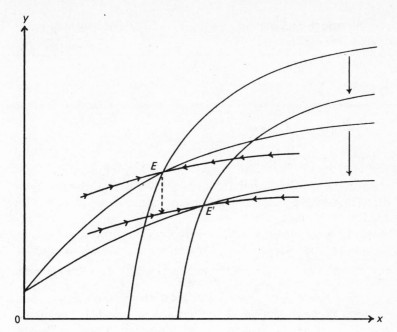

Fig. 2a. Case (i) $\sigma + \eta > 1$.

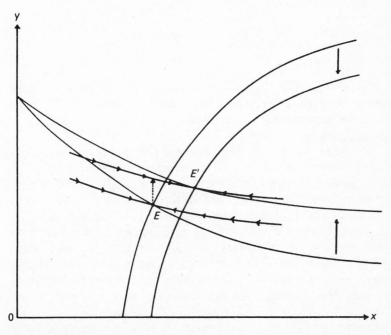

Fig. 2b. Case (ii) $\sigma + \eta < 1$.

rise in τ on the growth rate of public capital and on that of consumption is given by the following two equations:

$$\frac{\partial(\dot{g}(0, \tau)/g(0, \tau))}{\partial \tau} = \frac{\phi}{x} > 0,$$

$$\frac{\partial(\dot{c}(0, \tau)/c(0, \tau))}{\partial \tau} = -\frac{\phi - \phi' x}{\sigma} < 0,$$

from (3) and (5). Accordingly, the growth rate of consumption increases gradually and that of public capital decreases gradually. The growth rate of private capital is smaller than that of consumption. Figure 3a describes these transitional dynamics.

In case (ii), $\sigma + \eta < 1$, when τ rises, the graph of (8) shifts downward as in case (i); however, the graph of (9) shifts upward, contrary to case (i). Figure 2b depicts these shifts. From proposition 4, y initially jumps upward and then decreases, contrary to case (i), and x increases. Therefore, $\dot{x}/x = \dot{g}/g - \dot{k}/k > 0$ and $\dot{y}/y = \dot{c}/c - \dot{k}/k < 0$ on the transitional path. The initial level of consumption jumps upward in case (ii). The initial impact of a rise in τ on the growth rate of consumption and on that of public capital in case (ii) are the same as in case (i). In case (ii), the impact on the growth rate of private capital is given by:

$$\frac{\partial(\dot{k}(0, \tau)/k(0, \tau))}{\partial \tau} = -\phi - \frac{\partial y(0, \tau)}{\partial \tau} < 0,$$

from (4) and (6). Therefore, in case (ii) the growth rates of these variables behave in the same way as in case (i); however, the growth rate of private capital is greater than that of consumption, contrary to case (i). Figure 3b depicts these transitional dynamics.

Let us also note that in the short run, the rise in the tax rate has a positive effect on consumption in case (ii), contrary to the usual case. The response of present consumption to the change in τ consists of two effects; the intertemporal substitution effect and the income effect. In both cases (i) and (ii), the income effects are negative since the growth rate is reduced by this tax change. However, there is an opposite intertemporal substitution effect. An increase in τ causes the interest rate at time zero, $(1 - \tau)(1 - \eta) \phi(x(0, \tau))$, to decline since $x(0, \tau)$ cannot jump. Then, due to the increases in x^*, the interest rate gradually increases toward the new steady-growth value although the new value is lower than that of the original level; see equation (5) and proposition 3. Hence, the intertemporal substitution effect works to increase present consumption and to decrease future consumption. Since in case (ii) the elasticity of intertemporal

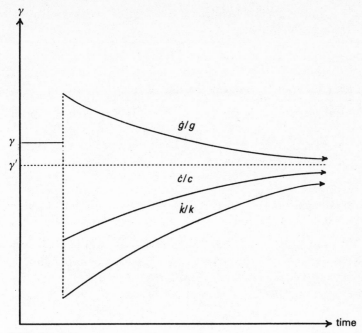

Fig. 3a. Case (i) $\sigma + \eta > 1$.

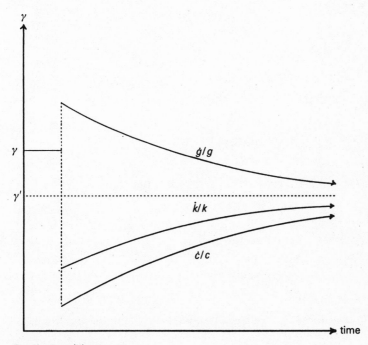

Fig. 3b. Case (ii) $\sigma + \eta < 1$.

substitution $1/\sigma$ is large, the intertemporal substitution effect dominates, increasing present consumption.

V. The Welfare Effect of Changing the Tax Rate

Let us now examine the welfare effect of changing the tax rate from a constant level.

Barro (1990) obtains an important result on the welfare aspect of public policy, that is, he derives the following result regarding optimal policy:

Barro's result. *Maximizing the growth rate of the economy is equivalent to maximizing social welfare.*

It is important to investigate whether or not this result still holds in our model. In Barro's model, there are no transitional dynamics and therefore the economy is always on a balanced growth path. In contrast, since our model has transitional dynamics, it is not clear whether Barro's result still holds.

For simplicity suppose that $\sigma = 1$, that is, the utility function takes the log-linear form:

$$\int_0^\infty [\ln c] e^{-\rho t} \, dt. \tag{15}$$

Let us now obtain the welfare effect of changing the tax rate. From the household's optimal condition (5) we get:

$$c(t, \tau) = c(0, \tau) exp \int_0^t [(1 - \tau)(1 - \eta)\phi(x(s, \tau)) - \rho] \, ds, \tag{16}$$

Substituting (16) into (15) gives the indirect utility function U:

$$U = \int_0^\infty [\ln c(0, \tau)] e^{-\rho t} \, dt$$

$$+ \int_0^\infty \int_0^t [(1 - \tau)(1 - \eta)\phi(x(s, \tau)) - \rho] \, ds \cdot e^{-\rho t} \, dt. \tag{17}$$

Thus the lifetime utility depends on the initial consumption and the time path of x. Following Judd (1982), we differentiate (17) with respect to τ, and derive the formula for the welfare effect caused by a change in the tax rate:

$$
\frac{dU}{d\tau} = \frac{c_\tau(0, \tau)}{\rho c(0, \tau)}
$$

$$
+ \int_0^\infty \int_0^t [(1 - \tau)(1 - \eta)\phi'(x^*)x_\tau(s, \tau) - (1 - \eta)\phi(x^*)]\, ds \cdot e^{-\rho t}\, dt. \tag{18}
$$

In equation (18), $c_\tau(t, \tau)$ and $x_\tau(t, \tau)$ represent the partial derivatives of $c(t, \tau)$ and $x(t, \tau)$ with respect to the change in τ which occurs at $t = 0$. The effect of the tax change on $x(s, \tau)$ is given by:

$$
x_\tau(s, \tau) = x_\tau^* \cdot (1 - e^{\mu s}), \tag{19}
$$

where μ is the negative eigenvalue of the system.[13] In obtaining (19) we use $x_\tau(0, \tau) = 0$. Substituting (19) into (18) gives:

$$
\frac{dU}{d\tau} = \frac{c_\tau(0, \tau)}{\rho c(0, \tau)}
$$

$$
+ \int_0^\infty \int_0^t [\{(1 - \tau)(1 - \eta)\phi'(x^*)x_\tau^* - (1 - \eta)\phi(x^*)\} \tag{20}
$$

$$
- (1 - \tau)(1 - \eta)\phi'(x^*)x_\tau^* \cdot e^{\mu s}]\, ds \cdot e^{-\rho t}\, dt.
$$

Our purpose in this section is not to obtain the optimal tax schedule but to investigate whether Barro's (1990) result holds in our model. In Barro's model the optimal tax rate is constant over time. Therefore, in order to prove that Barro's result does not hold in our model, it is sufficient to show that changing the tax rate from Barro's optimal rate gives non-zero welfare effects.

When τ is equal to η initially, it follows from (14) and the definition of η that $(1 - \tau)(1 - \eta)\phi'(x^*)x_\tau^* - (1 - \eta)\phi(x^*) = 0$. Hence, (20) reduces to:

$$
\left.\frac{dU}{d\tau}\right|_{\tau = \eta} = \frac{c_\tau(0, \tau)}{\rho c(0, \tau)} - \int_0^\infty \left[(1 - \tau)(1 - \eta)\phi'(x^*)x_\tau^* \cdot \frac{1}{\mu}(e^{\mu t} - 1) \right] e^{-\rho t}\, dt. \tag{21}
$$

---

[12] This formula is obtained by the Taylor expansion around the steady state. Essentially the same formula is derived by Judd (1982) and Ono and Shibata (1992) in exogenous growth models. The procedure is described in detail in both of these studies.

[13] See footnote 12.

Note that from (12) an increase in the tax rate always raises the public capital–private capital ratio in the long run. Furthermore, setting $\sigma = 1$ in proposition 4 we get:

$$y_\tau(0, \eta) < 0.$$

Hence, from the fact that $c \equiv yk$ and $k_\tau(0, \eta) = 0$, it follows that $c_\tau(0, \eta) = y_\tau(0, \eta) k(0, \eta) < 0$, implying that the first term of the r.h.s. of (21) is negative. Since $x_\tau^* \equiv x_\tau(\infty, \eta) > 0$ from (12) and $(e^{\mu t} - 1) \le 0$, the second term of the r.h.s. of (21) is also negative. Thus we get:

$$\left. \frac{dU}{d\tau} \right|_{\tau = \eta} < 0. \tag{22}$$

This implies that reducing the tax rate from the rate which attains the maximum national growth rate increases the agents' lifetime welfare. Hence, the welfare maximizing policy is not equivalent to maximizing the growth rate of the economy. The existence of transitional dynamics causes a difference in the welfare aspect of public policy to arise between Barro's model and ours.

Note that even if we evaluate the derivative of (18) at $\tau \ge \eta$ the same result can be obtained. From (5) and proposition 3, if $\tau \ge \eta$ it follows that $(1 - \tau)(1 - \eta)\phi'(x^*)x_\tau^* - (1 - \eta)\phi(x^*) \le 0$. Proposition 4 implies that $y_\tau(0, \tau) < 0$ when $\tau \ge \eta$ and $\sigma = 1$. Hence the sign of (18) is negative if $\tau \ge \eta$. From the above argument we have the following proposition.

Proposition 5. *Suppose that η is constant and that $\sigma = 1$. Then the optimal tax rate is lower than the rate which attains the maximum growth rate of the economy.*

This proposition differs from Barro's result due to the existence of transitional dynamics. This difference is important since it implies that policy makers' work is more complex than simply maximizing the growth rate of the economy.

In this context, we may also make the following remark on the existence of externalities:

Remark. Since public capital is associated with externalities, the privately determined value of economic growth becomes suboptimal. We can show that if households take the accumulation of public capital into account, then the long-run growth rate of the economy is larger than that of market equilibrium analyzed in this paper. This case is analyzed by Futagami, Morita and Shibata (1992).

VI. Concluding Remarks

Developing an endogenous growth model with public capital, we have derived the following results. First, under mild conditions, there exists a unique steady-growth equilibrium, and there is a unique transitional path converging to the steady-growth equilibrium. Second, the long-run growth rate of market equilibrium is maximized when the rate of income tax equals the elasticity of output with respect to public capital in the case where this elasticity is constant. Third, the tax rate which maximizes the growth rate of the economy is not equal to the rate which maximizes national welfare. The optimal (constant) tax rate is lower than the rate which maximizes the growth rate of the economy under the log-linear utility.

Finally, we would like to consider the direction of future research. Based on our analysis, it can be seen that for countries with identical tax rates but at different points on the transitional path, there will be a relationship where relatively low growth rates of public capital will be associated with relatively high growth rates of consumption. Since Barro's (1990) empirical analysis assumes countries to be in a steady state, the existence of this correlation on the transitional path is not taken into consideration. We should reexamine Barro's empirical results by explicitly considering the transitional path. This is an important topic for future research.

Appendix

In this appendix, we prove proposition 4 by using Judd's method. Differentiating (6) and (7) with respect to τ around the new stationary state, we obtain the following:

$$\begin{bmatrix} \dot{x}_\tau \\ \dot{y}_\tau \end{bmatrix} = \begin{bmatrix} [-(1-\tau)\phi' + \tau(\phi'x^* - \phi)/x^{*2} & x^* \\ [-(1-\tau)(\phi' + \phi''x^*/\sigma)]y^* & y^* \end{bmatrix} \begin{bmatrix} x_\tau \\ y_\tau \end{bmatrix} + \begin{bmatrix} \phi(1+x^*) \\ y^*\phi(\sigma+\eta-1)/\sigma \end{bmatrix}, \quad (A1)$$

where $x_\tau \equiv \partial x(t, \tau)/\partial \tau$ and $y_\tau \equiv \partial y(t, \tau)/\partial \tau$, respectively. Here, we denote the coefficient matrix as follows:

$$J \equiv \begin{bmatrix} a_{11} & a_{12} \\ a_{21} & a_{22} \end{bmatrix}.$$

Since the Jacobian matrix of this system is the same as matrix J in the text, it has one negative eigenvalue μ and one positive eigenvalue λ. Hence, this system has a unique bounded solution. Take the Laplace transformations of $x(t)$ and $y(t)$ and denote them $X(s)$ and $Y(s)$, respectively. For example, $X(s) \equiv \int_0^\infty x(t)e^{-st}\, dt$. This converts system (A1) into the following algebraic equation:

$$\begin{bmatrix} sX_\tau \\ sY_\tau - y_\tau(0, \tau) \end{bmatrix} = \begin{bmatrix} a_{11}\, a_{12} \\ a_{21}\, a_{22} \end{bmatrix} \begin{bmatrix} X_\tau \\ Y_\tau \end{bmatrix} + \begin{bmatrix} \phi(1+x^*)/s \\ y^* \phi(\sigma+\eta-1)/s\sigma \end{bmatrix},$$

or:

$$\begin{bmatrix} X_\tau \\ Y_\tau \end{bmatrix} = (sI - J)^{-1} \begin{bmatrix} \phi(1+x^*)/s \\ y_\tau(0, \tau) + y^* \phi(\sigma+\eta-1)/s\sigma \end{bmatrix},$$

where we have used $x_\tau(0, \tau) = 0$ because $\dot{x}$ is a predetermined variable. The system has a bounded solution; hence, it must be bounded even when $s = \lambda$, but $sI - J$ becomes singular when $s = \lambda$. This is possible only if the following relation holds:

$$a_{21}\phi(1+x^*)/\lambda + (\lambda - a_{11})[y_\tau(0, \tau) + y^*\phi(\sigma+\eta-1)/\sigma\lambda] = 0. \tag{A2}$$

Since $\phi = x^\eta$, we get $a_{21} = -(1-\tau)(\sigma+\eta-1)\eta x^{*\eta-1}y^*/\sigma$. Therefore, by rearranging the terms, we can obtain:

$$y_\tau(0, \tau) = y^*\phi[(1-\tau)\eta x^{*\eta-1}(1+x^*) + a_{11} - \lambda](1-\sigma-\eta)/(a_{11} - \lambda)\sigma\lambda. \tag{A3}$$

Finally, the terms in the square bracket of (A3) become $(\eta-\tau)x^{*\eta-1} - \lambda$. Accordingly, because a_{11} is negative, when η is smaller than τ, the relation in proposition 4 holds.

References

Abe, K.: Tariff reform in a small open economy with public production. *International Economic Review 33*, 209–22, 1991.

Arrow, K. J. & Kurz, M.: *Public Investment, the Rate of Return, and Optimal Fiscal Policy.* Johns Hopkins University Press, Baltimore, 1970.

Aschauer, D. A.: Is public expenditure productive? *Journal of Monetary Economics 23*, 177–200, 1989.

Atkinson, A. B. & Stiglitz, J. E.: *Lectures on Public Economics.* McGraw-Hill, New York, 1980.

Barro, R. J.: Government spending in a simple model of endogenous growth. *Journal of Political Economy 98*, 103–25, 1990.

Barro, R. J. & Sala-i-Martin, X.: Public finance in models of economic growth. *Review of Economic Studies 59*, 645–61, 1992.

Chamley, C.: Optimal taxation of capital income in general equilibrium with infinite lives. *Econometrica 54*, 607–22, 1986.

Futagami, K., Morita, Y. & Shibata, A.: Dynamic analysis of an endogenous growth model with public capital. DP 13, Faculty of Economics, Ritsumeikan University, 1992.

Futagami, K. & Mino, K.: Infrastructure and long-run growth with threshold externalities. Mimeo, Ritsumeikan and Tohoku Universities, 1992.

Iwamoto, Y.: An evaluation of public investment policy in postwar Japan (in Japanese). Economic Review 41, 250–61, 1990.

Jones, L. E. & Manuelli, R.: A convex model of equilibrium growth: Theory and policy implications. *Journal of Political Economy 98*, 1008–38, 1990.

Judd, K. L.: An alternative to steady state comparisons in perfect foresight models. *Economics Letters 10*, 55–9, 1982.

Judd, K. L.: Short-run analysis of fiscal policy in a simple perfect foresight model. *Journal of Political Economy 93*, 298–319, 1985.

King, R. & Rebelo, S.: Public policy and economic growth: Developing neoclassical implications. *Journal of Political Economy 98*, 126–50, 1990.

Lee, J.: Optimal magnitude and composition of government spending. *Journal of the Japanese and International Economies 6*, 423–39, 1992.

Lucas, R. E.: On the mechanics of economic development. *Journal of Monetary Economics 22*, 3–42, 1988.

Mino, K.: Analysis of a two-sector model of endogenous growth with capital income taxation. Faculty of Economics DP, Tohoku University, 1990a.

Mino, K.: Accumulation of public capital and long-run growth. Mimeo, Tohoku University 1990b.

Mulligan, C. B. & Sala-i-Martin, X.: Transitional dynamics in two-sector models of endogenous growth. NBER WP 3986, 1992.

Ono, Y. & Shibata, A.: Spill-over effects of supply-side changes in a two-country economy with capital accumulation. *Journal of International Economics 33*, 127–46, 1992.

Rebelo, S.: Long run policy analysis and long run growth. *Journal of Political Economy 99*, 500–21, 1991.

Romer, P.: Increasing returns and long-run growth. *Journal of Political Economy 94*, 1002–37, 1986.

Uzawa, H.: Sur la théorie économique du capital collectif social. Cahiers du seminaire d'économetrie, 103–22, 1974. Reprinted as Chapter 19 in H. Uzawa, *Preference, Production and Capital*, Cambridge University Press, New York, 1988.

Index

238   *Index*